AMERICAN FIGHTS & FIGHTERS SERIES

South American Fights & Fighters

"THE POOR LITTLE GOVERNOR . . . DISTANCED HIS
FIERCE PURSUERS AT LAST"

AMERICAN FIGHTS & FIGHTERS SERIES

South American Fights & Fighters

The Conquistadors and Other Accounts of Adventure

Cyrus Townsend Brady

LEONAUR

South American Fights & Fighters
The Conquistadors and
Other Accounts of Adventure
by Cyrus Townsend Brady

First published under the title
South American Fights & Fighters
And Other Tales of Adventure

Leonaur is an imprint of Oakpast Ltd

Copyright in this form © 2011 Oakpast Ltd

ISBN: 978-0-85706-579-7 (hardcover)
ISBN: 978-0-85706-580-3 (softcover)

http://www.leonaur.com

Contents

To
GEORGE WILLIAM BEATTY
GOOD FELLOW, GOOD CITIZEN
GOOD FRIEND

Preface

The first part of this new volume of the *American Fights and Fighters Series* needs no special introduction. Partly to make this the same size as the other books, but more particularly because I especially desired to give a permanent place to some of the most dramatic and interesting episodes in our history—especially as most of them related to the Pacific and the Far West—the series of papers in part second was included.

The Yarn of the Essex, Whaler is abridged from a quaint account written by the Mate and published in an old volume which is long since out of print and very scarce. The papers on the *Tonquin, John Paul Jones,* and *The Great American Duellists* speak for themselves. The account of the battle of the Pitt River has never been published in book form heretofore. The last paper *On Being a Boy Out West* I inserted because I enjoy it myself, and because I have found that others young and old who have read it generally like it also.

Thanks are due and are hereby extended to the following magazines for permission to republish various articles which originally appeared in their pages: *Harper's, Munseys, The Cosmopolitan, Sunset* and *The New Era.*

I project another volume of the Series supplementing the two Indian volumes immediately preceding this one, but the information is hard to get, and the work amid many other demands upon my time, proceeds slowly.

Cyrus Townsend Brady.

St. George's Rectory,
Kansas City, Mo., February, 1910.

1

Panama and the Knights-Errant of Colonization

1. THE SPANISH MAIN

One of the commonly misunderstood phrases in the language is "the Spanish Main." To the ordinary individual it suggests the Caribbean Sea. Although Shakespeare in *Othello*, makes one of the gentlemen of Cyprus say that he "*cannot 'twixt heaven and main descry a sail*," and, therefore, with other poets, gives warrant to the application of the word to the ocean, "main" really refers to the other element. The Spanish Main was that portion of South American territory distinguished from Cuba, Hispaniola and the other islands, because it was on the main land.

When the Gulf of Mexico and the Caribbean Sea were a Spanish lake, the whole circle of territory, bordering thereon was the Spanish Main, but of late the title has been restricted to Central and South America. The *buccaneers* are those who made it famous. So the word brings up white-hot stories of battle, murder and sudden death.

The history of the Spanish Main begins in 1509, with the voyages of Ojeda and Nicuesa, which were the first definite and authorized attempts to colonize the mainland of South America.

The honour of being the first of the fifteenth-century navigators to set foot upon either of the two American continents, indisputably belongs to John Cabot, on June 24, 1497. Who was next to make a continental landfall, and in the more southerly latitudes, is a question which lies between Columbus and Amerigo Vespucci.

Fiske, in a very convincing argument awards the honour to Vespucci, whose first voyage (May 1497 to October 1498) carried him from the north coast of Honduras along the Gulf coast around Florida, and possibly as far north as the Chesapeake Bay, and to the Bahamas on his return.

Markham scouts this claim. Winsor neither agrees nor dissents. His verdict in the case is a Scottish one, "Not proven." Who shall decide when the doctors disagree? Let everyone choose for himself. As for me, I am inclined to agree with Fiske.

If it were not Vespucci, it certainly was Columbus on his third voyage (1498-1500). On this voyage, the chief of the navigators struck the South American shore off the mouth of the Orinoco and sailed westward along it for a short distance before turning to the northward. There he found so many pearls that he called it the "Pearl Coast." It is interesting to note that, however the question may be decided, all the honours go to Italy. Columbus was a Genoese. Cabot, although born in Genoa, had lived many years in Venice and had been made a citizen there; while Vespucci was a Florentine.

The first important expedition along the northern coast of South America was that of Ojeda in 1499-1500, in company with Juan de la Cosa, next to Columbus the most expert navigator and pilot of the age, and Vespucci, perhaps his equal in nautical science as he was his superior in other departments of polite learning. There were several other explorations of the Gulf coast, and its continuations on every side, during the same year, by one of the Pizons, who had accompanied Columbus on his first voyage; by Lepe; by Cabral, a Portuguese, and by Bastidas and La Cosa, who went for the first time as far to the westward as Porto Rico on the Isthmus of Darien.

On the fourth and last voyage of Columbus, he reached Honduras and thence sailed eastward and southward to the Gulf of Darien, having not the least idea that the shore line which he called Veragua was in fact the border of the famous Isthmus of Panama. There were a number of other voyages, including a further exploration by La Cosa and Vespucci, and a second by Ojeda in which an abortive attempt was made to found a colony; but most of the voyages were mere trading expeditions, slave-hunting enterprises or searches, generally fruitless, for gold and pearls. Ojeda reported after one of these voyages that the English were on the coast. Who these English were is unknown. The news, however, was sufficiently disquieting to Ferdinand, the Catholic—and also the Crafty!—who now ruled alone in Spain, and he determined to frustrate any possible English movement by planting colonies on the Spanish Main.

2. The Don Quixote of Discoveries and His Rival

Instantly two claimants for the honour of leading such an expedition presented themselves. The first Alonzo de Ojeda, the other Diego de Nicuesa. Two more extraordinary characters never went knight-erranting upon the seas. Ojeda was one of the prodigious men of a time which was fertile in notable characters. Although small in stature, he was a man of phenomenal strength and vigour. He could stand at the foot of the Giralda in Seville and throw an orange over it, a distance of two hundred and fifty feet from the earth![1]

Wishing to show his contempt for danger, on one occasion he ran out on a narrow beam projecting some twenty feet from the top of the same tower and there, in full view of Queen Isabella and her court, performed various gymnastic exercises, such as standing on one leg, *et cetera*, for the edification of the spectators, returning calmly and composedly to the tower when he had finished the exhibition.

He was a magnificent horseman, an accomplished knight and an able soldier. There was no limit to his daring. He went with Columbus on his second voyage, and, single-handed, effected the capture of a powerful Indian *cacique* named Caonabo, by a mixture of adroitness, audacity and courage.

Professing amity, he got access to the Indian, and, exhibiting some polished manacles, which he declared were badges of royalty, he offered to put them on the fierce but unsophisticated savage and then mount the chief on his own horse to show him off like a Spanish monarch to his subjects. The daring programme was carried out just exactly as it had been planned. When Ojeda had got the forest king safely fettered and mounted on his horse, he sprang up behind him, held him there firmly in spite of his efforts, and galloped off to Columbus with his astonished and disgusted captive.

Neither of the voyages was successful. With all of his personal prowess, he was an unsuccessful administrator. He was poor, not to say penniless. He had two powerful friends, however. One was Bishop Fonseca, who was charged with the administration of affairs in the Indies, and the other was stout old Juan de la Cosa. These two men made a very efficient combination at the Spanish court, especially as La Cosa had some money and was quite willing to put it up, a prime requisite for the mercenary and niggardly Ferdinand's favour.

The other claimant for the honour of leading the colony happened

1. At least, the assertion is gravely made by the ancient chroniclers. I wonder what kind of an outfielder he would have made today.

"Ojeda Galloped Off with His Astonished Captive"

"The Indians Poured a Rain of Poisoned Arrows"

to be another man small in stature, but also of great bodily strength, although he scarcely equalled his rival in that particular. Nicuesa had made a successful voyage to the Indies with Ovando, and had ample command of means. He was a gentleman by birth and station—Ojeda was that also—and was grand carver-in-chief to the King's uncle! Among his other qualities for successful colonization were a beautiful voice, a masterly touch on the guitar and an exquisite skill in equitation. He had even taught his horse to keep time to music. Whether or not he played that music himself on the back of the performing steed is not recorded.

Ferdinand was unable to decide between the rival claimants. Finally he determined to send out two expeditions. The Gulf of Uraba, now called the Gulf of Darien, was to be the dividing line between the two allotments of territory. Ojeda was to have that portion extending from the Gulf to the Cape de la Vela, which is just west of the Gulf of Venezuela. This territory was named new Andalusia. Nicuesa was to take that between the Gulf and the Cape Gracias á Dios off Honduras. This section was denominated Golden Castile. Each governor was to fit out his expedition at his own charges. Jamaica was given to both in common as a point of departure and a base of supplies.

The resources of Ojeda were small, but when he arrived at Santo Domingo with what he had been able to secure in the way of ships and men, he succeeded in inducing a lawyer named Encisco, commonly called the Bachelor[2] Encisco, to embark his fortune of several thousand gold *castellanos*, which he had gained in successful pleadings in the court in the litigious West Indies, in the enterprise. In it he was given a high position, something like that of District Judge.

With this re-enforcement, Ojeda and La Cosa equipped two small ships and two *brigantines* containing three hundred men and twelve horses.[3]

They were greatly chagrined when the imposing *armada* of Nicuesa, comprising four ships of different sizes, but much larger than any of Ojeda's, and two *brigantines* carrying seven hundred and fifty men, sailed into the harbour of Santo Domingo.

The two governors immediately began to quarrel. Ojeda finally

2. From the Spanish word *bachiller*, referring to an inferior degree in the legal profession.
3. In the absence of particular information, I suppose the ships to be small *caravels* of between fifty and sixty tons, and the *brigantines* much smaller, open, flat-bottomed boats with but one mast—although a modern *brigantine* is a two-masted vessel.

challenged Nicuesa to a duel which should determine the whole affair. Nicuesa, who had everything to lose and nothing to gain by fighting, but who could not well decline the challenge, said that he was willing to fight him if Ojeda would put up what would popularly be known today in the pugilistic circles as "a side bet" of five thousand *castellanos* to make the fight worthwhile.[4]

Poor Ojeda could not raise another *maravedi*, and as nobody would stake him, the duel was off. Diego Columbus, governor of Hispaniola, also interfered in the game to a certain extent by declaring that the Island of Jamaica was his, and that he would not allow anybody to make use of it. He sent there one Juan de Esquivel, with a party of men to take possession of it. Whereupon Ojeda stoutly declared that when he had time he would stop at that island and if Esquivel were there, he would cut off his head.

Finally on the 10th of November, 1509, Ojeda set sail, leaving Encisco to bring after him another ship with needed supplies. With Ojeda was Francisco Pizarro, a middle-aged soldier of fortune, who had not hitherto distinguished himself in any way. Hernando Cortez was to have gone along also, but fortunately for him, an inflammation of the knee kept him at home. Ojeda was in such a hurry to get to El Dorado—for it was in the territory to the southward of his allotment, that the mysterious city was supposed to be located—that he did not stop at Jamaica to take off Esquivel's head—a good thing for him, as it subsequently turned out.

Nicuesa would have followed Ojeda immediately, but his prodigal generosity had exhausted even his large resources, and he was detained by clamorous creditors, the law of the island being that no one could leave it in debt. The gallant little meat-carver laboured with success to settle various suits pending, and thought he had everything compounded; but just as he was about to sail he was arrested for another debt of five hundred *ducats*. A friend at last advanced the money for him and he got away ten days after Ojeda. It would have been a good thing if no friend had ever interfered and he had been detained indefinitely at Hispaniola.

3. THE ADVENTURES OF OJEDA

Ojeda made a landfall at what is known now as Cartagena. It was not a particularly good place for a settlement. There was no reason on

---

4. The *castellano* was valued at two dollars and fifty-six cents, but the purchasing power of that sum was much greater then than now. The *maravedi* was the equivalent of about one-third of a cent.

earth why they should stay there at all. La Cosa, who had been along the coast several times and knew it thoroughly, warned his youthful captain—to whom he was blindly and devotedly attached, by the way—that the place was extremely dangerous; that the inhabitants were fierce, brave and warlike, and that they had a weapon almost as effectual as the Spanish guns. That was the poisoned arrow. Ojeda thought he knew everything and he turned a deaf ear to all remonstrances. He hoped he might chance upon an opportunity of surprising an Indian village and capturing a lot of inoffensive inhabitants for slaves, already a very profitable part of voyaging to the Indies.

He landed without much difficulty, assembled the natives and read to them a perfectly absurd manifesto, which had been prepared in Spain for use in similar contingencies, summoning them to change their religion and to acknowledge the supremacy of Spain. Not one word of this did the natives understand and to it they responded with a volley of poisoned arrows. The Spanish considered this paper a most valuable document, and always went through the formality of having the publication of it attested by a notary public.

Ojeda seized some seventy-five captives, male and female, as slaves. They were sent on board the ships. The Indian warriors, infuriated beyond measure, now attacked in earnest the shore party, comprising seventy men, among whom were Ojeda and La Cosa. The latter, unable to prevent him, had considered it proper to go ashore with the hot-headed governor to restrain him so far as was possible. Ojeda impetuously attacked the Indians and, with part of his men, pursued them several miles inland to their town, of which he took possession.

The savages, in constantly increasing numbers, clustered around the town and attacked the Spaniards with terrible persistence. Ojeda and his followers took refuge in huts and enclosures and fought valiantly. Finally all were killed, or fatally wounded by the envenomed darts except Ojeda himself and a few men, who retreated to a small palisaded enclosure. Into this improvised fort the Indians poured a rain of poisoned arrows which soon struck down every one but the governor himself. Being small of stature and extremely agile, and being provided with a large target or shield, he was able successfully to fend off the deadly arrows from his person. It was only a question of time before the Indians would get him and he would die in the frightful agony which his men experienced after being infected with the poison upon the arrow-points. In his extremity, he was rescued by La Cosa who had kept in hand a moiety of the shore party.

The advent of La Cosa saved Ojeda. Infuriated at the slaughter of his men, Ojeda rashly and intemperately threw himself upon the savages, at once disappearing from the view of La Cosa and his men, who were soon surrounded and engaged in a desperate battle on their own account. They, too, took refuge in the building, from which they were forced to tear away the thatched roof that might have shielded them from the poisoned arrows, in fear lest the Indians might set it on fire. And they in turn were also reduced to the direst of straits. One after another was killed, and finally La Cosa himself, who had been desperately wounded before, received a mortal hurt; while but one man remained on his feet.

Possibly thinking that they had killed the whole party, and withdrawing to turn their attention to Ojeda, furiously ranging the forest alone, the Indians left the two surviving Spaniards unmolested, whereupon the dying La Cosa bade his comrade leave him, and if possible get word to Ojeda of the fate which had overtaken him. This man succeeded in getting back to the shore and apprised the men there of the frightful disaster.

The ships cruised along the shore, sending parties into the bay at different points looking for Ojeda and any others who might have survived. A day or two after the battle they came across their unfortunate commander. He was lying on his back in a grove of mangroves, upheld from the water by the gnarled and twisted roots of one of the huge trees. He had his naked sword in his hand and his target on his arm, but he was completely prostrated and speechless. The men took him to a fire, revived him and finally brought him back to the ship.

Marvellous to relate, he had not a single wound upon him!

Great was the grief of the little squadron at this dolorous state of affairs. In the middle of it, the ships of Nicuesa hove in sight. Mindful of their previous quarrels, Ojeda decided to stay ashore until he found out what were Nicuesa's intentions toward him. Cautiously his men broke the news to Nicuesa. With magnanimity and courtesy delightful to contemplate, he at once declared that he had forgotten the quarrel and offered every assistance to Ojeda to enable him to avenge himself. Ojeda thereupon rejoined the squadron, and the two rivals embraced with many protestations of friendship amid the acclaim of their followers.

The next night, four hundred men were secretly assembled. They landed and marched to the Indian town, surrounded it and put it to the flames. The defenders fought with their usual resolution, and many of the Spaniards were killed by the poisonous arrows, but to no avail. The Indians were doomed, and the whole village perished then and there.

Nicuesa had landed some of his horses, and such was the terror inspired by those remarkable and unknown animals that several of the women who had escaped from the fire, when they caught sight of the frightful monsters, rushed back into the flames, preferring this horrible death rather than to meet the horses. The value of the plunder amounted to eighteen thousand dollars in modern money, the most of which Nicuesa took.

The two adventurers separated, Nicuesa bidding Ojeda farewell and striking boldly across the Caribbean for Veragua, which was the name Columbus had given to the Isthmian coast below Honduras; while Ojeda crept along the shore seeking a convenient spot to plant his colony. Finally he established himself at a place which he named San Sebastian. One of his ships was wrecked and many of his men were lost. Another was sent back to Santo Domingo with what little treasure they had gathered and with an appeal to Encisco to hurry up.

They made a rude fort on the shore, from which to prosecute their search for gold and slaves. The Indians, who also belonged to the poisoned-arrow fraternity, kept the fort in constant anxiety. Many were the conflicts between the Spaniards and the savages, and terrible were the losses inflicted by the invaders; but there seemed to be no limit to the number of Indians, while every Spaniard killed was a serious drain upon the little party. Man after man succumbed to the effects of the dreadful poison. Ojeda, who never spared himself in any way, never received a wound.

From their constant fighting, the savages got to recognize him as the leader and they used all their skill to compass destruction. Finally, they succeeded in decoying him into an ambush where four of their best men had been posted. Recklessly exposing themselves, the Indians at close range opened fire upon their prisoner with arrows. Three of the arrows he caught on his buckler, but the fourth pierced his thigh. It is surmised that Ojeda attended to the four Indians before taking cognizance of his wound. The arrow, of course, was poisoned, and unless something could be done, it meant death.

He resorted to a truly heroic expedient. He caused two iron plates to be heated white-hot and then directed the surgeon to apply the plates to the wound, one at the entrance and the other at the exit of the arrow. The surgeon, appalled by the idea of such torture, refused to do so, and it was not until Ojeda threatened to hang him with his own hands that he consented. Ojeda bore the frightful agony without a murmur or a quiver, such was his extraordinary endurance. It was the custom in that day to bind patients who were operated upon surgically, that their involuntary movements might not disconcert the doctors and cause them to wound where they hoped to cure. Ojeda refused even to be bound. The remedy was efficacious, although the heat of the iron, in the language of the ancient chronicler, so entered his system that they used a barrel of vinegar to cool him off.

Ojeda was very much dejected by the fact that he had been wounded. It seemed to him that the Virgin, his patron, had deserted him. The little band, by this time reduced to less than one hundred people, was in desperate straits. Starvation stared it in the face when fortunately assistance came. One Bernardino de Talavera, with seventy congenial cut-throats, absconding debtors and escaped criminals, from Hispaniola, had seized a Genoese trading-ship loaded with provisions and had luckily reached San Sebastian in her. They sold these provisions to Ojeda and his men at exorbitant prices, for some of the hard-earned treasure which they had amassed with their great expenditure of life and health.

There was no place else for Talavera and his gang to go, so they stayed at San Sebastian. The supply of provisions was soon exhausted, and finally it was evident that, as Encisco had not appeared with any re-enforcements or supplies, someone must go back to Hispaniola to bring rescue to the party. Ojeda offered to do this himself. Giving the charge of affairs at San Sebastian to Francisco Pizarro, who promised to remain there for fifty days for the expected help, he embarked with Talavera.

Naturally Ojeda considered himself in charge of the ship; naturally Talavera did not. Ojeda, endeavouring to direct things, was seized and put in chains by the crew. He promptly challenged the whole crew to a duel, offering to fight them two at a time in succession until he had gone through the ship, of which he expected thereby to become the master; although what he would have done with seventy dead pirates on the ship is hard to see. The men refused this wager of battle, but fortune favoured this doughty little cavalier, for presently a great storm arose. As neither Talavera nor any of the men were navigators or seamen, they had to release Ojeda. He took charge. Once he was in charge, they never succeeded in ousting him.

In spite of his seamanship, the caravel was wrecked on the island of Cuba. They were forced to make their way along the shore, which was then unsettled by Spain. Under the leadership of Ojeda the party struggled eastward under conditions of extreme hardship. When they were most desperate, Ojeda, who had appealed daily to his little picture of the Virgin, which he always carried with him, and had not ceased to urge the others to do likewise, made a vow to establish a shrine and leave the picture at the first Indian village they came to if they got succour there.

Sure enough, they did reach a place called Cueyabos, where they were hospitably received by the Indians, and where Ojeda, fulfilling his vow, erected a log hut, or shrine, in the recess of which he left, with much regret, the picture of the Virgin which had accompanied him on his wanderings and adventures. Means were found to send word to Jamaica, still under the governorship of Esquivel, whose head Ojeda had threatened to cut off when he met him. Magnanimously forgetting the purpose of the broken adventurer, Esquivel despatched a ship to bring him to Jamaica. We may be perfectly sure that Ojeda said nothing about the decapitation when the generous hearted Esquivel received him with open arms. Ojeda with Talavera and his comrades were sent back to Santo Domingo. There Talavera and the principal men of his crew were tried for piracy and executed.

Ojeda found that Encisco had gone. He was penniless, discredited and thoroughly downcast by his ill fortune. No one would advance him anything to send succour to San Sebastian. His indomitable spirit was at last broken by his misfortunes. He lingered for a short time in constantly increasing ill health, being taken care of by the good Franciscans, until he died in the monastery. Some authorities say he became a monk, others deny it; it certainly is quite possible. At any rate, before he died he put on the habit of the order, and after his death, by his own direction, his body was buried before the gate, so that those who passed through it would have to step over his remains. Such was the tardy humility with which he endeavoured to make up for the arrogance and pride of his exciting life.

4. Enter One Vasco Nuñez de Balboa

Encisco, coasting along the shore with a large ship, carrying re-enforcements and loaded with provisions for the party, easily followed the course of Ojeda's wanderings, and finally ran across the final remnants of his expedition in the harbour of Cartagena. The remnant was crowded into a single small, unseaworthy brigantine under the command of Francisco Pizarro.

Pizarro had scrupulously kept faith with Ojeda. He had done more. He had waited fifty days, and then, finding that the two brigantines left to him were not large enough to contain his whole party, by mutual agreement of the survivors clung to the death-laden spot until a sufficient number had been killed or had died to enable them to get away in the two ships. They did not have to wait long, for death was busy, and a few weeks after the expiration of the appointed time they were all on board.

There is something terrific to the imagination in the thought of that body of men sitting down and grimly waiting until enough of them should die to enable the rest to get away! What must have been the emotions that filled their breasts as the days dragged on? No one knew whether the result of the delay would enable him to leave, or cause his bones to rot on the shore. Cruel, fierce, implacable as were these Spaniards, there is something Homeric about them in such crises as these.

That was not the end of their misfortunes, for one of the two brigantines was capsized. The old chroniclers say that the boat was struck by a great fish. That is a fish story, which, like most fish stories, it is difficult to credit. At any rate, sink it did, with all on board, and Pizarro and about thirty men were all that were left of the gallant three hundred who had followed the doughty Ojeda in the first attempt to colonize South America.

Encisco was for hanging them at once, believing that they had murdered and deserted Ojeda, but they were able to convince him at last of the strict legality of their proceedings. Taking command of the expedition himself, as being next in rank to Ojeda, the Bachelor led them back to San Sebastian. Unfortunately, before the unloading of his ship could be begun, she struck a rock and was lost; and the last state of the men, therefore, was as bad as the first.

Among the men who had come with Encisco was a certain Vasco Nuñez, commonly called Balboa. He had been with Bastidas and La Cosa on their voyage to the Isthmus nine years before. The voyage had been a profitable one and Balboa had made money out of it. He had lost all his money, however, and had eked out a scanty living on a farm at Hispaniola, which he had been unable to leave because he was in debt to everybody. The authorities were very strict in searching every vessel that cleared from Santo Domingo, for absconders. The search was usually conducted after the vessel had got to sea, too!

Balboa caused himself to be conveyed aboard the ship in a provision cask. No one suspected anything, and when the officers of the boat had withdrawn from the ship and Hispaniola was well down astern, he came forth. Encisco, who was a pettifogger of the most pronounced type, would have dealt harshly with him, but there was nothing to do after all. Balboa could not be sent back, and besides, he was considered a very valuable re-enforcement on account of his known experience and courage.

It was he who now came to the rescue of the wretched colonists at San Sebastian by telling them that across the Gulf of Darien there was an Indian tribe with many villages and much gold. Furthermore, these Indians, unfortunately for them, were not acquainted with the use of poisoned arrows. Balboa urged them to go there. His suggestion was received with cheers. The *brigantines*, and such other vessels as they could construct quickly, were got ready and the whole party took advantage of the favourable season to cross the Gulf of Darien to the other side, to the present territory of Panama which has been so prominent in the public eye of late. This was Nicuesa's domain, but nobody considered that at the time.

They found the Indian villages which Balboa had mentioned, fought a desperate battle with Cacique Cemaco, captured the place, and discovered quantities of gold *castellanos* (upward of twenty-five thousand dollars). They built a fort, and laid out a town called Maria de la Antigua del Darien—the name being almost bigger than the town! Balboa was in high favour by this time, and when Encisco got into trouble by decreeing various oppressive regulations and vexatious restrictions, attending to things in general with a high hand, they calmly deposed him on the ground that he had no authority to act, since they were on the territory of Nicuesa. To this logic, which was irrefutable, poor Encisco could make no reply. Pending the arrival of Nicuesa they elected Balboa and one Zamudio, a Biscayan, to take charge of affairs.

The time passed in hunting and gathering treasure, not unprofitably and, as they had plenty to eat, not unpleasantly.

5 The Desperate Straits of Nicuesa

Now let us return to Nicuesa. Making a landfall, Nicuesa, with a small *caravel*, attended by the two *brigantines*, coasted along the shore seeking a favourable point for settlement. The large ships, by his orders, kept well out to sea. During a storm, Nicuesa put out to sea himself, imagining that the *brigantines* under the charge of Lope de Olano, second in command would follow him. When morning broke and the storm disappeared there were no signs of the ships or *brigantines*.

Nicuesa ran along the shore to search for them, got himself embayed in the mouth of a small river, swollen by recent rains, and upon the sudden subsidence of the water coincident with the ebb of the tide, his ship took ground, fell over on her bilge and was completely wrecked. The men on board barely escaped with their lives to the shore. They had saved nothing except what they wore, the few arms they carried and one small boat.

Putting Diego de Ribero and three sailors in the boat and directing them to coast along the shore, Nicuesa with the rest struggled westward in search of the two *brigantines* and the other three ships. They toiled through interminable forests and morasses for several days, living on what they could pick up in the way of roots and grasses, without discovering any signs of the missing vessels. Coming to an arm of the sea, supposed to be Chiriqui Lagoon off Costa Rica, in the course of their journeyings, they decided to cross it in a small boat rather than make the long detour necessary to get to what they believed to be the other side. They were ferried over to the opposite shore in the boat, and to their dismay discovered that they were upon an almost desert island.

It was too late and they were too tired, to go farther that night, so they resolved to pass the night on the island. In the morning they were appalled to find that the little boat, with Ribero and the three sailors, was gone. They were marooned on a desert island with practically nothing to eat and nothing but brackish swamp water to drink. The sailors they believed to have abandoned them. They gave way to transports of despair. Some in their grief threw themselves down and died forthwith. Others sought to prolong life by eating herbs, roots and the like.

They were reduced to the condition of wild animals, when a sail whitened the horizon, and presently the two brigantines dropped anchor near the island. Ribero was no recreant. He had been convinced that Nicuesa was going farther and farther from the ships with every step that he took, and, unable to persuade him of that fact, he deliberately took matters into his own hands and retraced his course. The event justified his decision, for he soon found the *brigantines* and the other ships. Olano does not seem to have bestirred himself very vigorously to seek for Nicuesa, perhaps because he hoped to command himself; but when Ribero made his report he at once made for the island, which he reached just in time to save the miserable remnant from dying of starvation.

As soon as he could command himself, Nicuesa, whose easy temper and generous disposition had left him under the hardships and misfortunes he had sustained, sentenced Olano to death. By the pleas of his comrades, the sentence was mitigated, and the wretched man was bound in chains and forced to grind corn for the rest of the party—when there was any to grind.

To follow Nicuesa's career further would be simply to chronicle the story of increasing disaster. He lost ship after ship and man after man. Finally reduced in number to one hundred men, one of the sailors, which had been with Columbus remembered the location of Porto Rico as being a haven where they might establish themselves in a fertile and beautiful country, well-watered and healthy. Columbus had left an anchor under the tree to mark the place, and when they reached it they found that the anchor had remained undisturbed all the years. They were attacked by the Indians there, and after losing twenty killed, were forced to put to sea in two small *brigantines* and a *caravel*, which they had made from the wrecks of their ships. Coasting along the shore, they came at last to an open roadstead where they could debark.

"In the name of God," said the disheartened Nicuesa, "let us stop here."

There they landed, called the place after their leader's exclamation, Nombre de Dios. The caravel, with a crew of the strongest, was despatched for succour, and was never heard of again.

One day, the colonists of Antigua were surprised by the sound of a cannon shot. They fired their own weapons in reply, and soon two ships carrying re-enforcements for Nicuesa under Rodrigo de Colmenares, dropped anchor in front of the town.

By this time the colonists had divided into factions, some favouring the existing *régime*, others inclining toward the still busy Encisco, others desirous of putting themselves under the command of Nicuesa, whose generosity and sunny disposition were still affectionately remembered. The arrival of Colmenares and his party, gave the Nicuesa faction a decided preponderance; and, taking things in their own hands, they determined to despatch one of the ships, with two representatives of the colony, up the coast in search of the governor. This expedition found Nicuesa without much difficulty. Again the rescuing ship arrived just in time. In a few days more, the miserable body of men, reduced now to less than sixty, would have perished of starvation.

Nicuesa's spirit had not been chastened by his unparalleled misfortunes. He not only accepted the proffered command of the colony—which was no more than his right, since it was established on his own territory—but he did more. When he heard that the colonists had amassed a great amount of gold by trading and thieving, he harshly declared that, as they had no legitimate right there, he would take their portion for himself; that he would stop further enterprises on their part—in short, he boastfully declared his intention of carrying things with a high hand in a way well calculated to infuriate his voluntary subjects. So arrogant was his bearing and so tactless and injudicious his talk, that the envoys from Antigua fled in the night with one of the ships and reported the situation to the colony. Olano, still in chains, found means to communicate with his friends in the other party. Naturally he painted the probable conduct of the governor in anything but flattering colours.

All this was most impolitic in Nicuesa. He seemed to have forgotten that profound political principle which suggests that a firm seat in the saddle should be acquired before any attempts should be made to lead the procession. The fable of *King Stork and the Frogs* was applicable to the situation of the colonists.

In this contingency they did not know quite what to do. It was Balboa who came to their rescue again. He suggested that, although they had invited him, they need not permit Nicuesa to land. Accordingly, when Nicuesa hove in sight in the other ship, full of determination to carry things in his own way, they prevented him from coming ashore.

Greatly astonished, he modified his tone somewhat, but to no avail. It was finally decided among the colonists to allow him to land in order to seize his person. Arrangements were made accordingly, and the unsuspicious Nicuesa debarked from his ship the day after his arrival. He was immediately surrounded by a crowd of excited soldiers menacing and threatening him. It was impossible for him to make headway against them.

He turned and fled. Among his other gubernatorial accomplishments was a remarkable fleetness of foot. The poor little governor scampered over the sands at a great pace. He distanced his fierce pursuers at last and escaped to the temporary shelter of the woods.

Balboa, a gentleman by birth and by inclination as well—who had, according to some accounts, endeavoured to compose the differences between Nicuesa and the colonists—was greatly touched and mortified at seeing so brave a cavalier reduced to such an undignified and desperate extremity. He secretly sought Nicuesa that night and proffered him his services. Then he strove valiantly to bring about an adjustment between the fugitive and the brutal soldiery, but in vain.

Nicuesa, abandoning all his pretensions, at last begged them to receive him, if not as a governor, at least as a companion-at-arms, a volunteer. But nothing, neither the influence of Balboa nor the entreaties of Nicuesa, could mitigate the anger of the colonists. They would not have the little governor with them on any terms. They would have killed him then and there, but Balboa, by resorting to harsh measures, even causing one man to be flogged for his insolence, at last changed that purpose into another—which, to be sure, was scarcely less hazardous for Nicuesa.

He was to be given a ship and sent away forever from the Isthmus. Seventeen adherents offered manfully to share his fate. Protesting against the legality of the action, appealing to them to give him a chance for humanity's sake, poor Nicuesa was hurried aboard a small, crazy bark, the weakest of the wretched *brigantines* in the harbour. This was a boat so carelessly constructed that the calking of the seams had been done with a blunt iron. With little or no provisions, Nicuesa and his faithful seventeen were forced to put to sea amid the jeers and mockery of the men on shore. The date was March 1, 1511. According to the chroniclers, the last words that those left on the island heard Nicuesa say were, "*Show thy face, O Lord, and we shall be saved.*" [5]

A pathetic and noble departure!

Into the misty deep then vanished poor Nicuesa and his faithful followers on that bright sunny spring morning. And none of them ever came back to tell the tale of what became of them. Did they die of starvation in their crazy *brigantine*, drifting on and on while they rotted in the blazing sun, until her seams opened and she sank? Did they founder in one of the sudden and fierce storms which sometimes swept that coast? Did the deadly *teredo* bore the ship's timbers full of holes, until she went down with all on board? Were they cast on shore to become the prey of Indians whose enmity they had provoked by

---

5. Evidently he was quoting the exquisite measures of the Eightieth Psalm, one of the most touching appeals of David the Poet-King, in which he says over and over again, "*Turn us again, O God, and cause Thy Face to shine, and we shall be saved.*"

their own conduct? No one ever knew.

It was reported that years afterward on the coast of Veragua some wandering adventurers found this legend, almost undecipherable, cut in the bark of a tree, "*Aqui anduvo el desdichado Diego de Nicuesa*," which may be translated, "Here was lost the unfortunate Diego de Nicuesa." But the statement is not credited. The fate of the gallant little gentleman is one of the mysteries of the sea.

Of the original eleven hundred men who sailed with the two governors there remained perhaps thirty of Ojeda's and forty of Nicuesa's at Antigua with Encisco's command. This was the net result of the first two years of effort at the beginning of government in South America on the Isthmus of Panama, with its ocean on the other side still undreamed of. What these men did there, and how Balboa rose to further prominence, his great exploits, and finally how unkind Fate also overtook him, will form the subject of the next paper.

2

Panama, Balboa and a Forgotten Romance

1. THE COMING OF THE DEVASTATOR

This is the romantic history of Vasco Nuñez de Balboa, the most knightly and gentle of the Spanish discoverers, and one who would fain have been true to the humble Indian girl who had won his heart, even though his life and liberty were at stake. It is almost the only love story in early Spanish-American history, and the account of it, veracious though it is, reads like a novel or a play.

After Diego de Nicuesa had sailed away from Antigua on that enforced voyage from which he never returned, Vasco Nuñez de Balboa was supreme on the Isthmus. Encisco, however, remained to make trouble. In order to secure internal peace before prosecuting some further expeditions, Balboa determined to send him back to Spain, as the easiest way of getting rid of his importunities and complaints.

A more truculent commander would have no difficulty in inventing a pretext for taking off his head. A more prudent captain would have realized that Encisco with his trained mouth could do very much more harm to him in Spain than he could in Darien. Balboa thought to nullify that possibility, however, by sending Valdivia, with a present, to Hispaniola, and Zamudio with the Bachelor to Spain to lay the state of affairs before the King. Encisco was a much better advocate than Balboa's friend Zamudio, and the King of Spain credited the one and disbelieved the other. He determined to appoint a new governor for the Isthmus, and decided that Balboa should be proceeded against rigorously for nearly all the crimes in the Decalogue, the most serious accusation being that to him was due the death of poor Nicuesa. For by this time everybody was sure that the poor little meat-carver was no more.

An enterprise against the French which had been declared off filled Spain with needy cavaliers who had started out for an adventure and were greatly desirous of having one. Encisco and Zamudio had both enflamed the minds of the Spanish people with fabulous stories of the riches of Darien. It was curiously believed that gold was so plentiful that it could be fished up in nets from the rivers. Such a piscatorial prospect was enough to unlock the coffers of a prince as selfish as Ferdinand. He was willing to risk fifty thousand *ducats* in the adventure, which was to be conducted on a grand scale. No such expedition to America had ever been prepared before as that destined for Darien.

Among the many claimants for its command, he picked out an old cavalier named Pedro Arias de Avila, called by the Spaniards Pedrarias.[1]

This Pedrarias was seventy-two years old. He was of good birth and rich, and was the father of a large and interesting family, which he prudently left behind him in Spain. His wife, however, insisted on going with him to the New World. Whether or not this was a proof of wifely devotion—and if it was, it is the only thing in history to his credit—or of an unwillingness to trust Pedrarias out of her sight, which is more likely, is not known. At any rate, she went along.

Pedrarias, up to the time of his departure from Spain, had enjoyed two nick-names, El Galan and El Justador. He had been a bold and dashing cavalier in his youth, a famous tilter in tournaments in his middle age, and a hard-fighting soldier all his life. His patron was Bishop Fonseca. Whatever qualities he might possess for the important work about to be devolved upon him would be developed later.

His expedition included from fifteen hundred to two thousand souls, and there were at least as many more who wanted to go and could not for lack of accommodations. The number of ships varies in different accounts from nineteen to twenty-five. The appointments both of the general expedition and the cavaliers themselves were magnificent in the extreme. Many afterward distinguished in America went in Pedrarias's command, chief among them being De Soto. Among others were Quevedo, the newly appointed Bishop of Darien, and Espinosa, the judge.

---

1. In the English chronicles he is often spoken of as Davila, which is near enough to *Diabolo* to make one wish that the latter *sobriquet* had been his own. It would have been much more apposite.

The first fleet set sail on the 11th of April, 1514, and arrived at Antigua without mishap on the 29th of June in the same year. The colony at that place, which had been regularly laid out as a town with fortifications and with some degree at least of European comfort, numbered some three hundred hard-bitten soldiers. The principle of the survival of the fittest had resulted in the selection of the best men from all the previous expeditions. They would have been a dangerous body to antagonize. Pedrarias was in some doubt as to how Balboa would receive him. He dissembled his intentions toward him, therefore, and sent an officer ashore to announce the meaning of the flotilla which whitened the waters of the bay.

The officer found Balboa, dressed in a suit of *pajamas* engaged in superintending the roofing of a house. The officer, brilliant in silk and satin and polished armour, was astonished at the simplicity of Vasco Nuñez's appearance. He courteously delivered his message, however, to the effect that yonder was the fleet of Don Pedro Arias de Avila, the new Governor of Darien.

Balboa calmly bade the messenger tell Pedrarias that he could come ashore in safety and that he was very welcome. Balboa was something of a dissembler himself on occasion, as you will see. Pedrarias thereupon debarked in great state with his men, and, as soon as he firmly got himself established on shore, arrested Balboa and presented him for trial before Espinosa for the death of Nicuesa.

2. The Greatest Exploit since Columbus's Voyage

During all this long interval, Balboa had not been idle. A singular change had taken place in his character. He had entered upon the adventure in his famous barrel on Encisco's ship as a reckless, improvident, roisterous, careless, hare-brained scapegrace. Responsibility and opportunity had sobered and elevated him. While he had lost none of his dash and daring and brilliancy, yet he had become a wise, a prudent and a most successful captain. Judged by the high standard of the modern times, Balboa was cruel and ruthless enough to merit our severe condemnation. Judged by his environments and contrasted with any other of the Spanish conquistadores he was an angel of light.

He seems to have remained always a generous, affectionate, openhearted soldier. He had conducted a number of expeditions after the departure of Nicuesa to different parts of the Isthmus, and he amassed much treasure thereby, but he always so managed affairs that he left the Indian chiefs in possession of their territory and firmly attached

"BALBOA. ENGAGED IN SUPERINTENDING THE ROOFING
OF A HOUSE"

"THE EXPEDITION HAD TO FIGHT ITS WAY THROUGH
TRIBES OF WARLIKE AND FEROCIOUS MOUNTAINEERS"

to him personally. There was no indiscriminate murder, outrage or plunder in his train, and the Isthmus was fairly peaceable. Balboa had tamed the tempers of the fierce soldiery under him to a remarkable degree, and they had actually descended to cultivating the soil between periods of gold-hunting and pearl-fishing. The men under him were devotedly attached to him as a rule, although here and there a malcontent, unruly soldier, restless under the iron discipline, hated his captain.

Fortunately he had been warned by a letter from Zamudio, who had found means to send it *via* Hispaniola, of the threatening purpose of Pedrarias and the great expedition. Balboa stood well with the authorities in Hispaniola. Diego Columbus had given him a commission as Vice-Governor of Darien, so that as Darien was clearly within Diego Columbus's jurisdiction, Balboa was strictly under authority. The news in Zamudio's letter was very disconcerting. Like every Spaniard, Vasco Nuñez knew that he could expect little mercy and scant justice from a trial conducted under such auspices as Pedrarias's. He determined, therefore, to secure himself in his position by some splendid achievement, which would so work upon the feelings of the King that he would be unable, for very gratitude, to press hard upon him.

The exploit that he meditated and proposed to accomplish was the discovery of the ocean upon the other side of the Isthmus. When Nicuesa came down from Nombre de Dios, he left there a little handful of men. Balboa sent an expedition to rescue them and brought them down to Antigua. Either on that expedition or on another shortly afterward, two white men painted as Indians discovered themselves to Balboa in the forest. They proved to be Spaniards who had fled from Nicuesa to escape punishment for some fault they had committed and had sought safety in the territory of an Indian chief named Careta, the *Cacique* of Cueva. They had been hospitably received and adopted into the tribe. In requital for their entertainment, they offered to betray the Indians if Vasco Nuñez, the new governor, would condone their past offenses. They filled the minds of the Spaniards, alike covetous and hungry, with stories of great treasures and what was equally valuable, abundant provisions, in Careta's village.

Balboa immediately consented. The act of treachery was consummated and the chief captured. All that, of course, was very bad, but the difference between Balboa and the men of his time is seen in his after conduct. Instead of putting the unfortunate chieftain to death and taking his people for slaves, Balboa released him. The reason he released him was because of a woman—a woman who enters vitally into the subsequent history of Vasco Nuñez, and indeed of the whole of South America. This was the beautiful daughter of the chief. Anxious to propitiate his captor, Careta offered Balboa this flower of the family to wife. Balboa saw her, loved her and took her to himself. They were married in accordance with the Indian custom; which, of course, was not considered in the least degree binding by the Spaniards of that time. But it is to Balboa's credit that he remained faithful to this Indian girl. Indeed, if he had not been so much attached to her it is probable that he might have lived to do even greater things than he did.

In his excursions throughout the Isthmus, Balboa had met a chief called Comagre. As everywhere, the first desire of the Spanish was gold. The metal had no commercial value to the Indians. They used it simply to make ornaments, and when it was not taken from them by force, they were cheerfully willing to exchange it for beads, trinkets, hawks' bells, and any other petty trifles. Comagre was the father of a numerous family of stalwart sons. The oldest, observing the Spaniards brawling and fighting—"brabbling," Peter Martyr calls it—about the division of gold, with an astonishing degree of intrepidity knocked over the scales at last and dashed the stuff on the ground in contempt. He made amends for his action by telling them of a country where gold, like Falstaff's reasons, was as plenty as blackberries. Incidentally he gave them the news that Darien was an isthmus, and that the other side was swept by a vaster sea than that which washed its eastern shore.

These tidings inspired Balboa and his men. They talked long and earnestly with the Indians and fully satisfied themselves of the existence of a great sea and of a far-off country abounding in treasure on the other side. Could it be that mysterious Cipango of Marco Polo, search for which had been the object of Columbus's voyage? The way there was discussed and the difficulties of the journey estimated, and it was finally decided that at least one thousand Spaniards would be required safely to cross the Isthmus.

Balboa had sent an account of this conversation to Spain, asking for the one thousand men. The account reached there long before Pedrarias sailed, and to it, in fact, was largely due the extensive expedition. Now when Balboa learned from Zamudio of what was intended toward him in Spain, he determined to undertake the discovery himself. He set forth from Antigua the 1st of September, 1513, with a hundred and ninety chosen men, accompanied by a pack of bloodhounds, very useful in fighting savages, and a train of Indian slaves. Francisco Pizarro was his second in command. All this in lieu of the one thousand Spaniards for which he had asked, which was not thought to be too great a number.

The difficulties to be overcome were almost incredible. The expedition had to fight its way through tribes of warlike and ferocious mountaineers. If it was not to be dogged by a trail of pestilent hatreds, the antagonisms evoked by its advance must be composed in every Indian village or tribe before it progressed farther. Aside from these things, the topographical difficulties were immense. The Spaniards were armour-clad, as usual, and heavily burdened. Their way led through thick and overgrown and pathless jungles or across lofty and broken mountain-ranges, which could be surmounted only after the most exhausting labour. The distance as the crow flies, was short, less than fifty miles, but nearly a month elapsed before they approached the end of their journey.

Balboa's enthusiasm and courage had surmounted every obstacle. He made friends with the chiefs through whose territories he passed, if they were willing to be friends. If they chose to be enemies, he fought them, he conquered them and then made friends with them then. Such a singular mixture of courage, adroitness and statesmanship was he that everywhere he prevailed by one method or another. Finally, in the territory of a chief named Quarequa, he reached the foot of the mountain range from the summit of which his guides advised him that he could see the object of his expedition.

There were but sixty-seven men capable of ascending that mountain. The toil and hardship of the journey had incapacitated the others. Next to Balboa, among the sixty-seven, was Francisco Pizarro. Early on the morning of the 25th of September, 1513, the little company began the ascent of the Sierra. It was still morning when they surmounted it and reached the top. Before them rose a little cone, or crest, which hid the view toward the south. "There," said the guides, "from the top of yon rock, you can see the ocean." Bidding his men halt where they were, Vasco Nuñez went forward alone and surmounted the little elevation.

A magnificent prospect was embraced in his view. The tree-clad mountains sloped gently away from his feet, and on the far horizon glittered a line of silver which attested the accuracy of the claim of the Indians as to the existence of a great sea on the other side of what he knew now to be an isthmus. Balboa named the body of water that he could see far away, flashing in the sunlight of that bright morning, "the Sea of the South," or "the South Sea." [2]

Drawing his sword, he took possession of it in the name of Castile and Leon. Then he summoned his soldiers. Pizarro in the lead they were soon assembled at his side. In silent awe they gazed, as if they were looking upon a vision. Finally someone broke into the words of a chant, and on that peak in Darien those men sang the "*Te Deum Laudamus*."

Somehow the dramatic quality of that supreme moment in the life of Balboa has impressed itself upon the minds of the successive generations that have read of it since that day. It stands as one of the great episodes of history. That little band of ragged, weather-beaten, hard-bitten soldiers, under the leadership of the most lovable and gallant of the Spaniards of his time, on that lonely mountain peak rising above the almost limitless sea of trackless verdure, gazing upon the great ocean whose waters extended before them for thousands and thousands of miles, attracts the attention and fires the imagination.

Your truly great man may disguise his imaginative qualities from the unthinking public eye, but his greatness is in proportion to his imagination. Balboa, with the centuries behind him, shading his eye and staring at the water:

———*Dipt into the future far as human eye could see,*
Saw the visions of the world, and all the wonder that would be.

He saw Peru with its riches; he saw fabled Cathay; he saw the uttermost isles of the distant sea. His imagination took the wings of the morning and soared over worlds and countries that no one but he had ever dreamed of, all to be the fiefs of the King of Castile. It is interesting to note that it must have been to Balboa, of all men, that some adequate idea of the real size of the earth first came.

Well, they gazed their fill; then, with much toil, they cut down trees, dragged them to the top of the mountain and erected a huge cross which they stayed by piles of stones. Then they went down the mountain-side and sought the beach. It was no easy task to find it, either. It was not until some days had passed that one of the several parties broke through the jungle and stood upon the shore. When they were all assembled, the tide was at low ebb. A long space of muddy beach lay between them and the water. They sat down under the trees and waited until the tide was at flood, and then, on the 29th of

---

2. It was Magellan who gave it the inappropriate name of "Pacific."

"He took possession of the sea in the name of
Castile and Leon"

"He threw the sacred volume to the ground in
a violent rage"

September, with a banner displaying the Virgin and Child above the arms of Spain in one hand and withdrawn sword in the other, Balboa marched solemnly into the rolling surf that broke about his waist and took formal possession of the ocean, and all the shores, wheresoever they might be, which were washed by its waters, for Ferdinand of Aragon, and his daughter Joanna of Castile, and their successors in Spain. Truly a prodigious claim, but one which for a time Spain came perilously near establishing and maintaining.[3]

Before they left the shore they found some canoes and voyaged over to a little island in the bay, which they called San Miguel, since it was that saint's day, and where they were nearly all swept away by the rising tide. They went back to Antigua by another route, somewhat less difficult, fighting and making peace as before, and amassing treasure the while. Great was the joy of the colonists who had been left behind, when Balboa and his men rejoined them. Those who had stayed behind shared equally with those who had gone. The King's royal fifth was scrupulously set aside and Balboa at once dispatched a ship, under a trusted adherent named Arbolancha, to acquaint the King with his marvellous discovery, and to bring back re-enforcements and permission to venture upon the great sea in quest of the fabled golden land toward the south.

3. "Furor Domini"

Unfortunately for Vasco Nuñez, Arbolancha arrived just two months after Pedrarias had sailed. The discovery of the Pacific was the greatest single exploit since the voyage of Columbus. It was impossible for the King to proceed further against Balboa under such circumstances. Arbolancha was graciously received, therefore, and after his story had been heard a ship was sent back to Darien instructing Pedrarias to let Balboa alone, appointing him an *adelantado*, or governor of the islands he had discovered in the South Sea, and all such countries as he might discover beyond.

All this, however took time, and Balboa was having a hard time with Pedrarias. In spite of all the skill of the envenomed Enciso, who had been appointed the public prosecutor in Pedrarias's administration, Balboa was at last acquitted of having been concerned in the death of Nicuesa. Pedrarias, furious at the verdict, made living a burden to poor Vasco Nuñez by civil suits which ate up all his property.

---

3. Today not one foot of territory bordering on that sea belongs to Spain. The American flag flies over the Philippines—shall I say forever?

It had not fared well with the expedition of Pedrarias, either, for in six weeks after they landed, over seven hundred of his unacclimated men were dead of fever and other diseases, incident to their lack of precaution and the unhealthy climate of the Isthmus. They had been buried in their brocades, as has been pithily remarked, and forgotten. The condition of the survivors was also precarious. They were starving in their silks and satins.

Pedrarias, however, did not lack courage. He sent the survivors hunting for treasures. Under different captains he dispatched them far and wide through the Isthmus to gather gold, pearls, and food. They turned its pleasant valleys and its noble hills into earthly hells. Murder, outrage and rapine flourished unchecked, even encouraged and rewarded. All the good work of Balboa in pacifying the natives and laying the foundation for a wise and kindly rule was undone in a few months.

Such cruelties had never before been practised in any part of the New World settled by the Spaniards. I do not suppose the men under Pedrarias were any worse than others. Indeed, they were better than some of them, but they took their cue from their terrible commander. Fiske calls him "a two-legged tiger." That he was an old man seems to add to the horror which the story of his course inspires. The recklessness of an unthinking young man may be better understood than the cold, calculating fury and ferocity of threescore and ten. To his previous appellations, a third was added. Men called him, "*Furor Domini*"— "The Scourge of God." Not Attila himself, to whom the title was originally applied, was more ruthless and more terrible.

Balboa remonstrated, but to no avail. He wrote letter after letter to the king, depicting the results of Pedrarias' actions, and some tidings of his successive communications, came trickling back to the governor, who had been especially cautioned by the King to deal mercifully with the inhabitants and set them an example of Christian kindness and gentleness that they might be won to the religion of Jesus thereby! Pedrarias was furious against Balboa, and would have withheld the King's dispatches acknowledging the discovery of the South Sea by appointing him *adelantado*; but the Bishop of Darien, whose friendship Balboa had gained, protested and the dispatches were finally delivered. The good Bishop did more. He brought about a composition of the bitter quarrel between Balboa and Pedrarias. A marriage was arranged between the eldest daughter of Pedrarias and Balboa. Balboa still loved his Indian wife; it is evident that he never intended to marry the

42

daughter of Pedrarias, and that he entered upon the engagement simply to quiet the old man and secure his countenance and assistance for the undertaking he projected to the mysterious golden land toward the south. There was a public betrothal which effected the reconciliation. And now Pedrarias could not do enough for Balboa, whom he called his "dear son."

4. THE END OF BALBOA

Balboa, therefore, proposed to Pedrarias that he should immediately set forth upon the South Sea voyage. Inasmuch as Pedrarias was to be supreme in the New World and as Balboa was only a provincial governor under him, the old reprobate at last consented.

Balboa decided that four ships, *brigantines*, would be needed for his expedition. The only timber fit for shipping, of which the Spaniards were aware, grew on the eastern side of the Isthmus. It would be necessary, therefore, to cut and work up the frames and timbers of the ships on the eastern side, then carry the material across the Isthmus, and there put it together. Vasco Nuñez reconnoitred the ground and decided to start his ship-building operations at a new settlement called Ada. The timber when cut and worked had to be carried sixteen miles away to the top of the mountain, then down the other slope, to a convenient spot on the River Valsa, where the keels were to be laid, the frames put together, the shipbuilding completed, and the boats launched on the river, which was navigable to the sea.

This amazing undertaking was carried out as planned. There were two setbacks before the work was completed. In one case, after the frames had been made and carried with prodigious toil to the other side of the mountain, they were discovered to be full of worms and had to be thrown away. After they had been replaced, and while the men were building the *brigantines*, a flood washed every vestige of their labour into the river. But, as before, nothing could daunt Balboa. Finally, after labours and disappointments enough to crush the heart of an ordinary man, two of the *brigantines* were launched in the river. Most of the carrying had been done by Indians, over two thousand of whom died under the tremendous exactions of the work.

Embarking upon the two *brigantines*, Balboa soon reached the Pacific, where he was presently joined by the two remaining boats as they were completed. He had now four fairly serviceable ships and three hundred of the best men of the New World under his command. He was well equipped and well provisioned for the voyage and lacked only a little iron and a little pitch, which, of course, would have to be brought to him from Ada on the other side of the Isthmus. The lack of that little iron and that little pitch proved the undoing of Vasco Nuñez. If he had been able to obtain them or if he had sailed away without them, he might have been the conqueror of Peru; in which case that unhappy country would have been spared the hideous excesses and the frightful internal brawls and revolutions which afterward almost ruined it under the long rule of the ferocious Pizarros. Balboa would have done better from a military standpoint than his successors, and as a statesman as well as a soldier the results of his policy would have been felt for generations.

History goes on to state that while he was waiting for the pitch and iron, word was brought to him that Pedrarias was to be superseded in his government. This would have been delightful tidings under any other circumstances, but now that a reconciliation had been patched up between him and the governor, he rightly felt that the arrival of a new governor might materially alter the existing state of affairs. Therefore, he determined to send a party of four adherents across the mountains to Ada to find out if the rumours were true.

If Pedrarias was supplanted the messengers were to return immediately, and without further delay they would at once set sail. If Pedrarias was still there, well and good. There would be no occasion for such precipitate action and they could wait for the pitch and iron. He was discussing this matter with some friends on a rainy day in 1517—the month and the date not being determinable now. The sentry attached to the governor's quarters, driven to the shelter of the house by the storm, overheard a part of this harmless conversation. There is nothing so dangerous as a half-truth; it is worse than a whole lie. The soldier who had aforetime felt the weight of Balboa's heavy hand for some dereliction of duty, catching sentences here and there, fancied he detected treachery to Pedrarias and thought he saw an opportunity of revenging himself, and of currying favour with the governor, by reporting it at the first convenient opportunity.

Now, there lived at Ada at the time one Andres Garavito. This man was Balboa's bitter enemy. He had presumed to make dishonourable overtures to Balboa's Indian wife. The woman had indignantly repulsed his advances and had made them known to her husband. Balboa had sternly reproved Garavito and threatened him with death. Garavito had nourished his hatred, and had sought opportunity to injure his former captain. The men sent by Balboa to Ada to find out the state of affairs were very maladroit in their manoeuvres, and their peculiar actions awakened the suspicions of Pedrarias. The first one who entered the town was seized and cast into prison. The others thereupon came openly to Ada and declared their purposes. This seems to have quieted, temporarily, the suspicions of Pedrarias; but the implacable Garavito, taking opportunity, when the governor's mind was unsettled and hesitant, assured him that Balboa had not the slightest intention whatever of marrying Pedrarias's daughter; that he was devoted to his Indian wife, and intended to remain true to her; that it was his purpose to sail to the South Sea, establish a kingdom and make himself independent of Pedrarias.

The old animosity and anger of the governor awoke on the instant. There was no truth in the accusations except in so far as it regarded Vasco Nuñez's attachment to his Indian wife, and indeed Balboa had never given any public refusal to abide by the marital engagement which he had entered into; but there was just enough probability in Garavito's tale to carry conviction to the ferocious tyrant. He instantly determined upon Balboa's death. Detaining his envoys, he sent him a very courteous and affectionate letter, entreating him to come to Ada to receive some further instructions before he set forth on the South Sea.

Among the many friends of Balboa was the notary Arguello who had embarked his fortune in the projected expedition. He prepared a warning to Vasco Nuñez, which unfortunately fell into the hands of Pedrarias and resulted in his being clapped into prison with the rest. Balboa unsuspiciously complied with the governor's request, and, attended by a small escort, immediately set forth for Ada.

He was arrested on the way by a company of soldiers headed by Francisco Pizarro, who had nothing to do with the subsequent transactions, and simply acted under orders, as any other soldier would have done. Balboa was thrown into prison and heavily ironed; he was tried for treason against the King and Pedrarias. The testimony of the soldier who had listened in the rainstorm was brought forward, and, in spite of a noble defense, Balboa was declared guilty.

Espinosa, who was his judge, was so dissatisfied with the verdict, however, that he personally besought Pedrarias to mitigate the sentence. The stern old tyrant refused to interfere, nor would he entertain Balboa's appeal to Spain. "He has sinned," he said tersely; "death to him!" Four of his companions—three of them men who had been imprisoned at Ada, and the notary who had endeavored to warn him—were sentenced to death.

It was evening before the preparations for the execution were completed. Balboa faced death as dauntlessly as he had faced life. Pedrarias was hated in Ada and Darien; Balboa was loved. If the veterans of Antigua had not been on the other side of the Isthmus, Balboa would have been rescued. As it was, the troops of Pedrarias awed the people of Ada and the judicial murder went forward.

Balboa was as composed when he mounted the scaffold as he had been when he welcomed Pedrarias. A proclamation was made that he was a traitor, and with his last breath he denied this and asserted his innocence. When the axe fell that severed his head, the noblest Spaniard of the time, and one who ranks with those of any time, was judicially murdered. One after the other, the three companions, equally as dauntless, suffered the unjust penalty. The fourth execution had taken place in the swift twilight of the tropical latitude and the darkness was already closing down upon the town when the last man mounted the scaffold. This was the notary, Arguello, who had interfered to save Balboa. He seems to have been beloved by the inhabitants of the town, for they awakened from their horror, and some of consideration among them appealed personally to Pedrarias, who had watched the execution from a latticed window, to reprieve the last victim. "He shall die," said the governor sternly, "if I have to kill him with my own hand."

So, to the future sorrow of America, and to the great diminution of the glory and peace of Spain, and the world, passed to his death the gallant, the dauntless, the noble-hearted Balboa. Pedrarias lived until his eighty-ninth year, and died in his bed at Panama; which town had been first visited by one of his captains, Tello de Guzman, founded by Espinosa and upbuilt by himself.

There are times when a belief in an old-fashioned Calvinistic hell of fire and brimstone is an extremely comforting doctrine, irrespective of theological bias. Else how should we dispose of Nero, Tiberius, Torquemada, and gentlemen of their stripe? Wherever such a company may be congregated, Pedro Arias de Avila is entitled to a high and exclusive place.

3

Peru and the Pizarros

A Study in Retribution
"They that take the sword shall perish by the sword."

1. THE CHIEF SCION OF A FAMOUS FAMILY

The reader will look in vain on the map of modern Spain for the ancient province of Estremadura, yet it is a spot which, in that it was the birthplace of the conquerors of Peru and Mexico—to say nothing of the discoverer of the Mississippi—contributed more to the glory of Spain than any other province in the Iberian peninsula. In 1883, the ancient territory was divided into the two present existing states of Badajoz and Caceres. In the latter of these lies the important mountain town of Trujillo.

Living there in the last half of the fifteenth century was an obscure personage named Gonzalo Pizarro. He was a gentleman whose lineage was ancient, whose circumstances were narrow and whose morals were loose. By profession he was a soldier who had gained some experience in the wars under the "Great Captain," Gonsalvo de Cordova. History would take no note of this *vagrom* and obscure cavalier had it not been for his children. Four sons there were whose qualities and opportunities were such as to have enabled them to play a somewhat large part in the world's affairs in their day. How many unconsidered other progeny, male or female, there may have been, God alone knows—possibly, nay probably, a goodly number.

The eldest son was named Francisco. His mother, who was not married to his father—indeed not married to anybody at any time so far as I can find out—was a peasant woman named Francisca Gonzales. Francisco was born about the year 1471. His advent was not of sufficient importance to have been recorded, apparently, and the exact

47

date of his terrestrial appearance is a matter of conjecture, with the guesses ranging between 1470 and 1478. A few years after the arrival of Francisco, there was born to Gonzales, and this time by his lawful wife, name unknown, a second son, Hernando. By the woman Gonzales, a score of years later, this promiscuous father had two more illegitimate sons, one of whom he named Gonzalo after himself, and the third he called Juan. Francisca Gonzales also bore a fourth son, of whom Gonzalo Pizarro was not the father, who was known as Martin de Alcántara. Thus Hernando, the second, was legitimate; Gonzalo and Juan were his illegitimate half-brethren, having the same father but a different mother; while Alcántara was a uterine brother to the three illegitimate Pizarros, having the same mother but a different father. There must have been marvellous qualities in the original Pizarro, for such a family is rarely to be met with in history.

Such a mixed state of affairs was not so shocking in those days as it would be at present. I do not find that anybody cast any stones at the Pizarros on account of these irregularities in their birth. In fact, they had plenty of companions in their anomalous social relations, and it is a speaking commentary on the times that nobody seemed to consider it as especially disgraceful or even very remarkable.

Hernando, the second son, received a good education for the day. The others were thrown mainly on their own resources. Legend says that Francisco was suckled by a sow. The statement may be dismissed as a fable, but it is more than probable that the assertion that he was a swineherd is correct. It is certain that to the day of his death he could neither read nor write. He never even learned to sign his own name, yet he was a man of qualities who made a great figure in history in spite of these disabilities, leaving behind him an immortal if unenviable name.

His career was humble and obscure to the vanishing point for forty years, of which practically nothing is known. It is alleged that he made a campaign in Italy with his father, but this is doubtful. A father who left him to tend the swine, who did nothing for his education, would not have bothered to take him a-soldiering.

We leave the field of conjecture, however, and meet him in far-off America in 1510 as an officer under Alonzo de Ojeda—that Don Quixote among discoverers. His qualities had obtained for him some preferment, for when Ojeda left the miserable remnants of his colony at San Sebastian on the Gulf of Darien, and returned to Cuba for help, Pizarro was put in charge, with instructions to wait a certain time, and if succour did not reach him to leave. He waited the required time, indeed waited longer, until enough people died to enable the brigantine that had been left with them to carry the survivors, and then sailed away. He was a member of Encisco's expedition to Darien, in which he fell in with the youthful and romantic Vasco Nuñez de Balboa. With Balboa he marched across the Isthmus, and was the second white man to look upon the Great South Sea in 1513. Subsequently, he was an officer under that American Nero, Pedro Arias de Avila, commonly called Pedrarias, the founder and Governor of Panama, the conqueror of Nicaragua and parts adjacent. Oviedo says that between his seventieth year, which was his age when he came to America, and his eighty-sixth year, when he died, the infamous Pedrarias caused more than two million Indians to be put to death, besides a numerous lot of his own countrymen. If we lop off two ciphers, the record is still bad enough.

In 1515, Pizarro and Morales, by direction of Pedrarias, made an expedition to the south of the Gulf of San Miguel, into the territory of a chieftain named Biru, from whom they early got into the habit of calling the vague land believed to exist in the South Sea, the "Land of Biru," or Peru. It was on this expedition that the Spaniards, hotly pursued by the natives, stabbed their captives one by one and left them dying at intervals in the pathway to check pursuit. The practice was effective enough and the action throws an interesting light on the Spanish *conquistador* in general and Pizarro in particular.

It fell to the lot of Pizarro also to arrest his old captain, Balboa, just as the latter was about to sail on a voyage of discovery to the fabulous gold country of Peru in 1517.[1] When Balboa and Pizarro had crossed the Isthmus six years before, the son of the Cacique Comagre, observing their avidity for gold, told them that it abounded in a mysterious land far toward the south, and the young Indian made a little clay image of a llama further to describe the country.

To conquer that El Dorado had been Balboa's cherished dream. Well would it have been for the country had not the jealousy of Pedrarias cut short Balboa's career by taking off his head, thus forcing the enterprise to be undertaken by men of coarser mould and meaner clay. It does not appear that Pizarro had any hand in the judicial murder of Balboa, and no reflection can be made on his conduct for the

1. "What is this, Francisco Pizarro?" Balboa asked, in great astonishment, of his former lieutenant and comrade, meeting him and his soldiers on the way with the order of arrest. "You were not wont to come out in this fashion to receive me!"

arrest, which was simply a matter of military duty, probably as distasteful to Pizarro as it was surprising to Balboa.

2. THE TERRIBLE PERSISTENCE OF PIZARRO

In 1519, Pizarro was living in Panama in rather straightened circumstances. His life had been a failure. A soldier of fortune, he possessed little but his sword. He was discontented, and although now nearly fifty years of age, he still had ambition. With remembrance of what he had heard the young Indian chief tell Balboa, constantly inciting him to a further grapple with hitherto coy and elusive fortune, he formed a partnership with another poverty-stricken but enterprising veteran named Diego de Almagro, whose parentage was as obscure as Pizarro's—indeed more so, for he is reputed to have been a foundling, although Oviedo describes him as the son of a Spanish labouring man. The two men supplemented each other.

Pizarro, although astute and circumspect, was taciturn and chary of speech, though fluent enough on occasion; he was slow in making up his mind, too, but when it was made up, resolute and tenacious of his purpose. Almagro was quick, impulsive, generous, frank in manner, "wonderfully skilled in gaining the hearts of men," but sadly deficient in other qualities of leadership. Both were experienced soldiers, as brave as lions and nearly as cruel as Pedrarias himself—being indeed worthy disciples of his school.

The two penniless, middle-aged soldiers of fortune determined to undertake the conquest of that distant empire—a stupendous resolution. Being almost without means, they were forced to enlarge the company by taking on a third partner, a priest named Luque, who had, or could command, the necessary funds. With the sanction of Pedrarias, who demanded and received a share, largely gratuitous, in the expedition, they bought two of the four vessels which Balboa had caused to be taken to pieces, transported them across the Isthmus, then set them up again, and relaunched in the Pacific. Enlisting one hundred men under his banner, Pizarro set sail with the first vessel on the 14th of November, 1524. Almagro was to follow after with re-enforcements and supplies in the second ship. One Andagoya had made a short excursion southward some time before, but they soon passed his latitude and were the first white men to cleave those southern seas.

With only their hopes to guide them, without pilot, chart or experience, being, I suspect, indifferent sailors and wretched navigators, they crept along the forbidding shore in a crazy little ship, landing from time to time, seeing no evidence of the empire, being indeed unable to penetrate the jungles far enough to find out much of anything about the countries they passed. Finally, at one place, that they afterwards called "Starvation Harbor," the men rebelled and demanded to be led back. They had seen and heard little of importance. There seemed to be nothing before them but death by starvation.

Pizarro, however, who has been aptly described as "terribly persistent," refused to return. He sent the ship back to the Isles of Pearls for provisions, and grimly clung to the camp on the desolate shore. When twenty of his men were dead of starvation, the ship came back with supplies. In one of their excursions, during this wait at Starvation Harbor, they had stumbled upon and surprised an Indian village in which they found some clumsy gold ornaments, with further tales of the El Dorado to the southward. Instead of yielding to the request of his men that they immediately return in the ship, therefore, the indomitable Spaniard made sail southward. He landed at various places, getting everywhere little food and less gold, but everywhere gaining more and more confirmation that the foundation of his dreams was not "the baseless fabric of a vision."

In one place they had a fierce battle with the Indians in which two of the Spaniards were killed and a large number wounded. Pizarro now determined to return to Panama with the little gold he had picked up and the large stories he had heard, there to recruit his band and to start out again. Almagro meanwhile had set forth with his ship with sixty or seventy additional adventurers. He easily followed the traces of Pizarro on the shore but the ships did not meet. Almagro went farther south than Pizarro.

At one landing-place he had a furious battle with the natives in which he lost an eye. He turned back after reaching the mouth of the river San Juan in about the fourth parallel of north latitude. He, too, had picked up some little treasure and a vast quantity of rumour to compensate for his lost optic and bitter experience. But the partners had little to show for their sufferings and expenditures but rumours and hopes.

Pedrarias in disgust withdrew from the expedition for a price, which, with the money necessary to send out a second expedition, was furnished through Luque by the Licentiate Espinosa. About September, 1526, with two ships, the two captains set forth once more. This time they had with them a capable pilot named Ruiz. They avoided the coast and steered direct for the mouth of the San Juan River.

Pizarro surprised a village here, carried off some of the natives, and a considerable amount of gold. This Almagro, as the best "persuader," took back to Panama in the hope that by exhibiting it he could gain much needed re-enforcements for their expedition.

The ships were very much undermanned. The experience of the first expedition, as related by the survivors, had been so horrible that it was with difficulty that they could get anybody to go with them on the second. Pizarro agreed to remain at the mouth of the river and examine the vicinity, while Ruiz with the second ship sailed southward to see what he could discover. Pizarro's men found no gold, although they explored the country with prodigious labour. Indians fell upon them, at one time killing fourteen who had stranded in a canoe on the bank of a river. Many other Spaniards perished, and all except Pizarro and a few of the stoutest hearts begged to return to Panama.

Ruiz came back just as they had begun to despair. He had crossed the Equator, the first European to cross it from the north, and had sailed half a degree south from the line.[2]

He brought back some Indians, further specimens of gold and silver ornaments, exquisitely woven woollen garments, *et cetera*, which he had taken from a craft cruising near the shore, which were proofs positive of the existence of the long-desired country.

Almagro now made his appearance with re-enforcements and the keels were soon turned to the south. Coasting along the shore, they saw increasing evidence of cultivation in the valleys and uplands, backed by the huge snow-crowned range of the Andes. Large villages appeared here and there. Finally, they anchored opposite a considerable town laid out in well-defined streets, containing about two thousand houses, many of them built of stone. From their position close to the shore they thought that they could make out that the inhabitants wore ornaments of gold. Several canoes approached the ship, one of them crowded with warriors carrying a species of gold mask as an ensign.

There appeared to be at least ten thousand warriors assembled on the shore but Pizarro landed with the few horses which he had brought along in the ship. A sharp engagement ensued, and the result might have been disastrous to the Spaniards had not one of them fallen from his horse during the fray. This diversion of what they considered a single animal into two, both living, alarmed the Indians so much, that they desisted from the attack and withdrew, the Spaniards

2. Magellan had crossed it from the south five years before.

taking advantage of the chance to return to the ships.

What to do next was the problem. They had not sufficient force or supplies with them to encounter the natives, or conquer or even explore the country. The expedition was about as meagrely equipped as it well could be and be an expedition at all. There were long discussions on the ships and a fierce quarrel between the two partners. Finally, it was composed outwardly, and it was decided that Pizarro should remain at the coast at some convenient point while Almagro, the traverser, went back for re-enforcements. Pizarro elected to pitch his camp on the little Island of Gallo which they had discovered. Those who were appointed to remain with him rebelled at the decision which left them marooned on a desolate island with no adequate provisions for their needs. Pizarro, however, insisted and Almagro sailed with the other ship. Shortly afterward, Pizarro sent the remaining ship with the most obstinate of the mutineers to Panama. A letter revealing their sad plight, which was concealed in a ball of cotton sent as a present to the wife of the governor by one of the men on the island of Gallo, was smuggled ashore at Panama when Almagro's ship reached that point, despite his vigilant efforts to allow no such communications to pass.

There was a new governor in Panama, Pedro de los Rios. Incensed by the loss of life and the hardships of the two expeditions, with the lack of definite and tangible results, and disregarding the remonstrances of Almagro, he dispatched two ships under one Pedro Tafur to bring them back. Life on the island of Gallo had been a hideous experience. Famine, disease and inclement weather had taken off many and had broken the spirit of the most of the rest of the band. Nothing could break that of Pizarro. When Tafur appeared, he refused to return. Drawing an east-and-west line upon the sand with his sword, he made a brief soldierly address to his men.

"Friends and comrades," he said, facing the south, "on that side of the line are toil, hunger, nakedness, the drenching storm, destruction and death. On this side," turning to the north, "are ease and pleasure. There lies Peru with its riches. Here, Panama with its poverty. Choose each man as best becomes a cavalier of Castile. For my part, I go to the south."

Such was the effect of his electrifying words, that, as he stepped over the line, a number of his comrades, led by Ruiz, the pilot, and Pedro de Candia, a Greek gunner, followed him. The number varies from thirteen to sixteen according to different authorities. The weight of evidence inclines me to the smaller number.[3]

Tafur raged and threatened, but Pizarro and his men persisted. They got themselves transferred to the Island of Gorgona where there were water and game and no inhabitants, and there they stayed while Tafur returned.

Less than a score of men marooned on a desert island in an unknown sea, opposite a desolate and forbidding coast, without a ship or any means of leaving the island, not knowing whether Almagro and Luque would be able to succour them; their position was indeed a desperate one. It shows, as nothing else could, the iron determination of the indomitable Spaniard. At that moment when Pizarro drew the line and stepped across it after that fiery address, he touched at the same time the *nadir* of his fortunes and the *zenith* of his fame. Surely it stands as one of the great dramatic incidents of history. The conquest of Peru turned upon that very instant, upon the determination of that moment; and upon the conquest of Peru depended more things in the future history of the earth than were dreamed of in the narrow philosophy of any Spaniard there present, or of any other man in existence in that long-past day.

Peru has played a tremendously important part in the affairs of men. It was the treasure of Peru that armed the soldiers of Alva and laid the keels of the Armada. It was the treasure of Peru that relieved the Spanish people of the necessity of wresting a national revenue out

---

3. Prescott, to whose remarkable accuracy, considering the time in which he wrote, the authorities at his command, and the disabilities under which he laboured, I am glad to testify, in view of the prevalent opinion that his books are literature and not history, says thirteen; Helps says fifteen, while Markham and Fiske say sixteen. Kirk verifies Prescott's conclusion with a good argument. One thing there is to which no one but Prescott seems to have called attention or explained. Everybody says Ruiz, the old pilot, was the first to follow Pizarro across the line. If so, he must have stepped back again, probably at Pizarro's request, for six months later we find him leaving Panama in charge of the ship which took Pizarro and his devoted subordinates off the Island of Gorgona. Ruiz could only have reached Panama in Tafur's ship. Certain it is that only thirteen men were ennobled for their heroic constancy on the Island of Gallo, as we shall see later. The three names added to Prescott's list are put there on the authority of Garcilasso de la Vega, the son of a Spanish cavalier and an Inca princess. Two of the three men he mentions he claims told him personally that they had been of the heroic band which had refused to abandon Pizarro. Such claims made by men who may really believe them to be true after the event, are not rare in history.

Whatever the exact number, there were but a handful. The rest, choosing Panama, remained on the north side of the line, and I have no doubt regretted their decision for the rest of their lives.

of a soil by agriculture; which abrogated the auxiliary of agriculture, manufactures; which precluded the possibility of the corollary of the other two, commerce. It was the treasure of Peru that permitted the Spanish people to indulge that passion for religious bigotry which was stifling to liberty and throttling to development, and which put them hopelessly out of touch with the onward and progressive movement of humanity in one of the most vital periods and movements in history. It was the treasure of Peru that kindled the fires of the Inquisition, in which the best blood of the nation lighted it to its downfall, and blazed the way for Manila and Santiago. Philip II, and his decadent and infamous successors depended upon the mines of Potosi and the mines of Potosi hung upon Pizarro and his line in the sand. The base-born, ignorant, cruel soldier wrecked in one moment a nation, made and unmade empires, and changed the whole course of the world.

It was largely the Spanish zeal and intolerance that developed and made perfect the Reformation, for no great cause has ever won success without opposition, nay, persecution. "The blood of the martyr," says St. Augustine, "is the seed of the church."

To return to the situation. Tafur presently reached Panama and reported. The governor and the people of that city looked upon Pizarro as a madman. Luque and Almagro were unwearying in their efforts and importunities, however, and finally they wrung a reluctant permission from De los Rios for Ruiz and one small ship and a few men to go to the rescue, with the proviso that a return must be made within six months. One can imagine the joy with which the desperate adventurers on the island saw the sails of that ship whitening the horizon. Once more they set sail to the south, arriving finally before a large and populous town called Tumbez. Here they saw undoubted signs of the existence of a great empire in a high state of civilization. The little party had some pleasant intercourse with the natives of Tumbez.

They gathered a considerable amount of gold and silver, some of it exquisitely wrought by cunning artificers into the forms of beautiful and unknown plants and animals. There was no possible doubt as to the truth of their golden dreams. The empire of Peru in all its magnificence lay before them.

Too meagre a force to embrace the opportunity, there was nothing to do but to return to Panama. There it was agreed that Pizarro, with De Candia, should go over to Spain, taking with him Peruvians and treasures, tell what he had seen, and secure the royal countenance and support for their future undertaking, while Almagro and Luque remained at Panama preparing for the final expedition. Pizarro had no sooner set foot in Spain than he was arrested for debt on some ancient charge by Encisco, but he was too big a man, now, for such petty persecution and he was at once released and ordered to present himself at court. The rough, blunt soldier, with his terrible yet romantic tale with its infinite possibilities, was received with astonishing cordiality. He gained a royal commission to discover and conquer the empire of Peru for Spain for the distance of two hundred leagues south of the Santiago River, and received the title of Governor and Captain-General with large powers and revenue appertaining, which it was easy for the crown to bestow since Pizarro had to get them himself.

Almagro, who justly felt himself slighted and his services inadequately valued, was made Governor of Tumbez; Luque was appointed Bishop for the same place and Protector of the Peruvians; Ruiz was named Grand Pilot of the Southern Ocean; De Candia, a General of Artillery; and every one of the thirteen who had crossed the line at Gallo was ennobled and made an Hidalgo of Spain.

Then Pizarro went back to Trujillo. Certainly it must have been a happy moment for the neglected bastard who had been a swineherd to return to his native village under such enviable conditions. He set sail for America early in 1530, with three ships. His four brothers came with him, the able Hernando being made second in command. Almagro and Luque were very much chagrined at the meagre reward that had fallen to them, and Almagro looked with deep antagonism upon the advent of the Pizarros, who, he realized instinctively, would undermine his influence with his partner. This hatred the new Pizarros repaid in kind. Some sort of peace, however, was patched up between them, and in January, 1531, with three small ships and one hundred and eighty-three men, including thirty-seven horses, Francisco set forth on his final voyage of conquest.

Nearly seven years had elapsed since the first attempt was made. As yet they had little but empty titles, large powers, purely potential, however, and drained purses to show for their heroic endeavour, but the persistence of Pizarro was about to triumph at last. After a voyage of thirteen days, the squadron arrived at San Mateo, where the horses and soldiers were landed and ordered to march along the shore southward, while the ships were sent back for re-enforcements which Almagro was gathering as usual. They returned with thirty more men and thirty-six additional horses. Arriving at the Gulf of Guayaquil,

Pizarro established himself on the island of Puna, opposite Tumbez, which he cleared of its inhabitants by a series of desperate battles. There he was re-enforced by a detachment of one hundred men with an additional number of horses under the command of young Hernando de Soto, another gallant Estremaduran, and quite the most attractive among this band of *desperadoes*, whose design was to loot an empire and proclaim the Holy Gospel of Christ as the Spanish people had received the same.

I have no doubt at all that the desire to propagate their religion was quite as real and as vividly present to them at all times as was their greed for gold. They had a zeal for God, but not according to knowledge; like the men of the Middle Ages who bore the cross on their hauberks, every Spaniard was a crusader. Aside from De Soto, there is no single character of all those, either Indian or Spaniard, who for fifteen years made Peru a bloody battle-ground, except the unfortunate young Inca Manco Capac, who is entitled to the least admiration or affection.

In April, 1532, Pizarro embarked his men on the ships and landed, not without some fierce fighting, at Tumbez, on the coast of Peru. At last the expedition was on solid ground and nothing prevented its further advance. On the 18th of May, therefore, they took up the march for the interior, little dreaming of the ultimate fate that awaited them all.

3. "A Communistic Despotism."

The empire of Peru well deserved the title of Magnificent. The highest civilization attained on the Western Hemisphere had been reached on this South American coast. A form of government unique in history had been developed and put in operation by a capable and enlightened people. It was a "communistic despotism," a community with a despot and a ruling class superimposed upon its socialism. The sway of these despots was exceedingly mild and gentle, even if absolute. With wonderful ingenuity and a rare capacity for organization, upon the ruins of an older civilization, they built the Inca Empire.

The Incas were the ruling tribe, the Emperor being the Inca par excellence. Their empire was as thoroughly organized as it is possible for a community to be. Indeed, it was organized to death; the Inca was the empire, and one source of the empire's speedy downfall was due to the fact that the national spirit of the Peruvians had been so crushed by the theocratic despotism of their rulers that they viewed the change of masters with more or less indifference. When the Incas conquered a country and people they so arranged affairs as to incorporate the people as part of the empire. They called their domains grandiloquently "the four quarters of the earth." They did not govern this great territory by brute force as did the Aztecs—although they knew how to use the sword if necessary—but by methods dictated by prudent and profound policy, productive of peaceful success. The mild government of the Incas was at once patriarchal, theocratic and despotic. Whatever it was, from the Incas' point of view it was absolute and satisfactory.

Prescott's account of the Inca civilization reads like a romance, yet it is practically borne out by all chroniclers who have discussed the subject, some of whom appear to desire to find the great American historian at fault. Large and populous cities existed, communication between which was had by great national roads traversing every part of the land. Vast herds of llamas were domesticated, from the hair of which the exquisitely woven cloth was made. Agriculture flourished. The country, upraised from the sea by the great range of mountains, afforded every variety of climate from temperate to tropic, and the diversified products of the soil corresponded with the opportunities presented. And every foot of space was utilized for a population of millions of industrious workers, with an economy and resourcefulness only emulated by the Chinese in the working of their country. Even the mountain-sides were terraced by tiny farms.

The Peruvians had made some progress in the arts, less in science. They lacked the art of writing, although they possessed a highly developed system of mnemonic aids in the form of curiously knotted and parti-coloured strings called *quipus*. Their literature, if the contradiction be permitted, was handed down like their history, by oral tradition.

Great as had been their achievements, however, they were in a curious state of arrested development. With the Peruvians, says Helps, "everything stopped short." They had not arrived at a finality anywhere, save perhaps in their mode of government. They could erect enormous time-defying buildings, but they knew of no way to roof them except by thatching them. Their roads were marvels of engineering construction, but they could not build bridges except frail ones made out of osier cables. No wheels ran along the smooth, well-paved, magnificent highways. They could refine gold and silver and make weapons of tempered copper, but they were entirely ignorant of the use of iron.

The greatest human development has depended upon that last metal. The great nations are those which have had the steel-tempered sword blades in their hands. They could administer a colony in a way to excite the admiration of the world, and yet not write a line. There is little probability that they would have progressed much beyond the state at which they had arrived, *for there was no individual liberty in the land*. That was the fatal defect in their system. It was the lack which put that touch of finality to their otherwise marvellously developed condition and which limited inexorably their civilization. The unchangeable conditions were stifling to ambition and paralyzing to achievement. The two things the country lacked were the two vital things to human progress and human success—letters and liberty.

The religious development of the Peruvians was very high. They worshipped an unknown Supreme Being and they worshipped him, it is conclusively demonstrated, without human sacrifice. Objectively they paid their chief adoration to the sun, moon and stars, and to the Inca as the child or earthly representative of the sun. Sun-worship is the noblest and highest of all the purely natural religions. When to this was superadded an instinctive feeling for a great First Cause, of which the solar magnificence was but a manifestation, the religion of the Peruvians is entitled to great respect.

Their history ran back into the mists of the past. At the time of the arrival of Pizarro, a curious condition, anomalous in their records, had arisen. Huayna Capac, one of the greatest monarchs of the Inca line, had extended his dominion by force of arms over the rich province of Quito, far to the north. He had taken as one of his *concubines* the daughter of the conquered monarch of Quito and by her had a son named Atahualpa.[4]

The son of the monarch by his sister, his only legal wife, or *Coya*—the irrevocable Peruvian method of providing for the Inca succession—was named Huascar. Huayna on his deathbed, after a glorious reign of forty years, made the fatal mistake of dividing his dominion between Huascar, to whom was given ancient Peru, and Atahualpa, who took Quito to the north. World-history, of which Huayna could have known nothing, has shown conclusively enough that such a policy has always brought about civil war, and this startling reversal of

4. Generally speaking, the Peruvians were monogamous, except in case of the Inca, who had as many wives as he wished, and who sometimes rewarded exceptional services by allowing some favoured adherent an extra wife.

Peruvian custom by a doting monarch on his deathbed produced the usual results.

The armies of Atahualpa, led by two famous soldiers called Quiz-Quiz and Chalcuchima, had met and defeated the troops of Huascar in a series of bloody battles. They had taken that unhappy monarch prisoner and, by a series of terrible massacres instigated by Atahualpa, had striven with large success to cut off the family of the unfortunate Inca root and branches. The land had been devastated by the fierceness of the internecine conflict, towns had been carried by storm, the inhabitants put to the sword; the ordinary course of events had been interrupted and agriculture had languished; the empire lay gasping under the paw of the Peruvian usurper when Pizarro landed upon the shore. The strife that was to ensue was between two base-born, cruel-hearted soldiers of fortune, one at the head of a little body of white men, but with all the prestige of their colour and development in warfare, and weapons, the other, the now undisputed monarch of a vast if prostrate and exhausted empire, at the head of great armies flushed with victory and eager for new conquests.

What would the result of the struggle be?

4. The Treacherous and Bloody Massacre of Caxamarca.

Having marched some thirty miles south of Tumbezin the pleasant spring weather, Pizarro, finding what he conceived to be a favourable location for a permanent colony, encamped his army, laid out and began to build a city, which he called San Miguel. The Spaniards were great builders and the city was planned and fortified on an extensive scale and the more important buildings erected, so that it was not until September that Pizarro considered his base of supplies had been made secure.

Meanwhile he had been assiduously seeking information on every hand concerning the internal dissensions in the Peruvian empire, so that he could undertake his conquest intelligently. On the 24th of September, 1532, the valiant little army was mustered and, after deducting a small garrison for San Miguel, those appointed for the expedition were found to include sixty-seven horsemen, three arquebusiers, twenty crossbowmen and eighty-seven footmen, in all one hundred and seventy-seven.[5]

They were accompanied by two pieces of small artillery called

---

5. The exact number varies with different authorities, none of whom, however, makes the total greater than two hundred.

falconets, each having a bore of two inches and carrying a shot weighing about a pound and a half, being, with the three *arquebusiers*, General De Candia's command. With this insignificant force, augmented, I suppose, by some Indian captives acting as pack-mules, Pizarro started out to conquer an empire conservatively estimated to contain from ten to twelve millions of people, supporting an army of disciplined soldiers whose numbers ran into the hundreds of thousands.

The Spanish forces were well equipped and in good condition, but as they left the sea-shore and advanced, without molestation, to be sure, through the populous country, some idea of the magnitude of their self-appointed task permeated the minds of the common soldiery, and evidences of hesitation, reluctance and dissension speedily appeared. The unwillingness of the men grew until Pizarro was forced to take notice of it. Halting on the fifth day in a pleasant valley, he met the emergency in his usual characteristic fashion. Parading the men, he addressed to them another of those fiery speeches for which he was famous, and the quality of which, from so illiterate a man, is amazingly high.

He painted anew the dangers before them, and then adroitly lightened the shadows of his picture by pointing to the rewards. He appealed to all that was best in humanity by saying that he wanted none but the bravest to go forward.[6]

He closed his address by offering to allow all who wished to do so to return to San Miguel, whose feeble garrison, he said, he should be glad to have re-enforced. And, with a subtler stroke of policy, he promised that those who went back should share in the rewards gained by their more constant brethren. But four infantrymen and five horsemen shamefacedly availed themselves of this permission. The rest enthusiastically clamoured to be led forward. Both mutiny and timidity were silenced forever in that band.

On a similar occasion, Cortes had burnt his ships. It is hard to decide which was the better expedient. Certainly Cortes was incomparably a much abler man than Pizarro, but somehow Pizarro managed to rise to the successive emergencies which confronted him, just the same.

---

6. Napoleon at Toulon succeeded in getting volunteers to man a particularly dangerous artillery outpost swept by the guns of the enemy, by the simple expedient of denominating the position as the "Battery of the Fearless," or the "Battery of those who are not afraid." Even better than Pizarro, this great Corsican soldier of fortune knew how to handle his men.

Greatly refreshed in spirits, the army, purged of the malcontents, proceeded cautiously on its way south. They were much elated from time to time at receiving envoys from Atahualpa, who coupled a superstitious reverence for the invaders as Children of the Sun with demands as to their purposes, and a request that they halt and wait the pleasure of the Inca. Pizarro dissembled his intentions and received them with fair words, but refusing to halt, kept steadily on, announcing his intention of visiting Atahualpa wherever he might be found.

Pursuing their journey, the Spaniards came early in November to the foot of the mountains. To the right of them, that is toward the south, extended a great well-paved road which led to the imperial capital of Cuzco. In front of them, a narrow path rose over the mountains. One was easy, the other hard. In spite of suggestions from his soldiery, Pizarro chose the hard way. He had announced his intention of visiting the Inca, and visit him he would although the way to the city of Cuzco was open and the place might easily be taken possession of. The seat of danger and the source of power were alike with the Inca, and not in Cuzco.

With sixty foot and forty horse, this old man, now past sixty years, led the way over the mountains, while his brother brought up the rear with the remainder. The passage was a terrible one, but the indomitable band, catching some of the spirit of their leader, surmounted all the obstacles, and a few days after from the summits of a mighty range, surveyed the fertile, beautiful plains spread out before them on the farther side of the mountain. Close at hand was the white-walled city, Caxamarca or Cajamarca, embowered in verdure in a fruitful valley. The place was an important position, well fortified and containing, under ordinary circumstances, a population of ten thousand. The reader should remember the name, for it was the scene of one of the most remarkable and determinative events in history. The conquest, in fact, was settled there.

Beyond the city, on the slopes of the hills, and divided from it by a river, over which a causeway led, stood the white tents of the fifty thousand soldiers of Atahualpa's army. The number of them filled the Spaniards with amazement, and in some cases with apprehension. There was no going back then, however; there was nothing to do but advance. At the hour when the bells of Holy Church in their home land were ringing vespers, in a cold driving rain mingled with sleet, the little *cortège* entered the city, which they found as the French found Moscow, deserted of its inhabitants. With the ready instinct of a soldier, Pizarro led his force to the public square, or Plaza, which was in the shape of a rude triangle surrounded on two sides by well-built, two-story houses of stone. On the other side, or base, rose a huge fortress with a tower overlooking the city on one hand and the Inca's camp on the other.

Without hesitation, the weary Spaniards made themselves at home in the vacant buildings around the square; guards were posted in order that the strictest watch might be kept, and other preparations made for defence. Here they prepared for the repose of the night. Meanwhile Hernando de Soto with twenty horse was sent as an ambassador to Atahualpa's camp. He had been gone but a short time when Pizarro, at the suggestion of his brother Hernando, who made the point that twenty horsemen were not sufficient for defence and too many to lose, despatched the latter with twenty more cavalrymen to re-enforce the first party.

The two cavaliers and their escort found the Inca in the midst of his camp. The monarch was seated and surrounded by a brilliant assemblage of nobles in magnificent vestments. He was guarded by a great army of soldiers armed with war-clubs, swords and spears of tempered copper, and bows and slings. He received the deputation with the impassivity of a stone image, vouchsafing no answer to their respectful address until it had been several times repeated. At last he declared he would visit the strangers on the morrow, and directed them to occupy the buildings in the public square, and none other until he came to make arrangements. His demeanour was cold and forbidding to the last degree. The results of the embassy were highly unsatisfactory. One incident connected with the interview is worthy of mention.

De Soto, who was a most accomplished cavalier, a perfect centaur in fact, noticing the amazed and somewhat alarmed glances of the Inca's men at the movements of his restless horse, suddenly determined to exhibit his skill at the *manège*. Striking spurs to his charger, he caused him to curvet and prance in the open before the Inca, showing at the same time his own horsemanship and the fiery impetuosity of the high-spirited animal. He concluded this performance—shall I say circus?—by dashing at full speed toward the Inca, reining in his steed with the utmost dexterity a few feet from the royal person. What the Inca thought of this has not been recorded. I imagine he must have been terribly affronted.

Some of his nobles and soldiers, less able to preserve their iron composure than their master, shrank back from the onrushing avalanche of steed and steel presented by De Soto and his horse. The Spaniards found their dead bodies the next day. It did not do to show cowardice in the presence of the Inca! They had been summarily executed by Atahualpa's order. Yet, I cannot think the Inca a man of surpassing bravery after all. Certainly he was not a man of sufficient ability worthily to hold the sceptre of so great an empire. He made a frightful mistake in not stopping the invaders where it would have been easy for him to do so, in the narrow defiles of the mountains, and he did not even yet seem to have decided in his own mind how he should treat them.

To be sure, according to some accounts, he looked upon them as belonging to the immortal gods, but there have been men brave enough in the defence of land and liberty to defy even the immortal gods! A vast deal of sympathy, indeed, has been wasted upon Atahualpa. Without doubt the Spaniards treated him abominably, and for that treatment the wretched monarch has claims to our consideration, but for his personal qualities or his past record, none. Helps explains his name as derived from two words meaning, "sweet valour!" Markham affirms that the words mean "A chance, or lucky, game-cock!" Neither appellation, in view of Atahualpa's history can be considered as especially apt or happy.

Much dissatisfied and thoroughly perturbed, De Soto and Hernando Pizarro returned to the city. Long and serious were the deliberations of the leaders that night. At length they arrived at a momentous decision, one for which they have been severely and justly censured, but which under the circumstances was the only possible decision which insured their safety. They had no business in that country. They had come there with the deliberate intention of looting it without regard to the rights of the inhabitants, and in that purpose lay the seeds of all their subsequent crimes, treachery, murder, outrage and all other abominations whatsoever. No surprise need be felt therefore, that they determined upon the seizure of the person of the Inca.

The example of Cortes with Montezuma was before them. I have no doubt that his amazing exploits in Mexico had been talked over frequently by every camp-fire in the New and the Old World, and many bold spirits had longed for an opportunity to emulate his doings. The Spaniards in Peru had already learned enough of the local conditions to realize that with the person of the Inca they could control the government. To seize him was black treachery, of course; but

64

being there, it was the only thing to do, from their point of view. The night was an anxious one and the morning found them engaged in preparations.

De Candia was posted with two small falconets and three *arquebusiers* on the roof of the fortress. His guns pointed toward the Inca's camp, though he had instructions to turn them on the square as soon as the Peruvians arrived. De Soto and Hernando Pizarro divided the horse between them and occupied the houses on the other side of the square with them. The infantry were distributed at various points of vantage. Pizarro reserved twenty of the trustiest blades for his own escort. The arms of the men were carefully looked to, and nothing that the skill or experience of the captains could suggest was left undone to promote the success of their hazardous and bold undertaking.

Mass was said with great solemnity by the priest of the expedition, Fra Vincente de Valverde, an iron-souled, fierce-hearted Dominican, meet ecclesiastic for such a band. Refreshments were then provided liberally for the soldiers—it is not so stated, but it may be presumed that some of them were in liquid shape—and then the whole party settled down to await developments. Nothing seemed to be going on in the Peruvian camp during the morning. The Inca moved toward the city in the afternoon, but stopped just outside the walls, to the great annoyance of the Spaniards, who had found the long wait a trying experience indeed.

Late in the afternoon, Pizarro received a message that Atahualpa had changed his mind and would not visit him until the following day. This did not suit his plans at all. He instantly returned an answer to the Inca, begging him not to defer his visit, saying that he had provided everything for his entertainment—which was quite true although in a very different sense from that conveyed by the words of his messenger—and requesting Atahualpa to arrange to sup with him without fail that night. Pizarro had previously assured the Inca that he would receive him as a "friend and brother"! What reasons actuated the Inca we have no means of ascertaining. Suffice it to say that he changed his mind and came.

A short time after sunset, therefore, the Inca, attended by a numerous retinue, entered the square. Atahualpa was borne aloft on a throne made of massive gold, supported on the shoulders of his attendants. He was dressed with barbaric magnificence in robes of exquisite texture, heavily embroidered and ornamented with gold and silver. Around his neck blazed a necklace of emeralds of wonderful size and great brilliancy. His forehead was hidden by a thick vivid scarlet fringe depending from a diadem almost to the eyebrows. This tassel (or *borla*, as the Spaniards called it; *llauta*, according to the Peruvians) was the supreme mark of the imperial dignity in that no one but the Inca could wear it. The Inca was surrounded by a gorgeously attired body of retainers who were preceded by hundreds of menials who cleared the streets of every obstacle which might impede the progress of their master, the Son of the Sun. The processions divided at the square, and the monarch was carried forward in the open. Not a Spaniard save the watchful sentries pacing the fort above, was to be seen.

"Where," asked Atahualpa, looking about in surprise, "are the strangers?"

At this moment, at the request of Pizarro, Father Valverde came forward in his canonicals, crucifix in one hand, breviary or Bible in the other.[7] He was attended by one of the Peruvians whom Pizarro had taken back to Spain, who was to act as interpreter. This precocious little rascal, named Felippo, was the best interpreter that could be found, which is saying little, for his Spanish was bad and mainly picked up in the camps from the rude soldiery, and his Peruvian was only an uncouth dialect of the highly inflected and most flexible and expressive Quichua, the language of the educated, indeed of the most of the people. Approaching the litter of the Inca, Valverde delivered an extraordinary address. He briefly explained the doctrines of the Christian religion to the astonished Peruvian, requiring him to conform to this religion and acknowledge the spiritual supremacy of the Pope, and at the same time to submit to the sway of his Imperial Majesty Charles V. It was a pretty heavy demand to spring upon a great monarch in the midst of his people, and it was not to be wondered at that Atahualpa rejected these requests with contempt.

The Inca answered the friar not without shrewdness. He had gathered the idea from Felippo's vile mistranslation that the Christians worshipped four Gods, *i.e.* the Trinity and the Pope. He declared that he himself worshipped one, and there was its sign and symbol—pointing to the declining sun; that he believed one God was better than four. He rejected indignantly the idea that he, "The Lord of the Four Quarters of the Earth," owed allegiance to any Charles V. or any other earthly monarch, of whom he had never heard and who had assuredly never heard of him either.

Valverde had referred to the book in his hand as he had spoken and

---

7. Authorities differ as to which it was. The matter is not material, anyway.

Atahualpa now asked to see it. The volume was a clasped one and he found it difficult to open. Valverde, probably thinking he could show him to unclasp the volume, stepped nearer to him. The Inca repulsed him with disdain. Wrenching open the covers he glanced rapidly at the book, and perhaps suddenly realizing the full sense of the insult which had been offered to him in the demands of the dogmatic and domineering Dominican, he threw the sacred volume to the ground in a violent rage.

"Tell your companions," he said, "that they shall give me an account of their doings in my land. I will not go hence until they have made me full satisfaction for all the wrongs they have committed!"

Then he turned and spoke to his people—the last word he was ever to address them as a free monarch from his throne. There was a loud murmur from the crowd.

Thereupon, according to some accounts, Valverde picked up the book through which Atahualpa had offered such a deadly insult to his religion and rushed back to Pizarro, exclaiming, "Do you not see that while we stand here wasting our breath in talking with this dog, full of pride as he is, the fields are filling with Indians? Set on at once! I absolve you for whatever you do!" I would fain do no man an injustice. Therefore, I also set down what other authorities say, namely, that Valverde simply told Pizarro what had occurred.

There is no dispute, however, as to what happened immediately. Pizarro stepped out from the doorway, and drawing a white scarf from his shoulders, threw it into the air. Instantly a shot roared from the fort above his head. The famous war-cry of the Spaniards, "St. Jago, and at them!" rang over every quarter of the square into which, with bared swords, couched lances and drawn bows, poured the mail-clad soldiery horse and foot.

They burst upon the astonished ranks of the unarmed Indians with the suddenness and swiftness of a tornado. From the roof above, the gunners discharged their bullets into the swaying, seething mass. With their wands of office, with their naked hands, with whatever they could seize, the Peruvians defended themselves. They rallied around the person of the Inca, freely offering their breasts to the Spanish blades with the vain attempt to protect their monarch.

Atahualpa sat upon his reeling throne gazing upon the bloody scene in a daze of surprise. Pizarro and the twenty chosen cut their way to the litter and, striking down the helpless bearers thereof, precipitated the Inca to the ground. The Spaniards were mad with carnage now, and were striking indiscriminately at any Indian. Then could be heard Pizarro's stern voice ringing above the *mêlée*, "Let no man who values his life strike at the Inca!" Such was the fierceness of his soldiery, however, that in his frenzied attempt to protect the monarch, Pizarro was wounded in one of his hands by his own men. As the Inca fell, he had been caught by Pizarro and supported, although a soldier named Estete snatched the imperial *llauta* from his head as he fell.

With the capture of the Inca, what little futile resistance the unarmed host had been able to make ceased. The Indians, relentlessly pursued by their bloody conquerors, fled in every direction, and, to anticipate events, the army deprived of its monarch and its generals, dispersed the next day without striking a blow. Indeed the army was helpless for offence while the Spaniards held the Inca as a hostage.

The estimates of the numbers slain in one half-hour's fighting in the square of Caxamarca vary from two to ten thousand. Whatever the number, it was great and horrible enough. An unparalleled act of treachery had been consummated, and Peru, in the space of thirty minutes had been conquered and Pizarro held it in the hollow of his hand. Not a Spaniard had been wounded except Pizarro himself, and his wound had been received from his own men while he tried to protect Atahualpa from the Spaniards' fury.

5. THE RANSOM AND MURDER OF THE INCA

Pizarro treated the Inca well enough, although he held him in rigorous captivity. Nobody else in Peru seemed to know what to do under the circumstances, and the Spaniards soon lost all apprehension of resistance. Quiz-Quiz and Chalcuchima still held Huascar a captive at Xuaca, a fortress between Caxamarca and Cuzco. Atahualpa, realizing how important such a man would be to the Spaniards, sent orders that he be put to death and the unfortunate deposed Inca was therefore executed by the two generals. Although he was captive, Atahualpa's orders were as implicitly obeyed as if he had been free. He was still the Inca, if only by the right of sword, and the forces of his generals were sufficiently great to render it impossible for the son of Huascar, named Manco Capac, who had escaped the massacre of his kinfolk and who was the legitimate heir to the throne, to claim the crown.

Pizarro, with a fine show of rectitude, affected to be horrified by this evidence of brutal cruelty, and although Atahualpa claimed no connection with the assassination of Huascar, it was impossible to acquit him of it. Greatly desiring his freedom, Atahualpa, who had observed the Spanish greed for gold, made an extraordinary proposition to Pizarro. They were together in a room twenty-two feet long by seventeen feet broad. Standing on his tiptoes and reaching as high as he could, probably about eight feet, for he was a tall man, Atahualpa offered to fill the room with gold to the height he had touched, if, when he had completed his undertaking, Pizarro would release him.

Pizarro jumped at the offer, and well he might for no such proposition had ever before been offered in the history of the world. The cubic contents enclosed by the figures mentioned are three thousand three hundred and sixty-six feet, or in round numbers, one hundred and twenty-five cubic yards. Such a treasure was even beyond the most delirious dreams of the conquerors.[8]

As soon as these astonishing terms had been formally accepted in writing by Pizarro, the Inca sent orders to all parts of his dominion for the people to bring in their treasures. He also directed the royal palaces and temples to be stripped, and his orders were obeyed. He had stipulated that he be allowed two months in which to raise the ransom and day after day a stream of Indians poured into the city loaded with treasure which dazzled the eyes of the astonished and delighted conquerors. Atahualpa had stipulated also that the gold was not to be smelted—that is, he would not be required to fill the spaces solidly with ingots, but that it should be put into the room just as it was brought in and allowed to take up as much space as was required, even though it might be in the shape of a manufactured article.

Some of the gold was in the shape of ingenious plants and animals, one especially beautiful object being the corn plant with blades of gold and tassels of silver. Pizarro, to his credit, ordered that some of these specimens of exquisite workmanship should be preserved intact. Much of the treasure was in the shape of plates or tiles, from the interior of the temples or palaces which did not take up much space. The great temple of the Sun at Cuzco had a heavy outside cornice, or moulding, of pure gold. It was stripped of this dazzling ornament

---

8. The ransom of King John II. of France, taken prisoner by the Black Prince, was three million golden crowns. The value of the ancient *ecu de la couronne* varied between $1.50 and $1.30, so that the ransom of John was between four and one-half and seven million dollars. Estimating the purchasing power of money in John's time at two and one-half times that of the present, we arrive at a ransom of between eleven and eighteen million dollars. If we split the difference and call the ransom fourteen and a half millions, we still find that the Christian monarch was slightly undervalued as compared with his heathen fellow in misery. However, all this is profitless, because the ransom of John was never paid.

"THEY BURST UPON THE RANKS
OF THE UNARMED INDIANS."

"The Three Pizarros . . . sallied out to meet them"

to satisfy the rapacity of the conquerors. There was also a vast quantity of silver which was stored in other chambers. Silver hardly counted in view of the deluge of the more precious metal.

Atahualpa did not quite succeed in filling the space, but he came so near it that Pizarro, in a formal agreement executed before a notary, declared that the Inca had paid his ransom and that he was released from any further obligation concerning it. That is the only release, however, which the unfortunate Inca ever got. Obviously, it was dangerous to turn loose such a man. Therefore, in spite of his legal quittance, he still was held in captivity. The Spaniards concluded finally that the only safe course was to get rid of him.

The ransom amounted in our money to over seventeen million dollars, according to Prescott; to nearly eighteen million dollars, according to Markham. Pizarro's personal share was seven hundred thousand dollars; Hernando received three hundred and fifty thousand dollars; De Soto two hundred and fifty thousand dollars. Each horse soldier received nearly one hundred thousand; the principal foot soldiers, fifty thousand, and the others smaller sums in accordance with their rank and service. The precious metals were so plentiful that for the time being they lost their value, for men cheerfully paid thousands of dollars for a horse. Indeed so bulky and unwieldly was the treasure with which the soldiers were loaded, that it is solemnly averred that creditors avoided their debtors fearing lest the latter should pay them what they owed in further heaps of the bulky treasure; and it is certainly a fact that even the animals shared in the opulence of the conquest, for the horses were shod with silver. Silver was cheaper and easier to get than iron.

While they were revelling in the treasure, dividing the spoils and deliberating what was to be done with Atahualpa, Almagro arrived with his re-enforcements. Naturally he and his men demanded a share of the booty. Great was their disgust and furious their anger when Pizarro and the other conquerors refused to give it up. Finally, the quarrels that ensued were composed by presenting Almagro and his followers certain sums, large in themselves though trifling in comparison with what Pizarro's men had received. Almagro's men were also given to understand that they could move on to the southwest at some convenient season and conquer another empire and take all they could for themselves. Unfortunately for them, there were no more empires like Peru on this or any other side of the world left them to conquer.

Hernando Pizarro was then dispatched to Spain to deliver the royal fifth to Charles, to give an account of the fortunes of the conquerors and to secure what further rewards and privileges he could for them. Atahualpa saw him leave with the greatest regret. He was a man of fierce, stern, implacable disposition, not a lovely character, according to any of the chroniclers, but he seems to have been fairer, and in his own way he had treated the unfortunate monarch better, than any of the others, unless it was De Soto. Possibly Hernando might have restrained his brother from the last infamy he was about to perpetrate if he had been there. Certainly De Soto would have sought to dissuade him. Pizarro realized this and got rid of De Soto by sending him away to investigate as to the truth of rumours that Atahualpa was conspiring to obtain his freedom. I have no doubt that he was so conspiring. I hope so, for if he was, it was about the only manly thing that he did. While De Soto was away, at the instigation of the soldiers, Pizarro with seeming reluctance, allowed Atahualpa to be brought to trial. I have no doubt that Pizarro instigated the soldiers himself. He was adroit enough to do it, and he would have no scruples whatever to deter him.

The Inca was tried on twelve charges, among which were included accusations that he had usurped the crown, and given its prerogatives to his friends (instead of to the Spaniards!). He was charged with being an idolator, an adulterer and a polygamist, and finally it was urged that he had endeavoured to incite an insurrection against the Spaniards. Such accusations came with a peculiarly bad grace from the conquerors. The whole thing, charges and all, would have been a farce had it not been for the certain grim and terrible outcome.

Felippo, the Infamous, was the only interpreter. He had made love to one of the Inca's wives, whom the Spaniards had allowed to share his captivity. Atahualpa, furiously affronted, desired to have him put to death, but Felippo was too important to the Spaniards, and he was spared. How Atahualpa's defence suffered from Felippo's interpretations under such circumstances may easily be imagined. In spite of the courageous opposition of a few of the self-appointed judges, the Inca was convicted and sentenced to death, Father Valverde concurring, in writing, with the sentence.

When the verdict of the court was communicated to Atahualpa, he did not receive it with any remarkable degree of fortitude. He is a pitiful rather than a heroic figure.

"What have I done," he cried, weeping, "what have my children done, that I should meet with such a fate?" Turning to Pizarro, he added, "And from your hands, too, who have met with friendship and kindness from my people, to whom I have given my treasure, who have received nothing but benefit from my hands!"

He besought the conqueror to spare his life, promising anything, even to double the enormous ransom he had already paid, and offering to guarantee in any appointed way the safety of every Spaniard in the army. Pedro Pizarro, a cousin of the conqueror, who has left an account of the interview, says that Pizarro was greatly affected by the touching appeal of the unfortunate monarch, and that he wept in turn also. However that may be, he refused to interfere. A man may weep and weep, to paraphrase Shakespeare, "*and be a villain!*" There was no help for it; Atahualpa had to die.

It was on the 29th of August, 1533. The trial and deliberations had occupied the whole day. It was two hours after sunset before they were ready to execute him in the great square of Caxamarca. The Spanish soldiers, fully armed, arranged themselves about a huge stake which had been planted in the square. Back of them were groups of terrified, awe-struck Peruvians, helplessly weeping and lamenting the fate of their monarch which they were powerless to prevent. Flickering torches held by the troops cast an uncertain light over the tragic scene. Atahualpa was led forth in fetters and chained to the stake. He showed little of the firmness and fortitude of a proud monarch or a brave man. How feebly he appears when contrasted with the great Aztec Guatemotzin, calmly enduring the tortures of the red-hot gridiron and resolutely refusing to gratify either his captors' lust for treasure or desire for revenge by vouchsafing them a single fact or a single moan.

By Inca's side was Valverde, who had been assiduous in his endeavors to make him a Christian. The friar was ready to offer such grim consolation as he could to the wretched Peruvian in whose death sentence he had concurred. Atahualpa had hitherto turned a deaf ear to all his importunities, but at the last moment Valverde told him that if he would consent to receive baptism, he should be strangled instead of burnt to death. Atahualpa asked Pizarro if this was true, and being assured that it was, he abjured his religion to avoid the agonies of fire, and was thereupon baptised under the name of Juan de Atahualpa. The name John was given to him because this baptism *in extremis* took place on St. John the Baptist's day. Rarely, if ever, has there been a more ghastly profanation of the Holy Sacrament of Regeneration!

Before he was garrotted, Atahualpa begged that his remains might be preserved at Quito with those of his mother's people. Then he turned to Pizarro and made a final request of that iron-hearted man, that he would look after and care for the Inca's little children. While he was strangled and his body was being burnt, the terrible soldiery could be heard muttering the magnificent words of the Apostolic Creed for the redemption of the soul of the monarch. Incidentally it may be noted that a little later the Spaniards burnt old Chalcuchima, of whom they had got possession by treacherous promises, at the stake. He did not embrace Christianity at the last moment, but died as he had lived, a soldier and a Peruvian.

The character of Atahualpa may be learned from his career. He was a cruel, ruthless usurper, neither magnanimous in victory nor resolute in defeat. As I have said, it is impossible to admire him, but no one can think of his fate and the treacheries of which he was a victim without being touched by his miseries. If he sowed the wind he reaped the whirlwind, and bad as he was, his conquerors were worse.

Pizarro placed the diadem on Toparca, a youthful brother of the late Inca. When he was alone with his attendants, the boy tore the *llauta* from his forehead, and trampled it under his foot, as no longer the badge of anything but infamy and shame, and in two short months he pined and died from the consciousness of his disgrace. Whereupon another Peruvian, Manco Capac, the legitimate heir of Huascar, appeared before Pizarro, made good his claim, and on the entry of the conquerors into Cuzco, was crowned Inca with all the ancient ceremonies. He soon realized that he was but a puppet in Pizarro's hands, however, and by and by he, too, made a bold stroke for freedom.

The conquest of Peru was complete. Charles V., dazzled by the report of Hernando Pizarro, and the substantial treasures placed before him, created Pizarro a Marquis of the country, confirmed him in the government of the country for two hundred and seventy leagues south of the Santiago River and gave Almagro authority to conquer everything beyond that limit. Almagro was very much dissatisfied with his share, but concluded, before he made any violent objections, to go to the south and find an El Dorado for himself.

Meanwhile Pizarro, who was almost as much of a builder as Rameses the Great, laid out the city of Lima and the Spaniards flocked into Peru from Spain in thousands. The natives were enslaved and the country divided into great estates, and Almagro and his discontented started for Chili. Hernando Pizarro, who was appointed governor of Cuzco, held young Manco in close confinement, and everything outwardly was as fine and lovely as a summer day. There was growing, however, a tremendous uprising in which hitherto somnolent Fate was about to lay her belated hands upon nearly all the actors of the great drama which had heretofore been so successfully played.

6. THE INCA AND THE PERUVIANS STRIKE VAINLY FOR FREEDOM

The city of Cuzco was, without doubt, the most superb capital on the American continent. Indeed, in many respects, it would have compared favourably with, let us say, Paris in the sixteenth century, with its narrow, crooked, unpaved filthy streets, its indifferent protections, and its utterly inadequate water and sewer system. The streets, which were broad and level, crossed each other at regular intervals at right angles. They were smoothly paved with large, carefully joined flagstones. The houses in the city were mainly built of stone. The palace of the Inca, which stood alone in the great square, was of marble. The temples and buildings for public assemblages, armories, granaries, storehouses, et cetera, were of great size. The stones used in their erection were of such dimensions that the Spanish marvelled at the engineering genius which could have quarried them and put them in place, just as the people of today are amazed at Baalbec and the pyramids. Stone conduits ran down each street, bringing delicious water to each doorway, and the city was traversed by two mountain streams crossed by bridges cut by watergates. That the cold, clear water might be kept pure and sweet, the beds of the rivers like those of the Euphrates at Babylon, had been paved.

The city was surrounded by walls and dominated by a great fortress called Sacsahuaman, which stood upon a steep and rocky hill overlooking the capital. On the side toward the city the fortress was practically impregnable on account of the precipitous slopes of the cliffs. The other side was defended by three stone walls laid out in zig-zag shape, with salient and re-entrant angles (demi-lunes), like an old-fashioned rail fence, with many doors, each closed by stone portcullis, in each wall. Within the walls was a citadel of three tall towers. The whole constituted a most formidable position.

While Francisco Pizarro was founding and laying out on a magnificent scale and with lavish generosity the city of Lima, near the seaboard, Hernando was made governor of Cuzco. Hernando was, without doubt, the most able and most admirable of the Pizarros, although his fame has been obscured by that of his elder brother. He had been directed by Charles V to treat the Inca and the people

76

with kindness, and, perhaps on that account, he had not exercised so rigorous a surveillance over the movements of young Manco as his ordinary prudence would have dictated. At any rate, the bold and youthful emperor found no difficulty in leaving his ancient capital. He repaired immediately to the Valley of Yucay, in the high mountains of the north-eastward of Cuzco. There had been brewing a vast conspiracy against the Spaniards for some time, and at the summons of the Inca, thither resorted the great chiefs of the Peruvians with their retainers and dependents, including their women and children.

The partisans of the two Inca half-brothers, who had not been slain, made common cause with each other. All internal differences were forgotten in the presence of the common enemy. They had much to revenge. Their treasures had been taken, their temples polluted, their religion profaned, their monarchs slain, their women outraged and the people forced into a degrading, exhausting slavery. Strange is it to recognize that human slavery was introduced into Peru by the Christians!

It is good to think that the manhood of the Peruvians was awakened at last. Manco, burning with fiery patriotic zeal, summoned his great vassals and subjects to his standard. "Death to the Spaniards!" were the watchwords that resounded with fierce war-cries among the mountains and hills. With ancient ceremonies, drinking from a common cup, they pledged their lives, their fortunes, and their sacred honour to their hereditary chief in defence of their altars and their fires, their native land.

Early in 1536 a vast army swept down through the mountain passes and made toward the ancient capital. The three Pizarros, Hernando, Juan and Gonzalo, put themselves at the head of their horsemen and sallied out to meet them. They killed numbers of Peruvians, but all their valour could not check the resistless force of the patriotic army. The Spaniards were swept back into the city, glad to escape with their lives before such overwhelming numbers; indeed, only a timely attack by a detachment in the rear of the Peruvians saved them from destruction then and there. Cuzco was at once invested. The Indians, with a heroism which cannot be too greatly commended, endeavoured to carry the place by assault.[9]

---

9. Query: Does the reader not wish that the Peruvians had succeeded? Indeed, how can the reader help wishing that? Yet would it have been better for the world if the Peruvians had succeeded in expelling the Spaniards, or would it have been worse? These questions afford matter for interesting speculation.

They set fire to the thatched roofs of their own houses, devoting their city to flames, like the Russians at Moscow, to compass the annihilation of the detested invaders. The wind favoured them, and a besom of flame swept over the devoted town until over one-half of it was laid in ruins. There were ninety Spanish horse in the city, probably as many foot, and a thousand Indian auxiliaries, but they were soldiers of the highest quality and led by three captains whose like for daring and skill are not often seen.

No one ever questioned the courage or the military ability of the Pizarros and certainly they exhibited both qualities in full measure during the siege. Of all the brothers, it is probable that Hernando was the most daring cavalier as well as the most capable captain, although in personal prowess his younger brothers were not a whit behind him. Indeed, Gonzalo was reckoned as the best lance in the New World. Stifled by the smoke, scorched by the flames, parched with heat, choked with thirst, exhausted with hunger, crazed from loss of sleep, yet battling with the energy of despair against overwhelming numbers of Indians, who, with a reckless disregard for life, hurled themselves upon the sword-points, the Spaniards after several days of the most terrific fighting, were forced into the square, which they held against their enemy by dint of the most heroic and continuous endeavours.

The Peruvians barricaded the streets with the debris of their ruined houses and sharpened stakes, and prepared to press home for a final attack. Although the slaughter among the Indians had been fearful, the odds against the Spaniards did not appear diminished, for it was learned afterward that there were more than one hundred thousand warriors engaged, and, with a host of followers and servants, the total aggregated at least eighty thousand more. And, indeed, the Spaniards mourned the death of many a brave cavalier and stout man-at-arms. In all the fighting the young Inca, in full war-gear of gold and silver, mounted on a captured horse, with a Spanish lance in his hand, had played a hero's dauntless part.

At the commencement of the siege there had been a discussion as to whether they should occupy the great fortress of Sacsahuaman, or not. Juan Pizarro had dissuaded the Spanish from the attempt, for, he said: "Our forces are too weak to hold both places. The city is the most important, and should it happen that we need the fortress we can take it any time." Without opposition the Indian High Priest had occupied it with a large body of men.

It was evident, at last, that the Spaniards would either have to retreat from their town or seize the fortress, which, now that they had been driven from the walls, commanded their position in the square. Most of the cavaliers were for retreat. There is no doubt that the horse could certainly have cut their way through the ranks of the besiegers, and have escaped, together with most of the foot as well.

Hernando was quite as persistent as his indomitable brother Francisco, however, and he talked equally as well to the soldiers. He made them a stirring address which he closed by declaring that he had been sent there to hold the town, and hold it he would if he had to hold it alone; that he would rather die there in the square with the consciousness that he had kept his trust than abandon the place. Juan and Gonzalo seconded his stirring appeal. It was resolved that the fortress should be taken. Hernando proposed to lead the assault in person, but Juan interposed with the remark that he had objected to its seizure in the first instance, and to him rightfully belonged the leadership of the forlorn hope to repair the error. Hernando consented.

Juan and Gonzalo, with their commands and fifty of their best horse, were detailed for the purpose. By Hernando's instructions they cut through the Indians and galloped headlong down the road in the direction of Lima. The Indians were deceived by the seeming dash of the horsemen through the lines and, supposing them to be in retreat, turned their attention to the Spaniards left in the square. The conflict which had been intermitted for a space began again with the utmost fury.

In the midst of it, Juan Pizarro, who had galloped about a league from the town and then made a long detour, suddenly appeared at Sacsahuaman. The Spaniards immediately rushed to the assault. This diversion caused the Indians, who had been literally forcing the Spaniards in the town up against the wall, and in the last ditch, as it were, to give ground. Thereupon the dauntless Hernando charged upon them, drove them out of the square, and succeeded in establishing communications with Juan and Gonzalo on the hill. He directed Juan to hold his position and make no attack, but Juan thought he saw an opportunity to gain the fortress, and at vespers the Spaniards rushed at the walls.

There were Indians not only within but without the walls, and the fighting was soon of the most sanguinary description. Juan Pizarro had been wounded previously in a skirmish and on account of this wound was unable to wear his *morion*. Hernando had especially cautioned him to be careful on this account; but the impetuous valour of the Pizarros was not to be restrained by considerations of any personal safety, and Juan was in the front rank of the storming party. They had cut their way through to the fort and were battling for entrance when a stone hurled from the tower struck Juan in the head, knocking him senseless. The wound was of such a character that two weeks afterward he died of it in great agony. He was the first to pay the penalty. History has preserved little concerning him, but some chroniclers have found him the highest-minded of the brothers—possibly because less is known about him! At any rate, he was a valiant soldier.

Gonzalo succeeded to the leadership, and although he and his men fought heroically, they were at last forced back from the fortress in spite of the fact that they had gained the outer walls. The fighting had transferred itself from the city to the hills, which was a sad tactical error on the part of the Peruvians, for they had force enough to overwhelm Hernando and his men in the city, while they held Juan and Gonzalo in play at Sacsahuaman, in which case all the Spaniards would eventually have fallen into their hands.

As night fell Hernando left the city and came up to the hill. The Spaniards busied themselves in making scaling-ladders, and in the morning, with the aid of the ladders, the assault was resumed with desperate fury. Wall after wall was carried, and finally the fighting ranged around the citadel. The Inca had sent five thousand of his best men to re-enforce the defenders, but the Spaniards succeeded in preventing their entrance to the fort which was now in a sorry plight. The ammunition—arrows, spears, stone, *et cetera*—of the garrison was almost spent. The Spanish attack was pressed as rigorously as at the beginning. The High Priest—priests have ever been among the first to incite people to war, and among the first to abandon the field of battle—fled with a great majority of his followers, and escaped by subterranean passages from the citadel, leaving but a few defenders to do or die.

First among them was a chief, whose name, unfortunately, has not been preserved. He was one of those, however, who had drunk of the cup and pledged himself in the mountains of Yucay. Driven from wall to wall and from tower to tower, he and his followers made a heroic defence. The Spanish chroniclers say that when this hero, whose exploits recall the half-mythical legends of the early Roman Republic, when men were as *demi*-gods, saw one of his men falter, he stabbed him and threw his body upon the Spaniards. At last he stood alone upon the last tower. The assailants offered him quarter, which he disdained. Shouting his war-cry of defiance, he dashed his sole remaining weapon in the faces of the escaladers and then hurled himself bodily upon them to die on their sword-points. Let him be remembered as a soldier, a patriot, and a gentleman.

The fortress was gained! Dismayed by the fearful loss that they had sustained, the Peruvians, who had fought so valiantly, if so unsuccessfully, withdrew temporarily. Hernando Pizarro was master of the situation. He employed the few days of respite given him in gathering supplies and strengthening his position. It was well that he did so, for in a short time the Peruvians once more appeared around the city, to which they laid a regular siege.

There was more sharp fighting, but nothing like the Homeric combats of the first investment. The Peruvians had risen all over the land. Detached parties of Spaniards had been cut off without mercy. Francisco Pizarro was besieged in Lima. Messengers and ships were despatched in every direction, craving assistance. Francisco did not know what had happened in Cuzco, and the brothers in that city began to despair of their being extricated from their terrible predicament. Help came to them from an unexpected source.

We left Almagro marching toward Chili. His was no lovely promenade through a pleasant, smiling, fertile, wealthy land. He traversed vast deserts under burning skies. He climbed lofty mountains in freezing cold and found nothing. In despair, he turned back to Peru. The limits assigned to Pizarro were not clear. Almagro claimed that the city of Cuzco was within his province, and determined to return and take it. On the way his little army, under the command of a very able soldier named Orgonez, met and defeated a large army of Peruvians. This, taken with the arrival of the harvest time, which must of necessity be gathered if the people were not to starve, caused the subsequent dissipation of the Peruvian army. The Inca maintained a fugitive court in the impregnable and secret fastnesses of the mountains, but the Peruvians never gave any more trouble to the Spaniards. They had spent themselves in this one fierce but futile blow. I am glad for the sake of their manhood that at least they had fought one great battle for their lands and liberties.

7. "The Men of Chili" and the Civil Wars

Almagro, assisted by treachery on the part of some of the Spaniards who hated the Pizarros, made himself master of the city, and, breaking his plighted word, seized Hernando and Gonzalo.

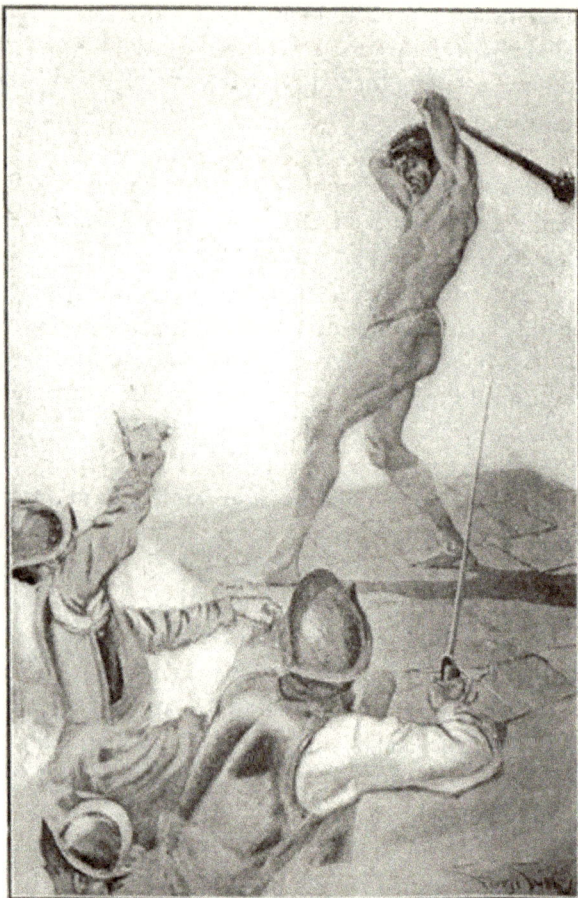

"HE THREW HIS SOLE REMAINING WEAPON
IN THE FACES OF THE ESCALADERS"

FERNANDO CORTES.

Meanwhile Francisco, the Marquis, had despatched a certain captain named Alvarado with a force to relieve Cuzco. Almagro marched out with his army and defeated the superior force of Alvarado in the battle of Abancay, in July, 1537, in which, through the generalship of Orgonez, Alvarado's troops were captured with little or no loss in Almagro's army. Almagro had left Gonzalo Pizarro behind in Cuzco, but had taken Hernando, heavily guarded, with him. Orgonez had urged Almagro to put both of them to death. "Dead men," he pithily remarked, "need no guards." On the principle of "*In for a penny, in for a pound*," Almagro was already deep enough in the bad graces of Francisco Pizarro, and he might as well be in deeper than he was, especially as the execution of Hernando would remove his worst enemy. But Almagro does not appear to have been an especially cruel man. He was an easy-going, careless, jovial, pleasure-loving soldier, and he spared the lives of the two brothers. Gonzalo escaped, and assembling a force, immediately took the field.

There had been a meeting between Francisco and Almagro. The latter got an inkling that there was treachery intended, and though the meeting had begun with embraces and tears, it was broken off abruptly and both the ancient partners prepared for an appeal to arms. Almagro had released Hernando on his promise to return immediately to Spain. This promise Hernando broke. Francisco made his brother commander of the army, and the forces of the two commanders met on the plains of Salinas on the 6th of April, 1538.

There were about seven hundred on one side, Pizarro's, and five hundred on the other, equally divided between horse and foot, with a few pieces of artillery in both armies. The men of Chili, as Almagro's forces were called, hated their former comrades, and Pizarro's men returned this feeling with such animosities as are engendered nowhere save in civil war. Victory finally attended Hernando Pizarro. He had fought in the ranks like a common soldier, save that he had been at great pains so to distinguish himself by his apparel that everyone could know him, so that all who sought him could find him. Orgonez was slain as he lay on the ground, wounded. Such was the close, fierce fighting that the killed alone numbered nearly two hundred, besides a proportionately greater number wounded.

Almagro had watched the battle from an adjacent hill. He was old and ill, broken down from excesses and dissipations. Unable to sit a horse, he had been carried thither on a litter. The sight of his routed army admonished him to try to escape. With great pain and difficulty he got upon a horse, but being pursued, the animal stumbled and Almagro fell to the ground. Some of Pizarro's men were about to dispatch him when Hernando interfered. He was taken prisoner to Cuzco and held in captivity for a while. Hernando had announced his intention of sending him to Spain for trial, but a conspiracy to effect his release, in which was our old friend De Candia, caused a change in his purposes. Almagro was tried on charges which were easily trumped up, was found guilty, of course, and in spite of his protestations and piteous appeals for life, he was strangled to death at night in his prison on the 8th of July, 1538, in the sixty-fifth year of his life. His head was then struck from his shoulders and both were exhibited in the great square at Cuzco. Vainglorious, ignorant, incompetent, yet cheerful, generous, frank, kindly and open-hearted, and badly treated by Pizarro and his brothers, he possibly deserved a better fate.

The Pizarro brothers affected to be overcome by the stern necessity which compelled poor Almagro's execution. As Francisco had done when he had killed Atahualpa, these two put on mourning and insisted upon being pall-bearers, and exhibited every outward manifestation of deep and abiding grief.

Almagro left a son, Diego, by an Indian woman, to whom he had not been married. This young man was under the guardianship of Pizarro at Lima. The sword of Damocles hung over his head for a while, but he was spared eventually and, the rebellion of Almagro having been cut down, the revolt of the Inca crushed, peace appeared once more to dwell in the land.

8. The Mean End of the Great Conquistador

But fate had not finished with the Pizarros as yet. Hernando was sent back to Spain to explain the situation, and Gonzalo despatched to Quito, of which province he was made governor. He had instructions to explore the country eastward to see if he could find another Peru. He made a marvellous march to the head-waters of the Amazon River, where he was deserted by one of his commanders, Orellana, who built a brigantine, sailed down the whole length of the Amazon, finally reaching Europe, while Gonzalo and those few of his wretched followers who survived the terrible hardships of that march, struggled back to Quito.

Francisco, the Marquis, was thus left alone in Peru. The position of the men of Chili was precarious. Although outwardly things were peaceful, yet they felt that at any time Pizarro might institute war against them. They got the young Almagro away from him, and a score of men under Juan de Rada, a stout-hearted veteran, mercenary soldier, determined to put the Marquis to death and proclaim the young Almagro as Lord and Dictator of Peru.

On Sunday afternoon, the 26th of June, 1541, De Rada and nineteen desperate men of Chili, met at De Rada's house in Lima. Pizarro had received a number of warnings which he had neglected, confident in the security of his position, but the existence of the conspiracy had been brought home to him with peculiar force that Sunday, and he had remained in his palace at Lima surrounded by a number of gentlemen devoted to his cause. At vespers—which seems to have been a favourite hour for nefarious deeds among the Spaniards—the assassins sallied forth from the home of De Rada and started for the palace.

Such was the indifference in which the people held the squabbles between the Pizarrists and the Almagrists, that it was casually remarked by many of them, as the assassins proceeded through the streets, that they were probably on their way to kill the governor. The governor was at supper on the second floor of his palace. There was a sudden tumult in the square below. The door was forced open and the Almagrists, shouting "Death to Pizarro!" rushed for the stairs. Most of the noble company with the old Marquis fled. The great conquistador at least had no thought of flight. There remained with him, however, two pages, his brother Martin de Alcántara, Francisco de Chaves, one of the immortal thirteen of Gallo, and another cavalier, named De Luna.

As they heard the clash of arms on the stairs and the shouting of the assailants, the Marquis ordered De Chaves to close the door; then he sprang to the wall, tore from it his corselet and endeavored to buckle it on his person. De Chaves unwisely attempted to parley, instead of closing the door and barring it. The assailants forced the entrance, cut down De Chaves, and burst into the room. Pizarro gave over the attempt to fasten his breastplate, and seizing a sword and spear, defended himself stoutly while pealing his war-cry: "Santiago!" through the palace. The two pages, fighting valiantly, were soon cut down. De Alcántara and De Luna were also killed, and finally, Pizarro, an old man over seventy years of age, stood alone before the murderers.

Such was the wonderful address of the sword play with which he defended himself that the conspirators were at a loss how to take him, until De Rada, ruthlessly seizing one of his comrades, pitilessly thrust him upon Pizarro's sword-point, and, before the old man could withdraw the weapon, cut him in the throat with his sword. Instantly Pizarro was struck by a dozen blades. He fell back upon the floor, but he was not yet dead, and with his own blood he marked a cross on the stones. It is alleged by some that he asked for a confessor, but that is hardly likely, for as he bent his head to press his lips upon the cross, one of the murderers, seizing a huge stone bowl, or earthen vessel, threw it upon his head and killed him. *Sic transit Pizarro!*

If he has been the subject of much severe censure, he has not lacked, especially of late, zealous defenders. I have endeavoured to treat him fairly in these sketches. Considering him in comparison with his contemporaries, Cortes surpassed him in ability, Hernando in executive capacity, Almagro in generosity, Balboa in gallantry, and De Soto in courtesy. On the other hand, he was inferior to none of them in bravery and resolution, and he made up for his lack of other qualities by a terrible and unexampled persistency. Nothing could swerve him from his determination. He had a faculty of rising to each successive crisis which confronted him, wresting victory from the most adverse circumstances in a way worthy of the highest admiration. He was not so cruel as Pedrarias, but he was ruthless enough and his fame is forever stained by atrocities and treacheries from which no personal or public success can redeem it. In passing judgment upon him, account must be taken of the humble circumstances of his early life, his lack of decent, healthy environment, his neglected youth, his total ignorance of polite learning. Take him all in all, in some things he was better and in other things no worse than his day and generation.

9. The Last of the Brethren

Hernando Pizarro was delayed on his voyage to Spain and some of Almagro's partisans got the ear of the King before he arrived. He was charged with having permitted by his carelessness the Peruvian uprising and having unlawfully taken the life of Almagro. The story of his desperate defence of Cusco was unavailing to mitigate the anger of the King at the anarchy and confusion—and incidentally the diminution of the royal revenue—which prevailed in Peru. Hernando was thrown into prison at Medina, and kept there for twenty-three long and weary years.

He had married his own niece, Francisca Pizarro, illegitimate daughter of the Marquis Francisco, by a daughter of the great Inca, Huayna Capac. The woman was a half-sister of Atahualpa and Huascar. By this questionable means, the family of the Pizarros, with certain dignities, restored for their Peruvian service, was perpetuated in Spain. Hernando died at the age of one hundred and four.

De Rada, after the assassination of Francisco, assembled the ancient partisans of Almagro. They swore fealty to the young Almagro, and immediately took the field against a new governor sent out by Charles V. to take charge of affairs in Peru. This Vaca de Castro, through his able lieutenants, Alvarado and Carvajal, defeated the forces of Almagro on the bloody and desperately fought field of Chapus, took the young man prisoner to Cuzco, and beheaded him forthwith. He met his death bravely, without beseeching or repining. Before the fate of the battle was decided, Almagro, suspecting that the gunner, De Candia, another of the thirteen who had adhered to his cause, was not serving his artillery with so good effect as he might, ran him through the body.

There remains but one of the brothers who gave Peru to Spain, the magnificent cavalier, Gonzalo. His fate may be briefly summarized. Another Viceroy, named Blasco Nuñez Vela, succeeded De Castro. He had orders to release the Peruvians from servitude, which meant that the conquerors and the thousands who had come after, would have been compelled to work. Led by Gonzalo, who had been rewarded for his services in the rebellion against Almagro by a domain in Peru which included the newly discovered mines of Potosi, which provided him with the sinews of war, the people rebelled against the Viceroy. Pizarro and his lieutenant, Carvajal, deposed and defeated the Viceroy in a battle near Quito on the 18th of January, 1546, the latter losing his life.

Gonzalo Pizarro was now the supreme lord of Peru, which included practically the whole of the South American coast from the Isthmus of Darien to the Straits of Magellan, for Valdivia, one of Francisco Pizarro's lieutenants, had partially conquered Chili at last.

The Spanish monarch, three thousand miles away, could do nothing by force. He sent an able and devoted ecclesiastic, Gasca by name, clothing him with dictatorial powers, to see what he could do. Gasca arrived at Panama, cunningly and tactfully won the captains of Gonzalo's navy to his side, went to Peru, assembled a force, and although Centeno, one of his lieutenants, was badly defeated by Gonzalo and Carvajal on the 26th of October, 1547, at Huarina, the bloodiest battle ever fought in Peru, finally gained strength enough to march to Cuzco, where Gonzalo had command of a large and splendidly equipped army. Gasca, by promising that the obnoxious laws concerning the

Indians should be repealed, and adroitly pointing out that those who adhered to Gonzalo were, in effect, in rebellion against their sovereign, had so undermined the allegiance of his men that Gonzalo, who had marched to the Valley of Xaquixaguana, found himself deserted on the eve of the battle by all but a handful of faithful retainers.

"What shall we do?" asked one of the devoted followers.

"Fall on them and die like Romans."

"I believe I should prefer to die like a Christian," said Gonzalo calmly.

Recognizing that it was all up with him, riding forward with Carvajal and the rest, he coolly surrendered himself to Gasca.

Carvajal was hung, drawn and quartered.

Gonzalo, the last of the brothers, was beheaded in the great square at Cuzco. He was magnificently arrayed as he rode to his death. His vast estates, including the mines of Potosi, had been confiscated and all his possessions were on his back. He met his fate with the courage of the family. Before he died he made a little address from the scaffold. Contrasting his present poverty with his former state, he asked those who had been his friends and who owed him anything, and also those who had been his enemies, to lay out some of the treasure they had gained through his family and himself in masses for the repose of his soul. Then he knelt down before a table bearing a crucifix, and prayed silently. At last he turned to the executioner and said:

"Do your duty with a steady hand!"

So he made a rather dramatic and picturesque exit there in the square at Cuzco, on that sunny morning in April, 1548. His head was exhibited at Lima with that of Carvajal. To it was attached this inscription:

This is the head of the traitor, Gonzalo Pizarro, who rebelled in Peru against his sovereign and battled against the royal standard at the Valley of Xaquixaguana.

There remains but one other person whose fate excites a passing interest, unless it be Bishop Valverde, who was killed, while on a journey, by the Peruvians, some years before; this is the last Inca, Manco Capac. When De Rada and his band started out to assassinate Pizarro, one of the soldiers, named Gomez Perez, made a detour as they crossed the square, to keep from getting his feet wet in a puddle of muddy water which had overflowed from one of the conduits.

"You shrink," cried De Rada, in contempt, "from wetting your feet, who are about to wade in the blood of the governor! Go back, we will have none of you."

He had not permitted Perez to take part in the assassination. This Perez, after the final defeat of the Almagrists, fled to the mountains where Manco still exercised a fugitive sway over such of his people as could escape the Spaniards. He was afterward pardoned and used as a medium of communication between Gasca and the Inca. The priest viceroy was anxious to be at peace with the Inca, but Manco refused to trust himself to the Spaniards.

Perez and he were playing bowls one day in the mountains. Perez either cheated, or in some way incensed the unfortunate Inca, who peremptorily reproved him, whereupon the Spaniard, in a fit of passion, hurled his heavy stone bowl at the last of the Incas, and killed him. That was the end of Perez, also, for the attendants of the young Inca stabbed him to death.

Thus all those who had borne a prominent part in the great adventures had gone to receive such certain reward as they merited; which reward was not counted out to them in the form of gold and silver, or stones of price. The sway in the new land of the king over the sea was absolute at last, and there was peace, such as it was, in Peru.

The Greatest Adventure in History

1. The Chief of all the Soldiers of Fortune

At the close of the fifteenth century, to be exact, in the year 1500, in the town of Painala, in the Province of Coatzacualco, one of the feudatory divisions of the great Aztec empire of Mexico, there was born a young girl who was destined to exercise upon the fortunes of her country an influence as great as it was baleful, as wonderful as it was unfortunate. She was the daughter of the Cacique of Tenepal, who was Lord of the town and province, a feoff of the Mexican Emperor Montezuma Xocoyotzin. This was the second Montezuma who had occupied the imperial throne and his last name means "The Younger," which he adopted to distinguish him from his predecessor in the empire.

This Lord of Painala, whose name has been forgotten, unfortunately for his country departed this life soon after the birth of his daughter, who was called Malinal because she was born on the twelfth day of the month, her name indicating that fact. His property naturally devolved upon the young daughter. Her mother assumed the office of guardian and regent of the state. This lady, whose name has also been lost in oblivion, did not long remain single. After her second marriage, which apparently took place with a somewhat indecent hurry, there was born to her and her new consort, a young son. To secure to this son the inheritance, she sold her little daughter, too young to realize the unfortunate transaction, to some traders of Xicalango, who in turn disposed of her to a coast tribe of Aztecs called the Tabascans. She lived in bondage with the Tabascans until she was nineteen years old. She developed into a woman of rare beauty and unusual intellect. Something of the power of high birth was evidently hers, for she escaped the degrading servitude of the time, and was carefully trained and prepared for some higher purpose. This girl was to be the instrument of the downfall of her native land.

Now it happened that when Malinal was nineteen years old, the rumour of a strange visitation ran up and down the shore among the people who dwelt upon the great Gulf of Mexico. Some remarkable beings, the like of whom had never been seen or heard of within the memory of living man, in some remarkable boats which absolutely transcended the imagination of the Aztecs, had been seen upon the coast and some of them had landed at different points. Also there had sifted from the south, from the Isthmus of Darien and the Panama States, some account of these white-skinned *demi*-gods. Just enough rumour was current to cause alarm and uneasiness in the Aztec Empire when the attention of the rulers was called to some definite facts.

On Good Friday, March 23, 1519, the dreaded and expected happened, for there landed at what is now the city of Vera Cruz, in the territory of the Tabascans, vassals of Montezuma, a party of these strange adventurers. They were led by a man of mature years, whose name was Fernando Cortes—sometimes written Hernando Cortes. Like Pizarro, whose history has been related, he was from the forgotten province of Estremadura. He was born in the year 1485, in the city of Medellin. He was seven years old when Columbus set sail upon that epoch-making voyage of discovery and he was thirty-four when he set foot for the first time on the shores of Mexico. In the intervening years much interesting and valuable experience had been enjoyed.

The parents of Cortes belonged to the provincial nobility. They were worthy and respectable subjects of the King of Spain. The old-fashioned adjectives, "poor, but honest" could be applied to them. The boy was a puny, sickly lad, whom they scarcely expected to reach man's estate. When he was fourteen years old they entered him in the great University of Salamanca where he took his degree as Bachelor of Laws, after a two years' course. The law, in Spain, was considered an entirely proper profession for the nobility, especially when the nobility were unable, through narrow circumstances, properly to support the profession of arms. Cortes, therefore, was in receipt of a liberal education for his day. His letters, some of which will be quoted hereafter, are evidences of his mental training. In some respects they are as interesting as are the famous Commentaries of Julius Caesar.

The young man, whose constitution improved as he grew older, until he eventually became the hardiest, most enduring and bravest of his company, which included the most intrepid men of the age, had no love for the humdrum profession of law. He desired to go to Italy and take service with Gonsalvo de Cordova, who is remembered, when he is remembered at all, as "The Great Captain"; but sickness prevented. Following that, his thoughts turned, as did those of so many Spanish youths who were of an adventurous disposition, toward the New World. After many setbacks, one of which was caused by a wound received by the hot-blooded young man while engaged in a love affair, and which left a permanent scar upon his upper lip, he finally landed at Santo Domingo in the Spring of 1504. From there he went to Cuba and served under one Diego Velasquez, the governor of that province in some fierce fighting in the island, and received as a reward from the governor, who was much attached to him, a large plantation with a number of Indians to work it. There he married and lived prosperously. What he had done before he arrived in Mexico counted little. What he did afterward gave him eternal fame as one, if not the greatest, of the conquerors and soldiers of fortune in all history. Sir Arthur Helps thus portrays him:

> Cortes, (he says), was an heroic adventurer, a very politic statesman, and an admirable soldier. He was cruel at times in conduct, but not in disposition; he was sincerely religious, profoundly dissembling, courteous, liberal, amorous, decisive. There was a certain grandeur in all his proceedings. He was fertile in resources; and, while he looked forward, he was at the same time almost madly audacious in his enterprises. This strange mixture of valour, religion, policy, and craft, was a peculiar product of the century.... There are two main points in his character which I shall dwell upon at the outset. These are his soldier-like qualities and his cruelty. As a commander, the only fault imputed to him, was his recklessness in exposing himself to the dangers of personal conflict with the enemy. But then, that is an error to be commonly noticed even in the greatest generals of that period; and Cortes, with this singular dexterity in arms, was naturally prone to fall into this error.
> As regards his peculiar qualifications as a commander, it may be observed, that, great as he was in carrying out large and difficult operations in actual warfare, he was not less so in attending to those minute details upon which so much of the efficiency of troops depends. His companion-in-arms, Bernal Diaz, says of

him, 'He would visit the hut of every soldier, see that his arms were ready at hand, and that he had his shoes on. Those whom he found had neglected anything in this way he severely reprimanded, and compared them to mangy sheep, whose own wool is too heavy for them.'

I have said that he was cruel in conduct, but not in disposition. This statement requires explanation. Cortes was a man who always determined to go through with the thing he had once resolved to do. Human beings, if they came in his way, were to be swept out of it, like any other material obstacles. He desired no man's death, but if people would come between him and success, they must bear the consequences. He did not particularly value human life. The ideas of the nineteenth century in that respect were unknown to him. He had come to conquer, to civilize, to convert (for he was really a devout man from his youth upward); and, as his chaplain takes care to tell us, knew many prayers and psalms of the choir by heart; and the lives of thousands of barbarians, for so he deemed them, were of no account in the balance of his mind, when set against the great objects he had in view. In saying this, I am not apologizing for this cruelty; I am only endeavouring to explain it.

Of all the generals who have been made known to us in history, or by fiction, Claverhouse, as represented by Sir Walter Scott, most closely resembles Cortes. Both of them thorough gentlemen, very dignified, very nice and precise in all their ways and habits, they were sadly indifferent to the severity of the means by which they compassed their ends; and bloody deeds sat easily, for the most part, upon their well-bred natures. I make these comments once for all; and shall hold myself excused from making further comments of a like nature when any of the cruelties of Cortes come before us—cruelties which one must ever deeply deplore on their own account, and bitterly regret as ineffaceable strains upon the fair fame and memory of a very great man... The conquest of Mexico could hardly have been achieved at this period under any man of less genius than that which belonged to Hernando Cortes. And even his genius would probably not have attempted the achievement, or would have failed in it, but for a singular concurrence of good and evil fortune, which contributed much to the ultimate success of his enterprise. Great difficulties and fearful conflicts of fortune not only stimulate to great attempts, but absolutely create the opportunities for them.

2. THE EXPEDITION TO MEXICO.

Reports brought back to Cuba by one Juan de Grijilva, who told of the populous and wealthy cities of the main land to the westward of Cuba, induced Velasquez to fit out an expedition for exploration, colonization or whatever might turn up. Casting about among his friends, followers, and acquaintances for a suitable leader, his choice after some hesitation devolved upon Cortes. This nascent captain had not lived at the provincial court of Velasquez without impressing his characteristics upon those with whom he came in contact. After the outfitting of the expedition had progressed considerably, Velasquez was warned that Cortes was of too high and resolved a spirit to be trusted with an independent command, and it was probable that upon this opportunity he would disregard his instructions and act for his own interests, without giving another thought to Velasquez and his backers.

Velasquez ignored the suggestions that he displace Cortes until it was too late. Cortes, learning that his enemies were undermining him with the governor, hastily completed his preparations and set sail a short time in advance of the arrival of the order displacing him from the command. His little squadron touched at a point in Cuba and was there overtaken by the missive from Velasquez, which Cortes absolutely disregarded. He had embarked his property and had persuaded his friends to invest and did not propose to be displaced by anybody or anything.

The expedition consisted of eleven ships. The flag was a small caravel of one hundred tons burden. There were three others of eighty tons each, and the seven remaining were small, undecked brigantines. Authorities vary as to the number of men in the expedition, but there were between five hundred and fifty and six hundred Spaniards, two hundred Indian servants, ten small pieces of artillery, four falconets and sixteen horses.

The truth must be admitted. There were three factors which contributed to the downfall of that vast empire against which this expedition of adventurers was launched. One of them was Cortes himself, the second was Malinal, and the third was the sixteen, doubtless sorry horses, loaded into the ships. Fiske says:

It was not enough that the Spanish soldier of that day was a bulldog for strength and courage, or that his armour was proof against stone arrows and lances, or that he wielded a Toledo blade that could cut through silken cushions, or that his *arquebus* and cannon were not only death-dealing weapons but objects of superstitious awe. More potent than all else together were those frightful monsters, the horses. Before these animals men, women, and children fled like sheep, or skulked and peeped from behind their walls in an ecstasy of terror. It was that paralyzing, blood-curdling fear of the supernatural, against which no amount of physical bravery, nothing in the world but modern knowledge, is of the slightest avail.

After touching at various places, in one of which they were lucky enough to find and release a Spanish captive named Geronimo de Aguilar, who had been wrecked on the Yucatan coast while on a voyage from the Spanish settlement in Darien and had been taken captive by the Mayas and held for several years. The hospitable Mayas had eaten most of the expedition. There were then but two alive. One had renounced his religion, married a Maya woman, and had been elected chieftain of the tribe, and accordingly refused to join Cortes. Aguilar was unfettered and glad of the opportunity. During his sojourn among the Mayas he had learned to speak their language fluently.

After landing at Tabasco on Good Friday, there was a great battle with the warlike inhabitants of that section, a battle which resulted in the complete discomfiture of the Tabascans. The artillery did much to bring this about, but was not especially terrifying to the aborigines because they crowded in such numbers around the Spaniards, and made such terrific outcries, beating on their drums the while, that they drowned out the noise of the cannonade; but when Cortes at the head of the horsemen sallied out from the woods, and fell upon them, the strange, terrifying spectacle presented by these mail-clad monsters and demons, took the heart out of the Tabascans, and they abandoned the contest, leaving, so the chroniclers say, countless numbers dead upon the field.

They knew when they had had enough, and immediately thereafter, they sued for peace. Cortes was graciously pleased to grant their request, and to accept as a peace-offering a score of slaves. Among them was Malinal. In the allotment of the slaves among the officers, she fell to the share of Alonzo de Puerto Carrero from whom Cortes speedily acquired her.

Of all the Indians present with Cortes, Malinal alone could speak two languages. The Tabascans spoke a sort of degenerate Maya, with which, as she had lived among them so long, she was of course perfectly familiar, at the same time she had not forgotten her native Mexican. It would have been impossible for Cortes to have communicated with the Mexicans without Malinal, for Aguilar could turn Spanish into Maya, and Malinal could turn Maya into Mexican. This means of communication, round about though it might be, was at once established. The intervention of Aguilar soon became unnecessary, for Malinal presently learned to speak pure Castilian with fluency and grace. She received instruction from the worthy priests who accompanied the expedition and was baptised under the name of Marina, and it is by that name that she is known in history. Her eminence is even greater than that unfortunate Florinda, whose father, to revenge her mistreatment by King Roderick, the Goth, sold Spain to Tarik, the Saracen, so many centuries before.

Marina learnt among other things to love Cortes, whose fortunes she followed and whom she served with an absolute, unquestioning, blind devotion and fidelity until the end. So absolute was this attachment of hers that Cortes became known to the Aztecs as the Lord of Marina. The Aztecs could not pronounce the letter R. Marina was therefore changed to Malina, which curiously enough was nearly her original name. The word "*Tzin*" is the Aztec name for Lord, consequently Cortes was called Malintzin, or more shortly Malinche, meaning, as has been stated, the Lord of Malina.

Sir Arthur Helps has this to say of her:

> Indeed her fidelity was assured by the love which she bore her master. Bernal Diaz says that she was handsome, clever, and eager to be useful (one that will have an oar in every boat), and she looked the great lady that she was.
>
> There was hardly any person in history to whom the ruin of that person's native land can be so distinctly brought home, as it can be to the wicked mother of Donna Marina. Cortes, valiant and skilful as he was in the use of the sword, was not less valiant (perhaps we might say, not less audacious) nor less skilful, in the use of the tongue. All the craft which he afterward showed in negotiations would have been profitless without a competent and trusty interpreter.... If a medal had been struck to commemorate the deeds of Cortes, the head of Donna Marina

should have been associated with that of Cortes on the face of the medal; for, without her aid, his conquest of Mexico would never have been accomplished.

3. THE RELIGION OF THE AZTECS

Now the Aztec Empire was a rather loose confederation of states bound together by allegiance to a common overlord, who had his capital across the mountains in the City of Mexico. It had been founded by the influx of an army of fierce marauders from the North who had overwhelmed the Toltecs who occupied the country and had attained a degree of civilization which is presumed to have been higher than that which displaced it. This Empire of Anahuac, as it was sometimes called, had endured for two centuries. It was a military despotism and the emperor was a military despot. His rule was the rule of fear. It subsisted by force of arms and terror was its cohering power. It had been extended by ruthless conquest alone until it comprised from eighteen hundred to two thousand square leagues, about two hundred thousand square miles of territory. The capital, situated on an island in the midst of a salt lake, was known as Tenochtitlan, or the City of Mexico, and what Rome was to the Italian states, or Carthage was to the north African literal, this city was to Anahuac, the empire of the Aztecs. The name Tenochtitlan is thus explained by Fiske:

When the Aztecs, hard pressed by foes, took refuge among these marshes, they came upon a sacrificial stone which they recognized as one upon which some years before one of their priests had immolated a captive chief. From a crevice in this stone, where a little earth was imbedded, there grew a cactus, upon which sat an eagle holding in its beak a serpent. A priest ingeniously interpreted this symbolism as a prophecy of signal and long-continued victory, and, forthwith diving into the lake, he had an interview with Tlaloc, the god of waters, who told him that upon that very spot the people were to build their town. The place was thereafter called Tenochtitlan, or "the place of the cactus-rock," but the name under which it afterward came to be best known was taken from Mexitl, one of the names of the war god Huitzilopochtli. The device of the rock, the cactus, with the eagle and the serpent, formed a tribal totem for the Aztecs, and has been adopted, as the coat-of-arms of the present Republic of Mexico.

Included in the sway of its emperor were many different tribes.

98

They were kept in submission by the strong and inexorable hand. There were a few tribes, however, which had not been subdued and which still maintained a more or less precarious independence. The subject peoples were only kept from open rebellion by the most rigorous and oppressive measures. There was jealousy, humiliation, hoped-for revenge throughout the entire empire.

Each tribe or people had its own local god, but there was a bond coherent in the general Mexican religion that had its centre of worship in the great city, and which all of them followed. This religion was one of the most ferocious, degrading and disgusting of any in history. It required human sacrifice on a larger scale than had ever before been practised. Cannibalism was universal. Captives of war were sacrificed to the gods and their bodies eaten. In Mexico, itself, with all its charm, with all its beauty, with all its luxuries, with all its verdure and wealth, there were huge pyramids of skulls. The priests were ferocious creatures, whose long black locks, never combed, were matted with blood, as they sacrificed to their awful war-god human hearts, still palpitating, torn from the victims a moment since alive. Fiske thus describes the temple pyramid and chief shrine in the great city:

> On the summit was a dreadful block of jasper, convex at the top, so that when the human victim was laid upon his back and held down, the breast was pushed upwards, ready for the priest to make one deep slashing cut and snatch out the heart. Near the sacrificial block were the altars, and sanctuaries of the gods, Tezcatlipoca, Huitzilopochtli, and others, with idols as hideous as their names. On these altars smoked fresh human hearts, of which the gods were fond, while other parts of the bodies were ready for the kitchens of the communal houses below. The gods were voracious as wolves, and the victims as numerous. In some cases the heart was thrust into the mouth of the idol with a golden spoon, in others the lips were simply daubed with blood. In the temple a great quantity of rattlesnakes, kept as sacred objects were fed with the entrails of the victims.
> Other parts of the body were given to the menagerie beasts, which were probably also kept for purposes of religious symbolism. Blood was also rubbed into the mouths of the carved serpents upon the jambs and lintels of the houses. The walls and floor of the great temple were clotted with blood and shreds of human flesh, and the smell was like that of a slaughter-house.

Just outside the temple, in front of the broad street which led across the causeway to Tlacopan, stood the *tzompantli*, which was an oblong parallelogram of earth and masonry, one hundred and fifty-four feet (long) at the base, ascended by thirty steps, on each of which were skulls.

Round the summit were upward of seventy raised poles about four feet apart, connected by numerous rows of cross-poles passed through holes in the masts, on each of which five skulls were filed, the sticks being passed through the temples. In the centre stood two towers, or columns, made of skulls and lime, the face of each skull being turned outwards, and giving a horrible appearance to the whole. This effect was heightened by leaving the heads of distinguished captives in their natural state, with hair and skin on. As the skulls decayed they fell from the towers or poles, and they were replaced by others, so that no vacant place was left.

Concerning the cruelty of the Spaniards, the contrast between the opposing religions must be considered. Ruthless as the conquerors were, there is no possible comparison between the most indifferent principles of the Christian Religion and the application of the awful principles of the Mexican religion. MacNutt, the author of the latest and best life of Cortes, makes this interesting comment on the Christianity of the Spanish adventurers of the time:

Soldier of Spain and soldier of the Cross, for the Cross was the standard of militant Christianity, of which Spain was the truest exponent, his religion, devoutly believed in, but intermittently practised, inspired his ideals, without sufficiently guiding his conduct. Ofttimes brutal, he was never vulgar, while as a lover of sheer daring and of danger for danger's sake, he has never been eclipsed....Sixteenth-century Spain produced a race of Christian warriors whose piety, born of an intense realization of, and love for a militant Christ, was of a martial complexion, beholding in the symbol of salvation—the Cross—the standard of Christendom around which the faithful must rally, and for whose protection and exaltation swords must be drawn and blood spilled if need be.

They were the children of the generation which had expelled the Moor from Spain, and had brought centuries of religious and patriotic warfare to a triumphant close, in which their country was finally united under the crown of Castile. From such forebears the generation of Cortes received its heritage of Christian chivalry. The discovery of a new world, peopled by barbarians, opened a fresh field to Spanish missionary zeal, in which the kingdom of God upon earth was to be extended and countless souls rescued from the obscene idolatries and debasing cannibalism which enslaved them.

In the Mexican Pantheon, however, there was one good god, named Quetzalcoatl. He was a Toltec deity, and was venerated as the god of the air. He was identified with the east wind which brought the fertilizing rains. Some historians and investigators explain him as purely a mythical personage. He was supposed to have appeared to the Toltecs long before the Aztecs came into the land. He was described in ancient traditions as a tall, white-faced, bearded man, whose dress differed from that of the aborigines and included a long white tunic, upon which were dark red crosses. His teachings enjoined chastity, charity, and penance. He had but one God and preached in the name of that God. He condemned human sacrifice and taught the nation agriculture, metal work and mechanics. He fixed their calendar so that it was much more reliable than either the Greek or the Roman. There were various legends as to his departure, one of them being that he sailed away across the sea upon a raft composed of serpents, and was wafted into the unknown East whence he had come.

His colour, his dress, his teachings, and his character, are all so symbolic of Christianity, they are so strange, so unique, so utterly without an explanation in anything else known of the Aztecs and Toltecs, that the conclusion that he was a Christian Bishop, wearing a *pallium* is almost irresistible. Why could not some Christian Bishop, voyaging along the shores of Europe, have been blown far out of his course by a long-continued easterly gale, finally have landed on the shores of Mexico and, having done what he could to teach the people, have built himself some kind of a ship and sailed eastward in the hope of once more revisiting his native land before he died. At any rate, such is the tradition. It was a tradition or legend which played no small part in the conquest about to be effected.

4. The March to Tenochtitlan

Into this loosely compact political and social organization, hard-headed, clear-sighted, iron-hearted, steel-clad Cortes precipitated himself. His was a mind at the same time capable of vast and comprehensive designs and a most minute attention to small details. For instance, he laid out the city of Vera Cruz at the place of his landing. He caused his men to elect a full corps of municipal officers from their number. To this organization he frankly resigned his commission and the power that he had by the appointment of Velasquez, which the latter had tried so hard to revoke. They immediately elected him captain-general of the expedition with vastly increased prerogatives and privileges. Thus he could now, in form at least, trace his authority to the crown, as represented by this new colonial municipality and he therefore had behind him the whole power of the expedition!

With a skill, which showed not only his adroitness, but his determination, he next caused his men to acquiesce in the scuttling of the ships which had conveyed them to Mexico! After saving the cordage, rigging and everything else that might be useful, which was carefully stored away in the little fort rapidly building, the vessels were destroyed beyond repair. Before this was done, Cortes offered to reserve one ship for certain malcontents and partisans of Velasquez in which they might return if they wished. Nobody took advantage of his offer.

By this bold and original stroke, he added to his expeditionary force some one hundred and twenty hardy mariners, who thereafter took part with the soldiery in all the hazards and undertakings. With, therefore, less than six hundred men, sixteen horses, ten small cannon, and one woman, Cortes prepared to undertake the conquest of this mighty empire. It was a small force, but its fighting quality was unsurpassed. Lew Wallace thus characterizes them:

> It is hardly worthwhile to eulogize the Christians who took part in Cortes's crusade. History has assumed their commemoration. I may say, however, they were men who had acquired fitness for the task by service in almost every clime. Some had tilted with the Moor under the walls of Granada; some had fought the Islamite on the blue Danube; some had performed the first Atlantic voyage with Columbus; all of them had hunted the Carib in the glades of Hispaniola. It is not enough to describe them as fortune-hunters, credulous, imaginative, tireless; neither is it enough to write them soldiers, bold, skilful, confident, cruel to enemies, gentle to each other. They were characters of the age in which they lived, unseen before, unseen since; knights errant, who believed in hippogriff and dragon, but sought them

only in lands of gold; missionaries, who complacently broke the body of the converted that Christ might the sooner receive his soul; palmers of pike and shield, who, in care of the Virgin, followed the morning round the world, assured that Heaven stooped lowest over the most profitable plantations.

Just what Cortes at first proposed to do is not quite clear. Indeed, he himself could not form any definite plan until the circumstances under which he would be compelled to act, should be more precisely ascertained. He was, therefore, an opportunist. For one thing, he made up his mind to lead his troops to the capital city willy-nilly, and there act as circumstances might determine. He was a statesman as well as a soldier. It did not take him long to fathom the peculiarities of the organization and composition of the Aztec Empire. He knew that discord existed and he had only to introduce himself to become a focus for the discontent and rebellion. By giving a secret impression that he was for either side, he could play one party against the other, as best suited his purposes. He came to bring freedom to the one, to promote the revolt of the other, check the oppression of the third, and destroy the presumption of the another tribe, or warring nation. So he caused his purposes to be declared.

Cortes's personal character was not by any means above reproach, yet withal he was a sincere and devoted Christian, strange and inexplicable as the paradox may seem, but it was an age of devoted Christians, whose devotion and principles fortunately were not translated into daily life. Neither Cortes nor any of his followers—perhaps not even the priests were of different opinion—thought any less of themselves or regarded themselves the less worthy Christians: if their conduct toward the native races did not manifest that continence, restraint and sympathy which their religion taught. Cortes was a child of his age; the other great men of his age were much like him in these things. Here and there a Las Casas appears, but he shines forth against a dark and universally extensive background. Such as the great apostles to the Indies were lonely exceptions indeed.

All the Spanish conquerors were cruel; but Cortes was not so cruel as many others. He was not to be compared to the ruthless Pizarro for instance. Save in daring and personal courage, he vastly surpassed the Lord of Peru in every quality which goes to make a man. Cortes was treacherous in his dealings with Montezuma and others, but the man of his age regarded very lightly the obligation of his word toward a savage. Indeed, it was a well-known principle that no faith was necessarily to be kept with either heretics or heathen and no oath was binding against the interests of the state. Cortes, of course, had all the contempt for the Aztecs that Caucasians usually have for inferior races, although in his letters, he tried his very best to be fair, to be just, even to be generous to these people he overcame; and no one can doubt the sincerity with which he desired to promote the spreading of the Christian religion.

They did things differently in those days. Not only did they believe that the religion of the heathen should be changed by force, but they believed that in some way they could constrain all people to accept Christianity. More blood has been shed in promoting the idea that the outsider should be compelled to come into the fold than from the misinterpretation of any other text in the sacred scriptures. If any civilized power in the world today should send an expeditionary force into a heathen country, which should signalize its arrival therein by the desecration of its temples and the destruction of its idols, the commander would be recalled at once. We have learned other methods, methods of persuasion, of reason, of love. The age of Cortes knew nothing of these methods, and he was only following out the common practice when he smashed with his battle-axe the hideous gods of the Mexicans, and washed and purified with clean water, the reeking, gory, ill-smelling slaughter-houses which were the Aztec Holy of Holies, and adorned them with crosses and images of the Blessed Virgin Mary. When Charles the IX. offered Henry of Navarre a choice of death, mass, or the Bastille on the night of Saint Bartholomew, he gave him one more chance than the early steel-clad militant missionary gave to the aborigines of the new world—for them there was no Bastille.

Making friends with the Tabascans, and leaving one hundred and fifty men to guard his base of supplies at Vera Cruz and to watch the coast, Cortes began his march toward Mexico on the sixteenth day of August, 1519. He proceeded with the greatest caution. Bernal Diaz, an old soldier, who afterward wrote a most vivid and graphic account of the conquest, of which he was no small part, says that they marched forward "with their beards on their shoulders," that is, looking from side to side, constantly. There was no hurry and there was no need to tire out the force which was thus facing the danger of a long, hard and rash adventure.

By the aid of Marina and Aguilar, Cortes speedily learned of places like Cempoalla, which were hostile to Montezuma and he took in as many of these places on his march as possible, always with incidents instructive and valuable. At Cempoalla, for instance, he met the tax-gatherers of Montezuma. He persuaded the Cempoallans to refuse payment of the tax—an action which would ordinarily have brought down upon them the fury of the Aztec monarch and would have resulted in their complete and utter extermination. He did more. He caused the Cacique of Cempoalla—a man so fat and gross, that, like "the little round belly" of Santa Claus, he "shook like a jelly" so that the Spaniards called him "The Trembler"—actually to raise his hand against the tax-gatherers and imprison them. They would undoubtedly have been sacrificed and eaten had not Cortes, secretly and by night released three of them and allowed them to go back to their royal master, after he had sent two into a safe ward at Vera Cruz.

Montezuma's messengers met him at every town. "Bearing rich gifts, they disclosed the possibilities of the *Hinterland* and germinated in the brain of Cortes the idea of conquest. One revelation was confirmed by another, and, as the evidence of Aztec wealth multiplied the proofs of internal disaffection throughout the empire stimulated the confidence of the brooding conqueror. Disloyalty among the Totonacs, treachery that only waited an opportunity in Texcoco, an ancient tradition of hate in Tlascala, and the superstition that obscured the judgment and paralyzed the action of the despotic ruler—these were the materials from which the astute invader evolved the machinery for his conquest."

Montezuma was in a pitiable state of superstitious indecision. It was popularly believed that Quetzalcoatl would someday return, and it was more than probable to the Aztec monarch and his counsellors that he might be reincarnated in the person of Cortes and his followers. Indeed, the common name for them among the Mexicans was Teules, which means gods. If Cortes was a god it was useless to fight against him. If he and his were men, they could of course be easily exterminated, but were they men? There were a few bold spirits who inclined to this belief, but not many. Besides, whatever the rest might be, the horsemen must be of divine origin. Cuitlahua, the brother of Montezuma, and one of the highest and most important of the Aztec rulers was for attacking them whatever the consequences, but he was alone in advising this. It was thought better to temporize. Perhaps later on it might be decided whether these strange beings were of common clay, and there would be plenty of time to exterminate them then.

Montezuma was therefore an opportunist, like Cortes, but there was a vast difference between them. Montezuma was a man of great ability, undoubtedly, or he never could have been chosen by the hereditary electors to the position he occupied, and he could never have held it if he had not been. He was a man over fifty years of age, and had maintained himself on the throne, in spite of many wars, in which he had been almost universally victorious. His judgment and his decision alike were paralyzed by superstition. He did the unwisest thing he could possibly have done. He sent messengers to Cortes, bearing rich gifts, gold, feather work, green stones, which the Spaniards thought were emeralds, vast treasures. He acknowledged in effect the wonderful wisdom of Cortes's overlord, the great emperor, Charles V., in whose name Cortes did everything, taking care always to have a notary to attest his proclamations to the Indians, but he told Cortes not to come to Mexico City. He said that he was poor, that the journey was a long and hard one; in short, he offered him every inducement to come with one hand, while he waved him back with the other.

Treasure was the only motive of the conquerors of Peru. Cortes was big enough and great enough to rise above that. He was after larger things than the mere filling of his purse, and on several occasions he relinquished his own share of the booty to the soldiery. He was an empire-builder, not a treasure-hunter.

As Cortes progressed through the country, the treasure sent by Montezuma grew in value, and the prohibitions, which by and by amounted to entreaties, increased in volume. We wonder what might have happened, if young Guatemoc, whom we shall hear of later had occupied the throne. Certainly, although the Spaniards would have died fighting, they would undoubtedly have been overwhelmed, and the conquest of Mexico might have been postponed for another generation or two. It was bound to happen anyway, sooner or later, as far as that goes.

5. THE REPUBLIC OF TLASCALA

Cortes's progress finally brought him to a remarkable tribe, whose friendship he succeeded in winning, and which must be added as the fourth factor, with himself, Marina, and the horses, as the cause of the downfall of Mexico. Curiously enough, this tribe had a sort of republican form of government. It is usually referred to as the Republic of Tlascala. It was an independent confederation composed of four separate states. The government consisted of a senate, composed

106

of the rulers of the four states or clans of the tribe. Tlascala was completely hemmed in by provinces of the Aztec Empire, with which it was always in a state of constant and bitter warfare. The inhabitants had no access to the sea, consequently they had never enjoyed the use of salt. They had no access to the lowlands, so they were without cotton, a fabric then universally used throughout the country. They had no trade or commerce. They were completely shut in and eternal vigilance was the price of their liberty. They lacked the arts, the grace, and the refinement of the Mexicans, but they were as hardy, as bold, as skilful in the use of arms, and as determined, as well as cruel, as the Aztecs. Neither Montezuma nor his predecessors with the power of millions had been able to make them acknowledge any sovereignty but their own. They were protected by the mountain ranges and here and there they had built high walls across the valley. Tlascala was a large and imposing city. Cortes thus describes it:

> This city is so extensive and so well worthy of admiration, that although I omit much that I could say of it, I feel assured that the little I shall say will be scarcely credited, for it is larger than Granada, and much stronger, and contains as many fine houses and a much larger population than that city did at the time of its capture; and it is much better supplied with the products of the earth, such as corn, and with fowls and game, fish from the rivers, various kinds of vegetables, and other excellent articles of food. There is in this city a market, in which every day thirty thousand people are engaged in buying and selling, besides many other merchants who are scattered about the city. The market contains a great variety of articles both of food and clothing, and all kinds of shoes for the feet; jewels of gold and silver, and precious stones, and ornaments of feathers, all as well arranged as they can possibly be found in any public squares or markets in the world.
>
> There is much earthenware of every style and a good quality, equal to the best Spanish manufacture. Wood, coal, edible and medicinal plants, are sold in great quantities. There are houses where they wash and shave the head as barbers, and also for baths. Finally, there is found among them a well-regulated police; the people are rational and well disposed, and altogether greatly superior to the most civilized African nations. The country abounds in level and beautiful valleys all tilled and

sown, without any part lying unimproved. In its constitution of government that has existed until the present time, it resembles the states of Venice, Genoa and Pisa; since the supreme authority is not reposed in one person. There are many nobles, all of whom reside in the city; the common people are labourers and the vassals of the nobility, but each one possesses land of his own, some more than others. In war all unite and have a voice in its management and direction. It may be supposed that they have tribunals of justice for the punishment of the guilty; since when one of the natives of the province stole some gold of a Spaniard, and I mentioned the circumstance to Magiscacin, the most powerful of the nobility, they made search for the thief, and traced him to a city in the neighbourhood called Churultecal (Cholula) from whence they brought him prisoner, and delivered him to me with the gold, saying that I must have him punished.

I acknowledged in suitable terms the pains they had taken in the matter, but remarked to them that since the prisoner was in their country, they should punish him according to their custom, and that I chose not to interfere with the punishment of their people while I remained among them. They thanked me and, taking the man, carried him to the great market, a town crier making public proclamations of his offense; they then placed him at the base of a structure resembling a theatre, which stands in the midst of the market-place, while the crier went to the top of the building, and with a loud voice again proclaimed his offense; whereupon the people beat him with sticks until he was dead. We likewise saw many persons in prison who were said to be confined for theft and other offenses they had committed. There are in this province, according to the report made by my order, five hundred thousand inhabitants, besides those in another smaller province adjacent to this, called Guazincango, who live in the manner, not subject to any native sovereign and are not less the vassals of Your Highness than the people of Tlascala.

Montezuma gave another reason for permitting the Tlascalans their liberty and independence. He said that he was allowing them to maintain their existence and remain a republic because everything else in the vicinity had been conquered; and as there was no field for the young warriors of the Aztec nation to obtain that military training which it was always best to learn by actual experience, he kept Tlascala in a state of enmity because it furnished him a place where he could get the human beings for sacrifices to his gods that he required and at the same time train his young soldiery. In other words, Tlascala was regarded as a sort of game preserve from a religious point of view. Doubtless, Tlascala did not acknowledge the justice, the propriety and the correctness of this attitude of scorn and contempt on the part of the Aztecs. The other tribes of Mexico bore the yoke uneasily, and cherished resentment, but even the enmity between the Jews and the Samaritans was not more bitter than the enmity between the Tlascalans and the people of the city of Anahuac.

When Cortes drew near Tlascala, the senate debated what course it should pursue toward him. One of the four regents, so called, of the republic was a man of great age, feeble and blind, but resolute of spirit. His name was Xicotencatl. He was all for war. He was opposed by a young man named Maxixcatzin. The debate between the two and the other participants was long and furious. Finally the desire of Xicotencatl prevailed in a modified form. There was a tribe occupying part of the Tlascalan territory and under Tlascalan rule called Otumies. It was decided to cause the Otumies to attack Cortes and his force. If Cortes was annihilated, the problem would be solved. If the Otumies were defeated their action would be disavowed by the Tlascalans and no harm would be done to anybody but the unfortunate Otumies, for whom no one in Tlascala felt any great concern.

The Otumies were placed in the front of the battle, but the Tlascalans themselves followed under the command of another Xicotencatl, son of the old regent, who was a tried and brilliant soldier. The battles along the coast had been more like massacres, but this was a real fight, and a number of Spaniards were killed, three horses also, more valuable than the men, were despatched, and at the close of the engagement the Spaniards had lost about fifty, a serious diminution of the forces of Cortes, but the unfortunate Otumies and the Tlascalans were overwhelmed with a fearful slaughter. Of course, the action of the Otumies was disavowed, Cortes was invited into Tlascala and an alliance between the Spaniards and the republic was consummated. The Tlascalans threw themselves, heart and soul, into the project, which they dimly perceived was in the mind of Cortes, the conquest of Mexico.

Nothing was said about all of this. Cortes simply declared his design to pay a friendly visit to Montezuma to whom he sent repeated and solemn assurances that he intended him no harm, that Montezuma could receive him with the utmost frankness and without fear and without anticipating any violence whatever on the part of the Spaniards. But the wise in Tlascala knew that a collision between the Spaniards and the Aztecs would be inevitable. They saw a chance to feed fat their ancient grudge, and to exact bitter revenge for all that they had suffered at the hands of the Aztecs.

To anticipate, they were faithful to the alliance and loyally carried out their part of the agreement in the resulting campaigns. Without them on several occasions Cortes' fortunes would have been even more desperate than they were. Montezuma's envoys, heartily detesting the Tlascalans, sought to persuade Cortes against any dealings with them whatsoever. They gave a very bad character to the dusky allies of the Spaniards and the Tlascalans returned the compliment in kind.

When his wounded had recovered, accompanied by a large army of Tlascalans under young Xicotencatl, Cortes set forth about the middle of October on the last stage of his wonderful journey. By this time, Montezuma had concluded to make a virtue out of a necessity, and he had sent word to him that he would welcome him to his capital. He received return reiterations of the statement that Cortes' intentions were entirely pacific, that he represented the greatest monarch in the world who lived beyond the seas, and all that he would require of Montezuma was the acknowledgment of his dependence in common with every earthly monarch upon this mysterious potentate across the ocean. This Montezuma was quite willing to give. He was also willing to pay any tribute exacted if only these children of the Sun would go away, and he could be left to the undisturbed enjoyment of his kingdom.

He suggested a way for Cortes to approach the capital. The Tlascalans did some scouting and informed Cortes that the way was filled with pitfalls, blocked with stones, and the opportunities for ambuscade were many and good. No one can blame Montezuma for taking these precautions, although he afterwards disowned any participation in them and said that the arrangements had been made by some irresponsible subjects, and Cortes passed it over.

The Tlascalans, who knew all the passes of the mountains, offered to lead Cortes and his followers by another way. Although he was warned not to trust them by the envoys of Montezuma, Cortes with that judgment of men which so distinguished him, elected the harder and shorter way across the mountains. Nature had made the pass a difficult one, but the indomitable Spaniards struggled over it, enduring terrible fatigue and periods of piercing cold. They got far above the timber line and approached the boundaries of eternal snow. It is characteristic of them, that on one point of their journey, they stopped and despatched a party under Ordaz to scale and explore the smoking volcano Popocatepetl, which with Ixtaccihuatl guarded the beautiful valley of Mexico. Ordaz and his twelve companions followed the guides as far as they would lead them and then they climbed far up the sides. They were unable to reach the top, but they accomplished a prodigious ascent, and Ordaz was afterwards allowed to add to his coat of arms a flaming volcano.

The summit of the mountain was at last passed, and the magnificent valley of Mexico opened to their view. It was a scene which caused even the hearts of these rugged and hardened adventurers to thrill with pleasure and satisfaction. No fairer land had ever burst upon human vision. The emerald verdure was broken by beautiful lakes, bordered by luxuriant vegetation, diversified by mountains and plateaus, while here and there magnificent cities glistened in the brilliant tropical sun among the sparkling waters. As far as one could see the land was under cultivation.

The descent of the mountains was easy, comparatively speaking, and the Spaniards, after some journeying, found themselves in the populous and wealthy city of Cholula, remarkable for the splendid pyramid temple—Teocalli—which rose in the centre of its encircling walls.

Here a plan was devolved to massacre the whole force which had been quartered in one of the vast palaces or houses of the town. The women and the children left the city in large numbers, a vast body of Mexican soldiers was secretly assembled nearby. The provisions, which had always been supplied them generously, were suddenly withdrawn. The suspicions of the Spaniards were of course awakened and extra good watch was kept. They did not know what to suspect, until a Cholulan woman, who had formed an acquaintance with Marina, told her of the purpose of the Mexicans, and advised her to flee from the Spanish camp if she valued her life. The faithful Marina immediately disclosed the whole plan to Cortes. He acted with remarkable celerity and decision. There were many Cholulan lords and attendants about the Spanish camp and there were many others in town, evidently to lull any suspicions which the Spaniards might feel and to make whatever excuse they could for the lack of provisions.

On one pretence or another, Cortes summoned the whole body to his house, which was a great rambling structure of many rooms and thick walls and enclosures. He got them assembled in one room and then proceeded to slaughter most of them, reserving only a few for use after the event had been determined. While this butchering was going on he sent others of his troops into the streets and squares of the town, where they killed without hesitation and without mercy all with whom they came in contact, including several bodies of soldiers who were more or less helpless without their leaders, whom Cortes had so craftily disposed of.

This was the celebrated massacre of Cholula. Whether it was justifiable or not, each reader must settle for himself. Cortes' situation then was certainly desperate; for that matter, it was desperate at all times. His life and the lives of his comrades hung upon a thread. He certainly had a right to protect himself. Personally, I do not think such a slaughter was necessary for his protection. However, Cortes thought so, and he was there. It was his life that was concerned, and not mine. Other monarchs in more civilized days have done practically the same as this, as for instance, the famous Barmecide feast, the wholesale assassination of the Abencerrages in Spain, the massacre of the Mamelukes by Napoleon in Egypt, and many others.

To be sure these massacres did not include the helpless inhabitants of the towns. However, with his usual policy, Cortes spared some of the Cholulan lords and when he had shown his power over them, he released them and told them to summon back the people who had left the city. He had no more trouble with the Cholulans after that victory, and he presently took up his journey toward Mexico.

Now, the City of Mexico to the Spaniards was one of the wonders of the world. They have described it in such terms as show the impression it made upon them, but they have not described it in such terms as to enable us to understand from their stories exactly what the city was. It was described as an island city. Some believed it to have been an enormous Pueblo city, such as may be seen in Arizona or New Mexico, surrounded by thousands of squalid huts. Others conjectured it as a city as beautiful as Venice, as great as Babylon, and as wonderful as hundred-gated Thebes.

Cortes shall tell himself the impression it made upon him in the next section which is lifted bodily from one of his famous letters to the emperor Charles V.

6. Cortes' Description of Mexico, written by his own hand to Charles V., Emperor of Germany and King of Spain

In order, most potent Sire, to convey to your Majesty a just conception of the great extent of this noble city of Temixtitan, and of the many rare and wonderful objects it contains; of the government and dominions of Muteczuma, the sovereign; of the religious rites and customs that prevail, and the order that exists in this as well as other cities, appertaining to his realm; it would require the labour of many accomplished writers, and much time for the completion of the task. I shall not be able to relate an hundredth part of what could be told respecting these matters; but I will endeavour to describe, in the best manner in my power, what I have myself seen; and, imperfectly as I may succeed in that attempt, I am fully aware that the account will appear so wonderful as to be deemed scarcely worthy of credit; since even we who have seen these things with our own eyes, are yet so amazed as to be unable to comprehend their reality. But your Majesty may be assured that if there is any fault in my relation, either in regard to the present subject, or to any other matters of which I shall give your Majesty an account, it will arise from too great brevity rather than extravagance or prolixity in the details; and it seems to me but just to my Prince and Sovereign to declare the truth in the clearest manner, without saying anything that would detract from it, or add to it.

Before I begin to describe this great city and the others already mentioned, it may be well for the better understanding of the subject to say something of the configuration of Mexico,[1] in which they are situated, it being the principal seat of Muteczuma's power. This province is in the form of a circle, surrounded on all sides by lofty and rugged mountains; its level surface comprises an area of about seventy leagues in circumference, including two lakes, that overspread nearly the whole valley, being navigated by boats more than fifty leagues round. One of these lakes contains fresh, and the other, which is the larger of the two, salt water. On one side of the lakes, in the middle of the valley, a range of highlands divides them from one another, with the exception of a narrow strait which lies between the highlands and

---

1. Cortes applies this name to the province in which the city, called by him Temixtitan, more properly Tenochtitlan, but now Mexico, was situated. Throughout this article the curious spelling of the great conqueror is retained as he wrote.

the lofty *sierras*. This strait is a bow-shot wide, and connects the two lakes; and by this means a trade is carried on by the cities and other settlement on the lakes in canoes, without the necessity of travelling by land. As the salt lake rises and falls with the tides like the sea, during the time of high water it pours into the other lake with the rapidity of a powerful stream; and on the other hand, when the tide has ebbed, the water runs from the fresh into the salt lake.

This great city of Temixtitan (Mexico) is situated in this salt lake, and from the main land to the denser parts of it, by which ever route one chooses to enter, the distance is two leagues. There are four avenues or entrances to the city, all of which are formed by artificial causeways, two spears' length in width. The city is as large as Seville or Cordova; its streets, I speak of principal ones, are very wide and straight; some of these, and all the inferior ones, are half land and half water, and are navigated by canoes. All the streets at intervals have openings, through which the water flows, crossing from one street to another; and at these openings, some of which are very wide, there are also very wide bridges, composed of large pieces of lumber, of great strength and well put together; on many of these bridges ten horses can go abreast. Foreseeing that if the inhabitants of this city should prove treacherous, they would possess great advantages from the manner in which the city is constructed, since by removing the bridges at the entrances and abandoning the place, they could leave us to perish by famine without our being able to reach the mainland—as soon as I had entered it, I made great haste to build four *brigantines*, which were soon finished, and were large enough to take ashore three hundred men and the horses, whenever it became necessary.

This city has many public squares, in which are situated the markets and other places for buying and selling. There is one square twice as large as that of the city of Salamanca, surrounded by *porticoes*, where are daily assembled more than sixty thousand souls, engaged in buying and selling; and where are found all kinds of merchandise that the world affords, embracing the necessities of life, as, for instance, articles of food, as well as jewels of gold, silver, lead, brass, copper, tin, precious stones, bones, shells, snails and feathers. There were also exposed for sale wrought and unwrought stone, bricks burnt and unburnt, timber hewn and unhewn of different sorts. There is a street for game, where every variety of birds found in the country is sold, as fowls, partridges, quails, wild ducks, fly-catchers, widgeons, turtle-doves, pigeons, reed-birds, parrots, sparrows, eagles, hawks, owls, and kestrels; they sell, likewise, the skins of some birds of prey, with their feathers, head and beak and claws.

There they also sold rabbits, hares, deer, and little dogs which are raised for eating and castrated. There is also an herb street, where may be obtained all sorts of roots and medicinal herbs that the country affords. There are apothecaries' shops, where prepared medicines, liquids, ointments, and plasters are sold; barber shops where they wash and shave the head; and restauranteurs that furnish food and drink at a certain price. There is also a class of men like those called in Castile porters, for carrying burdens. Wood and coal are seen in abundance, and *brasiers* of earthenware for burning coals; mats of various kinds for beds, others of a lighter sort for seats, and for halls and bedrooms. There are all kinds of green vegetables, especially onions, leeks, garlic, watercresses, nasturtium, borage, sorel, artichokes, and golden thistle-fruits also of numerous descriptions, amongst which are cherries and plums, similar to those in Spain; honey and wax from bees, and from the stalks of maize, which are as sweet as the sugar-cane; honey is also extracted from the plant called *maguey*,[2] which is superior to sweet or new wine; from the same plant they extract sugar and wine, which they also sell.

Different kinds of cotton thread of all colours in skeins are exposed for sale in one quarter of the market, which has the appearance of the silk market at Granada, although the former is supplied more abundantly. Painter's colours, as numerous as can be found in Spain, and as fine shades; deer-skins dressed and undressed, dyed different colours; earthenware of a large size and excellent quality; large and small jars, jugs, pots, bricks, and an endless variety of vessels, all made of fine clay, and all or most of them glazed and painted; maize or Indian corn, in the grain, and in the form of bread, preferred in the grain for its flavour to that of the other islands and *terra firma; pâtés* of birds and fish; great quantities of fish, fresh, salt, cooked and uncooked; the eggs of hens, geese and of all the other birds I have mentioned, in great abundance, and cakes made of eggs; finally, everything that can be found throughout the whole country is sold in the markets, comprising articles so numerous that, to avoid prolixity and because their names are not retained in my memory, or are unknown to me, I shall not attempt to enumerate them.

---

2. This is the plant known in this country under the name of the *Century Plant*, which is still much cultivated in Mexico for the purposes mentioned by Cortes. It usually flowers when eight or ten years old.

Every kind of merchandise is sold in a particular street or quarter assigned to it exclusively, and thus the best order is preserved. They sell everything by number or measure; at least, so far we have not observed them to sell anything by weight. There is a building in the great square that is used as an audience house, where ten or twelve persons, who are magistrates, sit and decide all controversies that arise in the market, and order delinquents to be punished. In the same square there are other persons who go constantly about among the people observing what is sold, and the measures used in selling; and they have been seen to break measures that were not true.

This great city contains a large number of temples[3] or houses for their idols, very handsome edifices, which are situated in the different districts and the suburbs; in the principal ones religious persons of each particular sect are constantly residing, for whose use, beside the houses containing the idols, there are other convenient habitations. All these persons dress in black and never cut or comb their hair from the time they enter the priesthood until they leave it; and all the sons of the principal inhabitants, both nobles and respectable citizens, are placed in the temples and wear the same dress from the age of seven or eight years until they are taken out to be married; which occurs more frequently with the firstborn, who inherits estates, than with the others. The priests are debarred from female society, nor is any woman permitted to enter the religious houses. They also abstain from eating certain kinds of food, more at some seasons of the year than others.

Among these temples there is one which far surpasses all the rest, whose grandeur of architectural details no human tongue is able to describe; for within its precincts, surrounded by a lofty wall, there is room for a town of five hundred families. Around the interior of this enclosure there are handsome edifices, containing large halls and corridors, in which the religious persons attached to the temple reside. There are full forty towers, which are lofty and well built, the largest of which has fifty steps leading to its main body, and is higher than the tower of the principal church at Seville. The stone and wood of which they are constructed are so well wrought in every part, that nothing could be better done, for the interior of the chapels containing the idols consists of curious imagery, wrought in stone, with plaster ceilings, and woodwork carved in relief, and painted with figures of

---

3. The original has the word *Mesquitas*, mosques; but as the term is applied in English exclusively to Mohammedan places of worship, one of more general application is used in the translation.

monsters and other objects. All these towers are the burial places of the nobles, and every chapel of them is dedicated to a particular idol, to which they pay their devotions.

There are three halls in this grand temple, which contain the principal idols; these are of wonderful extent and height, and admirable workmanship, adorned with figures sculptured in stone and wood; leading from the halls are chapels with very small doors, to which the light is not admitted, nor are any persons except the priests, and not all of them. In these chapels are the images or idols, although, as I have before said, many of them are also found on the outside; the principal ones, in which the people have greatest faith and confidence, I precipitated from their pedestals, and cast them down the steps of the temple, purifying the chapels in which they stood, as they were all polluted with human blood, shed in the sacrifices. In the place of these I put images of Our Lady and the Saints, which excited not a little feeling in Muteczuma and the inhabitants, who at first remonstrated, declaring that if my proceedings were known throughout the country, the people would rise against me; for they believed that their idols bestowed upon them all temporal good, and if they permitted them to be ill-treated, they would be angry and withhold their gifts, and by this means the people would be deprived of the fruits of the earth and die of famine.

I answered, through the interpreters, that they were deceived in expecting any favours from idols, the work of their own hands, formed of unclean things; and that they must learn there was but one God, the universal Lord of all, who had created the heavens and the earth, and all things else, and had made them and us; that He was without beginning and immortal, and that they were bound to adore and believe Him, and no other creature or thing. I said everything to them I could to divert them from their idolatries, and draw them to a knowledge of God our Lord. Muteczuma replied, the others assenting to what he said: "That they had already informed me that they were not the aborigines of the country, but that their ancestors had emigrated to it many years ago; and they fully believed, after so long an absence from their native land, they might have fallen into some errors; that I, having been recently arrived, must know better than themselves what they ought to believe; and that if I would instruct them in these matters, and make them understand the true faith, they would follow my directions, as being for the best."

Afterward Muteczuma and many of the principal citizens remained with me until I had removed the idols, purified the chapels, and placed images in them, manifesting apparent pleasure; and I forbade them sacrificing human beings to their idols, as they had been accustomed to do; because, besides being abhorrent in the sight of God, your sacred Majesty had prohibited it by law and commanded to put to death whoever should take the life of another. Thus, from that time, they refrained from the practice, and during the whole period of my abode in that city, they were never seen to kill or sacrifice a human being.

The figures of the idols in which these people believe surpass in stature a person of more than the ordinary size; some of them are composed of a mass of seeds and leguminous plants, such as are used for food, ground and mixed together, and kneaded with the blood of human hearts taken from the breasts of living persons, from which a paste is formed in a sufficient quantity to form large statues. When these are completed they make them offerings of the hearts of other victims, which they sacrifice to them, and besmear their faces with the blood. For everything they have an idol, consecrated by the use of the nations that in ancient times honoured the same gods. Thus they have an idol that they petition for victory in war; another for success in their labours; and so for everything in which they seek or desire prosperity, they have their idols, which they honour and serve.

This noble city contains many fine and magnificent houses; which may be accounted for from the fact that all the nobility of the country, who are the vassals of Muteczuma, have houses in the city, in which they reside a certain part of the year; and besides, there are numerous wealthy citizens who also possess fine houses. All these persons, in addition to the large and spacious apartments for ordinary purposes, have others, both upper and lower, that contain conservatories of flowers. Along one of the causeways that lead into the city are laid two pipes, constructed of masonry, each of which is two paces in width, and about five feet in height. An abundant supply of excellent water, forming a volume equal in bulk to the human body, is conveyed by one of these pipes, and distributed about the city, where it is used by the inhabitants for drinking and other purposes.

The other pipe, in the meantime, is kept empty until the former requires to be cleansed, when the water is let into it; and continues to be used until the cleansing is finished. As the water is necessarily carried over bridges on account of the salt water crossing its route, reservoirs resembling canals are constructed on the bridges, through which the fresh water is conveyed. These reservoirs are of the breadth of the body of an ox, and of the same length as the bridges. The whole city is thus served with water, which they carry in canoes through all the streets for sale, taking it from the aqueduct in the following manner: the canoes pass under the bridges on which the reservoirs are placed, when men stationed above fill them with water, for which service they are paid. At all the entrances of the city, and in those parts where the canoes are discharged, that is, where the greatest quantity of provisions is brought in, huts are erected and persons stationed as guards, who receive a *certum quid* for everything that enters. I know not whether the sovereign receives this duty or the city, as I have not yet been informed; but I believe that it appertains to the sovereign, as in the markets of other provinces a tax is collected for the benefit of their cacique.

In all the markets and public places of this city are seen daily many laborers and persons of various employments waiting for someone to hire them. The inhabitants of this city pay a greater regard to style in their mode of living, and are more attentive to elegance of dress and politeness of manners, than those of the other provinces and cities; since as the Cacique[4] Muteczuma has his residence in the capital, and all the nobility, his *vassals*, are in the constant habit of meeting there, a general courtesy of demeanour necessarily prevails. But not to be prolix in describing what relates to the affairs of this great city, although it is with difficulty that I refrain from proceeding. I will say no more than that the manners of the people, as shown in their intercourse with one another, are marked by as great an attention to the proprieties of life as in Spain, and good order is equally well observed; and considering that they are a barbarous people, without the knowledge of God, having no intercourse with civilized nations, these traits of character are worthy of admiration.

In regard to the domestic appointments of Muteczuma, and the wonderful grandeur and state he maintains, there is so much to be told, that I assure Your Majesty I do not know where to begin my relation, so as to be able to finish any part of it. For, as I have already stated, what can be more wonderful, than that a barbarous monarch, as he is,

4. The title invariably given to Muteczuma (or Montezuma) in these dispatches is simply *Señor*, in its sense of Lord or (to use an Indian word) *Cacique*; which is also given to the chiefs or governors of districts or provinces, whether independent or feudatories. The title of *Emperador* (Emperor), how generally applied to the Mexican ruler, is never conferred on him by Cortes, nor any other implying royalty, although in the beginning of this despatch, he assures Charles V. that the country is extensive enough to constitute an empire.

should have every object found in his dominions, imitated in gold, silver, precious stones and feathers?—the gold and silver being wrought so naturally as not to be surpassed by any smith in the world; the stone work executed with such perfection that is it difficult to conceive what instruments could have been used; and the feather work superior to the finest productions in wax and embroidery. The extent of Muteczuma's dominions has not been ascertained, since to whatever point he despatched his messengers, even two hundred leagues from his capital, his commands were obeyed, although some of his provinces were in the midst of countries with which he was at war.

But as nearly as I have been able to learn, his territories are equal in extent to Spain itself, for he sent messengers to the inhabitants of a city called Cumatan (requiring them to become subjects of Your Majesty), which is sixty leagues beyond that part of Putunchan watered by the river Grijalva, and two hundred and thirty leagues distant from the great city; and I sent some of our people a distance of one hundred and fifty leagues in the same direction. All the principal chiefs of these provinces, especially those in the vicinity of the capital, reside, as I have already stated, the greater part of the year in that great city, and all or most of them have their oldest sons in the service of Muteczuma.

There are fortified places in all the provinces, garrisoned with his own men, where are also stationed his governors and collectors of the rent and tribute, rendered him by every province; and an account is kept of what each is obliged to pay, as they have characters and figures made on paper that are used for this purpose. Each province renders a tribute of its own particular productions, so that the sovereign receives a great variety of articles from different quarters. No prince was ever more feared by his subjects, both in his presence and absence. He possessed out of the city as well as within, numerous villas, each of which had its peculiar sources of amusement, and all were constructed in the best possible manner for the use of a great prince and lord. Within the city his palaces were so wonderful that it is hardly possible to describe their beauty and extent; I can only say that in Spain there is nothing to equal them.

There was one palace somewhat inferior to the rest, attached to which was a beautiful garden with balconies extending over it, supported by marble columns, and having a floor formed of jasper elegantly laid. There were apartments in this palace sufficient to lodge two princes of the highest rank with their retinues. There were likewise belonging to it ten pools of water, in which were kept the different species of water birds found in this country, of which there is a great variety, all of which are domesticated; for the sea birds there were pools of salt water, and for the river birds, of fresh water. The water is let off at certain times to keep it pure, and is replenished by means of pipes. Each species of bird is supplied with the food natural to it, which it feeds upon when wild. Thus fish is given to birds that usually eat it; worms, maize and the finer seeds, to such as prefer them. And I assure Your Highness, that to the birds accustomed to eat fish, there is given the enormous quantity of ten *arrobas*[5] every day, taken in the salt lake. The emperor has three hundred men whose sole employment is to take care of these birds; and there are others whose only business is to attend to the birds that are in bad health.

Over the pools for the birds there are corridors and galleries to which Muteczuma resorts, and from which he can look out and amuse himself with the sight of them. There is an apartment in the same palace, in which are men, women, and children, whose faces, bodies, hair, eyebrows, and eyelashes are white from birth. The *cacique* has another very beautiful palace, with a large courtyard, paved with handsome flags, in the style of a chess-board. There were also cages, about nine feet in height and six paces square, each of which was half covered with a roof of tiles, and the other half had over it a wooden grate, skilfully made. Every cage contains a bird of prey, of all the species found in Spain, from the kestrel to the eagle, and many unknown there. There were a great number of each kind, and in the covered part of the cages there was a perch, and another on the outside of the grating, the former of which the birds used in the night-time, and when it rained; and the other enabled them to enjoy the sun and air.

To all these birds fowl were daily given for food, and nothing else. There were in the same palace several large halls on the ground floor, filled with immense cages built of heavy pieces of timber, well put together, in all or most of which were kept lions, tigers, wolves, foxes and a variety of animals of the cat tribe, in great numbers, which were also fed on fowls. The care of these animals and birds was assigned to three hundred men. There was another palace that contained a number of men and women of monstrous size, and also dwarfs, and crooked and ill-formed persons, each of which had their separate apartments. These also had their respective keepers. As to the other remarkable things that the ruler had in his city for amusement, I can only say that they were numerous and of various kinds.

5. Two hundred and fifty pounds weight.

121

He was served in the following manner. Every day as soon as it was light, six hundred nobles and men of rank were in attendance at the palace, who either sat or walked about the halls and galleries, and passed their time in conversation, but without entering the apartment where his person was. The servants and attendants of these nobles remained in the courtyards, of which there were two or three of great extent, and in the adjoining street, which was also spacious. They all remained in attendance from morning until night; and when his meals were served, the nobles were likewise served with equal profusion, and their servants and secretaries also had their allowance. Daily his larder and wine-cellar were open to all who wished to eat and drink. The meals were served by three or four hundred youths, who brought on an infinite variety of dishes; indeed, whenever he dined or supped the table was loaded with every kind of flesh, fish, fruit, and vegetables that the country provided.

As the climate is cold, they put a chafing-dish with live coals under every plate and dish to keep them warm. The meals were served in a large hall where Muteczuma was accustomed to eat, and the dishes quite filled the room, which was covered with mats and kept very clean. He sat on small cushions curiously wrought in leather. During the meals there were present, at a little distance from him, five or six elderly *caciques*, to whom he presented some of the food. And there was constantly in attendance one of the servants, who arranged and handed the dishes, and who received from others whatever was wanted for the supply of the table. Both at the beginning and end of every meal, they furnished water for the hands, and the napkins used on these occasions were never used a second time; this was the case also with the plates and dishes, which were not brought again, but new ones in place of them; it was also the same with the chafing dishes. He is also dressed every day in four different suits, entirely new, which he never wears a second time.

None of the *caciques* ever enter his palace with their feet covered, and when those for whom he sends enter his presence, they incline their heads and look down, bending their bodies; and when they address him they do not look in his face; this arises from excessive modesty and reverence. Whenever Muteczuma appeared in public, which was seldom the case, all those who accompanied him or whom he accidentally met in the streets, turned away without looking toward him, and others prostrated themselves until he passed. One of the nobles always preceded him on these occasions, carrying three slender rods erect, which I suppose was to give notice of the approach of his person. And when they descended from the litters, he took one of them in his hands, and held it until he reached the places where he was going. So many and various were the ceremonies and customs observed by those in the service of Muteczuma, that more space than I can spare would be required for the details, as well as a better memory than I have to recollect them; since no sultan or other infidel lord, of whom any knowledge now exists, ever had so much ceremonial in their courts.

7. The Meeting with Montezuma

It was early in the morning of November the 8th, 1519, when Cortes, at the head of his little army, rode over one of the long causeways and into the city to his first meeting with Montezuma. As no one can tell better than he what happened, I here insert his own account of the episode:

The next day after my arrival at this city, I departed on my route, and having proceeded half a league, I entered upon a causeway that extends two leagues through the centre of the salt lake, until it reaches the great city of Temixtitan (Mexico), which is built in the middle of the lake....

I pursued my course over the above-mentioned causeway, and having proceeded half a league before arriving at the body of the city of Temixtitan, I found at its intersection with another causeway, which extends from this point to *terra firma*, a very strong fortress with two towers, surrounded by a double wall, twelve feet in height, with an embattled parapet, which commands the two causeways, and has only two gates, one for the entering and the other for departure. There came to meet me at this place nearly a thousand of the principal inhabitants of the great city, all uniformly dressed according to their custom in very rich costumes; and as soon as they had come within speaking distance, each one, as he approached me, performed a salutation in much use among them, by placing his hand upon the ground and kissing it; and thus I was kept waiting about an hour, until all had performed the ceremony.

Connected with the city is a wooden bridge ten paces wide, where the causeway is open to allow the water free ingress and egress, as it rises and falls; and also for the security of the city, as they can remove the long and wide beams of which the bridge

123

is formed, and replace them whenever they wish; and there are many such bridges in different parts of the city, as Your Highness will perceive hereafter from the particular account I shall give of it.

When we had passed the bridge, the Señor Muteczuma came out to receive us, attended by about two hundred nobles, all barefooted, and dressed in livery, or a peculiar garb of fine cotton, richer than is usually worn; they came in two processions in close proximity to the houses on each side of the street, which is very wide and beautiful, and so straight that you can see from one end of it to the other, although it is two-thirds of a league in length, having on both sides large and elegant houses and temples. Muteczuma came through the centre of the street, attended by two lords, one upon his right and the other upon his left hand, one of whom was the same nobleman who, as I have mentioned, came to meet me in a litter, and the other was the brother of Muteczuma, lord of the city of Iztapalapa, which I had left the same day; all three were dressed in the same manner, except that Muteczuma wore shoes, while the others were without them.

He was supported in the arms of both, and as we approached, I alighted and advanced alone to salute him; but the two attendant lords stopped me to prevent my touching him, and they and he both performed the ceremony of kissing the ground; after which he directed his brother who accompanied him to remain with me; the latter accordingly took me by the arm, while Muteczuma, with his other attendant, walked a short distance in front of me, and after he had spoken to me, all the other nobles also came up to address me, and then went away in two processions with great regularity, one after the other, and in this manner returned to the city. At the time I advanced to speak to Muteczuma, I took off from myself a collar of pearls and glass diamonds, and put it around his neck.

After having proceeded along the street, one of his servants came bringing two collars formed of shell fish, enclosed in a roll of cloth, which were made from the shells of coloured prawns or periwinkles, held by them in great esteem; and from each collar depended eight golden prawns, finished in a very perfect manner and about a foot and a half in length. When these were brought Muteczuma turned toward me and put them around

124

my neck; he then returned along the street in the order already described, until he reached a very large and splendid palace, in which we were to be quartered, which had been fully prepared for our reception. He there took me by the hand and led me into a spacious saloon, in front of which was a court, through which we entered.

Having caused me to sit down on a piece of rich carpeting, which he had ordered to be made for himself, he told me to await his return there, and then went away. After a short space of time, when my people were all bestowed in their quarters, he returned with many and various jewels of gold and silver, feather work and five or six thousand pieces of cotton cloth, very rich and of varied texture and finish. After having presented these to me, he sat down on another piece of carpet they had placed for him near me, and being seated he discoursed as follows:

'It is now a long time since, by means of written records, we learned from our ancestors that neither myself nor any of those who inhabit this region were descended from its original inhabitants, but from strangers who emigrated hither from a very distant land; and we have also learned that a prince, whose vassals they all were, conducted our people into these parts, and then returned to his native land. He afterward came again to this country, after the lapse of much time, and found that his people had inter-married with the native inhabitants, by whom they had many children, and had built towns in which they resided; and when he desired them to return with him, they were unwilling to go, nor were they disposed to acknowledge him as their sovereign; so he departed from the country, and we have always heard that his descendants would come to conquer this land and reduce us to subjection as his *vassals*; and according to the direction from which you say you have come, namely the quarter where the sun rises, and from what you say of the great lord or king who sent you hither, we believe and are assured that he is our natural sovereign, especially as you say that it is a long time since you first had knowledge of us.

'Therefore, be assured that we will obey you, and acknowledge you for our sovereign in place of the great lord whom you mention, and that there shall be no default or deception on our part. And you have the power in all this land, I mean wherever my power extends, to command what is your pleasure, and it shall be done in obedience thereto, and all that we have is at your disposal. And since you are in your own proper land and your own house, rest and refresh yourself after the toils of your journey, and the conflicts in which you have been engaged, which have been brought upon you, as I well know, by all the people from Puntunchan to this place; and I am aware that the Cempoallans and the Tlascalans have told you much evil of me, but believe no more than you see with your own eyes, especially from those who are my enemies, some of whom were once my subjects, and having rebelled upon your arrival, make these statements to ingratiate themselves in your favour. These people, I know, have informed you that I possessed houses with walls of gold, and that my carpets and other things in common use were of the texture of gold; and that I was a god, or made myself one, and many other such things. The houses, as you see, are of stone and lime and earth.'

And then he opened his robes and showed his person to me, saying: 'You see that I am composed of flesh and bone like yourself, and that I am mortal and palpable to the touch,' at the same time pinching his arms and body with his hands. 'See,' he continued, 'how they have deceived you. It is true that I have some things of gold, which my ancestors have left me; all that I have is at your service whenever you wish it. I am now going to my other houses where I reside; you will be here provided with everything necessary for yourself and your people, and will suffer no embarrassment, as you are in your own house and country.'

I answered him in respect to all that he had said, expressing my acknowledgments, and adding whatever the occasion seemed to demand, especially endeavouring to confirm him in the belief that Your Majesty was the sovereign they had looked for; and after this he took his leave, and having gone, we were liberally supplied with fowls, bread, fruits and other things required for the use of our quarters. In this way I was for six days amply provided with all that was necessary, and visited by many of the nobility.

It throws a somewhat amusing light on the interview when we note that the presents exchanged were of great value on Montezuma's part, while the gift of Cortes was a collar of cheap imitation diamonds!

The emotions of the Spaniards at this singular meeting between the immeasurable distance of the past and present were so strong that even the rough soldier felt it.

> And when we beheld, (says Bernal Diaz), so many cities and towns rising up from the water, and other populous places situated on the *terra firma*, and that causeway, straight as a level, which went into Mexico, we remained astonished, and said to one another that it appeared like the enchanted castles which they tell of in the book of Amadis, by reason of the great towers, temples, and edifices which there were in the water, all of them work of masonry. Some of our soldiers asked if this that they saw was not a thing in a dream.

Fiske thus felicitously alludes to it:

> It may be well called the most romantic moment in all history, this moment when European eyes first rested upon that city of wonders, the chief ornament of a stage of social evolution two full ethnical periods behind their own. To say that it was like stepping back across the centuries to visit the Nineveh of Sennacherib or hundred-gated Thebes, is but inadequately to depict the situation, for it was a longer step than that. Such chances do not come twice to mankind, for when two grades of culture so widely severed are brought into contact, the stronger is apt to blight and crush the weaker where it does not amend and transform it.
>
> In spite of its foul abominations, one sometimes feels that one would like to recall the extinct state of society in order to study it. The devoted lover of history, who ransacks all sciences for aid toward understanding the course of human events, who knows in what unexpected ways one progress often illustrates other stages, will sometimes wish it were possible to resuscitate, even for one brief year, the vanished City of the Cactus Rock. Could such a work of enchantment be performed, however, our first feeling would doubtless be one of ineffable horror and disgust, like that of the knight in the old English ballad, who, folding in his arms a damsel of radiant beauty, finds himself in the embrace of a loathsome fiend.

What the emotions of the Mexicans were we have no account, but it is not difficult to imagine them. Amazement as at the visitation of a god, fear begot of this gross superstition, apprehension of what might be the result of the coming of these strange monsters, curiosity mingled with admiration; and as they looked at the long lines of fierce, dauntless, implacable Tlascalans who accompanied the Spaniards, their hereditary enemies, there must have swelled in their savage breasts feelings of deep and bitter hatred.

Outwardly, however, all was calm. The Spaniards marched through the flower-decked streets to the great palace of Ayxacatl, which had been assigned to them as a residence, and which was spacious and commodious enough to take them all in, bag and baggage, including their savage allies. It is one of the singular contradictions of the Aztec character that with all of their brutal religion and barbarism, they were passionately fond of flowers and like other barbarians rejoiced in colour.

Flowers were used in many of the religious festivals, and there is abundant evidence, moreover, that the Mexicans were very fond of them. This is illustrated in the perpetual reference to flowers in old Mexican poems:

They led me within a valley to a fertile spot, a flowery spot, where the dew spread out in glistening splendour, where I saw various lovely fragrant flowers, lovely odorous flowers, clothed with the dew, scattered around in rainbow glory; there they said to me, 'Pluck the flowers, whichever thou wishest; mayst thou, the singer, be glad, and give them to thy friends, to the chiefs, that they may rejoice on the earth.' So I gathered in the folds of my garments the various fragrant flowers, delicate, scented, delicious.

The will of Montezuma was supreme. Nothing dimmed the warmth and generosity of his splendid hospitality. There were no frowning looks, no mutterings of discontent, everything was joyous and pleasant, at least outwardly, yet not one of the Christians was blind to the peril in which he stood, or doubted that the least accident might precipitate an outbreak which would sweep them all from off the face of the earth.

For six days the Spaniards remained the guests of the Mexican Emperor. Visits were exchanged, religious discussions were indulged in, and Cortes was only constrained from overthrowing their idols in the temples which he visited, and substituting Christian emblems therein by force, by the prudent counsel of the worthy priests, men remarkable for their wisdom and their statesmanship, who accompanied him. Continual efforts were made to convert Montezuma, but without results.

That monarch, who was of a cheerful and jovial nature, professed great friendship for and interest in the Spaniards, whom he often visited and to whom he accorded many privileges. Such a condition of affairs, however, could not last very long. The suspense was intolerable to a man of action like Cortes and to the men who followed him as well. They were not good waiters. Something had to be done.

Into the mind of this Spanish soldier of fortune there leaped a bold design. He decided upon a course of action, as amazing in its character, so far-reaching in its result, that its conception and its execution almost thrust him into the ranks of the *demi*-gods. This project was nothing less than the seizure of the person of Montezuma in the midst of his capital, a city of three hundred thousand people, among whom were thousands of fierce and highly trained veteran warriors who counted their lives as nothing in the Emperor's need. Undoubtedly such an action was the basest of treachery, but Cortes had put himself in such a position that the nakedness of such an action did not prevail with him for a moment. He quieted his conscience with the old reasoning that Montezuma was a heathen, and that oaths to him were by no means binding.

Whether he quieted his conscience or not, something was necessary. He could not retire from Mexico after this ostensibly friendly visit. Such a withdrawal would not have suited his purposes at all, and it was more than possible that the moment he turned his back on the Aztec capital, he would be forced to fight for his life against conditions which would leave him little or no possibility of escape. It was really Montezuma's life and liberty or Cortes' life and liberty. In such an alternative, there was no hesitation.

8. THE SEIZURE OF THE EMPEROR

Occasion was soon found for the seizure. A chief on the sea coast had attacked and killed some of the men left at Vera Cruz. It was alleged that this was done by the orders of Montezuma. Cortes accompanied by the hardiest and bravest of his companions, and after a night of prayer—singular with what good consciences they could pray for the success of the most nefarious undertaking!—visited Montezuma, and accused him of having instigated the crime. Montezuma denied it, and despatched messengers to the offending cacique, directing that he be put under close arrest and brought to the capital. This was all any reasonable man could expect, but Cortes and his companions were not reasonable.

In spite of the fact that the prompt action of the Aztec had deprived them of the faintest pretext, they nevertheless at last declared to the unhappy monarch that he must accompany them to the *pueblo*, which he had assigned to them, and remain in the custody of the Spaniards until the matter had been decided. In vain Montezuma protested. His situation was unfortunate. He was surrounded by an intrepid body of steel-clad Spaniards, and although the room was filled with officers, courtiers and soldiers, he realized—indeed he was bluntly told—that the first act of hostility against the Spaniards would result in his immediate death. He made a virtue of a necessity, and complied with the Spaniards' demand. Forbidding his subjects, who were moved to tears—tears of rage and anger, most probably—to assist him, he submitted himself to the will of his captors, and went away with them. He had to go or he would have died then and there. Far better would it have been if he had chosen the nobler course, both for his fame and his empire.

The affairs of the government were carried on as usual by Montezuma, to whom his officers and his counsellors had free access. Cortes even permitted him to go to the Temple on occasion for the ordinary worship, but in every instance he was accompanied and practically surrounded by a body of one hundred completely armed and thoroughly resolute Spaniards. Cortes did not attempt to interfere in the least degree with the national administration, although it was patent to everybody that as he held the person of the Emperor, he could also command, if he so elected, the power of the empire.

Meanwhile, the *Cacique* Quahpopoca, who was guilty of the murder of the Spaniards on the coast, was brought into Mexico two weeks after the seizure of Montezuma. With a loyalty touchingly beautiful, he promptly declared that he had acted upon his own responsibility and that Montezuma had had nothing whatever to do with it, which was, of course, highly improbable. The official clearing of Montezuma was complete; nevertheless, despite the testimony of Quahpopoca, Cortes actually put the Mexican monarch in double irons. It is true, the irons were removed almost immediately, and he was treated as he had been during his two weeks' captivity, with the greatest possible respect and deference, but the irons had not merely clasped the wrists and ankles of the unfortunate Aztec. They had entered his soul.

Quahpopoca was burned in the public square. The heaping fagots which surrounded the stake were made of javelins and spears collected by Cortes with intrepid audacity and far-seeing prudence, from the public armoury. Vast numbers of them were used. The populace looked on in sullen and gloomy silence. Montezuma was not merely the ruler of the country, but in some senses he was a *deity*, and his capture, together with the capture of the great lords of his family, who, under ordinary circumstances would have succeeded to his throne, paralyzed the national, social, political and religious organization.

Cortes actually held his captive in this way until spring. The intervening months were not wasted. Expeditions were sent to all parts of the country to ascertain its resources and report upon them, so that, when the Spaniards took over the government, they would be prepared to administer it wisely and well. No such prudent and statesmanlike policy was inaugurated by any other conqueror. Cortes in this particular stands absolutely alone among the great adventurers, Spanish and otherwise. He was not a mere plunderer of the people, he was laying a foundation for an empire. Vast treasures were, nevertheless, collected. Messengers were despatched to Charles V. with the letters which have already been quoted and with the royal share of the booty, which was great enough to insure them a favourable reception.

What Cortes would have done further can only be surmised. Something happened suddenly which forced his hand. In the spring, Montezuma received word through an excellent corps of messengers which supplied him daily with information from all parts of the empire, of the arrival of a strange Spanish force on the coast. Mexico had no writing, but its messenger system was one of the best in the world. Messengers arrived daily from the farthest parts and confines of the Mexican empire, supplementing pictures, which the Mexicans drew very cleverly, with verbal accounts. Incidentally, there was no money in the empire, either. The art of coinage had not been attained.

9. The Revolt of the Capital

Cortes was naturally much interested and not a little perturbed by the news. Soon the exact tidings reached him from the commander at Vera Cruz, that the force consisted of some twelve hundred men, including eighty horse, all under the command of one Panfilo de Narvaez, which had been organized, equipped and sent out by Cortes' old enemy, Velasquez, with instructions to seize him and his companions and send them back to Cuba for trial. Narvaez was loud in his threats of what he was going to do with Cortes and how he was going to do it.

The great Spaniard acted with his usual promptness. He left in charge of the city one Pedro de Alvarado, called from his fair hair, To-natiuh, or the child of the sun. Committing the care of Montezuma to this cavalier and bidding him watch over him and guard him with his life, as the safety of all depended upon him, Cortes with some two hundred and fifty men made a dash for the coast. It was two hundred and fifty against five times that number, but with the two hundred and fifty was a man whose mere presence equalized conditions, while with the twelve hundred and fifty was another whose braggart foolishness diminished their superiority until, in the end, it really amounted to nothing!

Cortes actually surprised Narvaez in the town in which he had taken refuge and seized him after an attack—a night surprise of bold and audacious conception—by the two hundred and fifty against the twelve hundred which was completely successful. With Narvaez in Cortes's hands all opposition ceased on the part of the men. In one swoop Narvaez lost power, position and one eye, which had been knocked out during the contest, and Cortes found his following re-inforced by so great a number and quality that he had never dreamed of such a thing.

"You are, indeed, fortunate," said Narvaez to his conqueror, "in having captured me."

"It is," said Cortes carelessly, "the least of the things I have done in Mexico!"

While affairs were thus progressing favourably on the coast, the smouldering rebellion had at last broken out in Mexico, and Cortes received a message from Alvarado, bidding him return with all possible speed. There was not a braver soldier, a fiercer fighter, or a more reso-lute man in the following of Cortes than Pedro de Alvarado. When that has been said, however, practically all has been said that can be said in his favour. He was a rash, impetuous, reckless, head-long, tact-less, unscrupulous man, and brutal and cruel to a high degree.

His suspicions that the Aztecs, led by Montezuma, were conspiring to overwhelm his small force were aroused. It is probable that there was some truth in his apprehensions, although he could not point to anything very definite upon which to base them. He knew of but one way to deal with such a situation—by brute force. He waited until the great May Festival of the Aztecs was being held, and then fell upon them in the midst of their joyous play and slew six hundred, including many of the noblest chiefs of the land. The outbreak was instant and universal. The house of Ayxacatl was at once besieged, the influx of provisions was stopped, and the *pueblo* was surrounded by vast numbers of thoroughly enraged citizens. Neither the Spaniards nor the allies could leave the pueblo without being overwhelmed. Alvarado at last compelled Montezuma to show himself on the walls and bid the people stop fighting, to enable him to strengthen his position and hold it until the arrival of Cortes, and some fifteen hundred men, his own force and that of Narvaez combined.

When the conqueror met Alvarado he upbraided him and told him that he had behaved like a madman. There was little or no provision. Cortes now made the mistake of sending Cuitlahua, the brother of Montezuma, out into the city with instructions for him to have the markets opened at once and secure provisions for the Spaniards and their horses. Cuitlahua, being free, called the council of priests. This council at once deposed Montezuma and elected Cuitlahua emperor and priest in his place. The revolution and the religion now had a head.

The next morning an attack of such force was delivered that many of even the stoutest-hearted Spaniards quailed before it. The slaughter of the natives was terrific. The Spanish cannon opened long lanes through the crowded streets. The Spanish horse sallied forth and hacked and hewed broad pathways up the different avenues. Still, the attack was pressed and was as intrepid as if not a single Aztec had died. The roar that came up from every quarter of the city, from the house tops, from the crowded streets, from the Temples, was in itself enough to appal the bravest.

10. In God's Way

Finally Cortes resorted to Alvarado's expedient. He compelled the unhappy Montezuma to mount the walls of the palace and bid the people disperse. When he appeared in all his splendid panoply upon the roof of the palace there was a strange silence. He was no longer priest, he was no longer emperor, he was no longer a power, he was no longer a god, but some of the old divinity seemed to cling to him, to linger around him still. The situation was so tragic that even the

133

meanest soldier, Mexican or Spanish, felt its import. A long time the Aztec looked over his once smiling capital, and into the faces of his once subordinate people. Finally he began to address them. He bade them lay down their arms and disperse.

The people, led by the great lords and Montezuma's brother, Cuitlahua, and his nephew, Guatemoc, answered with a roar of rage, and the roar spread as the purport of the message was communicated to those further back. Montezuma stood appalled. The next instant a rain of missiles was actually launched at him and the Spaniards who stood by his side. A stone hurled, it is said by young Guatemoc, struck him in the forehead. He reeled and fell. With the bitter words: "Woman! woman!" ringing in his ears, he was carried away by the Spaniards. His face, says Lew Wallace, was the face of a man "breaking because he was in God's way!" He lived a few days after that, but he refused to eat, and repeatedly tore the bandages from his wounds until death put an end to his miseries. The stone that had struck him had broken his heart. Neither Cortes nor Montezuma himself knew that he had been deposed. Cortes and the principal Spaniards visited him and endeavoured to console him, but he turned his face to the wall and would have none of them. It was said afterward that he became a Christian, but it is most probably not true. He died as he had lived. Helps thus describes the scene and the great Montezuma's end:

He was surrounded by Spanish soldiers, and was at first received with all respect and honour by his people. When silence ensued, he addressed them in very loving words, bidding them discontinue the attack, and assuring them that the Spaniards would depart from Mexico. It is not probable that much of his discourse could have been heard by the raging multitude. But, on the other hand, he was able to hear what their leaders had to say, as four of the chiefs approached near him, and with tears addressed him, declaring their grief at his imprisonment. They told him that they had chosen his brother as their leader, that they had vowed to their gods not to cease fighting until the Spaniards were all destroyed, and that each day they prayed to their gods to keep him free and harmless. They added, that when their designs were accomplished, he should be much more their lord than heretofore, and that he should then pardon them.

Amongst the crowd, however, were, doubtless, men who viewed the conduct of Montezuma with intense disgust, or

THE DEATH OF MONTEZUMA.
FROM AN OLD ENGRAVING.

"He defended himself with his terrible spear"

who thought that they had already shown too much disrespect toward him ever to be pardoned. A shower of stones and arrows interrupted the parley; the Spanish soldiers had ceased for the moment to protect Montezuma with their shields; and he was severely wounded in the head and in two other places. The miserable monarch was borne away, having received his death-stroke; but whether it came from the wounds themselves, or from the indignity of being thus treated by his people, remains a doubtful point. It seems, however, that, to use some emphatic words which have been employed upon a similar occasion: 'He turned his face to the wall, and would be troubled no more.'

It is remarkable that he did not die like a Christian,[6] and I think this shows that he had more force of mind and purpose than the world has generally been inclined to give him credit for. To read Montezuma's character rightly, at this distance of time, and amidst such a wild perplexity of facts, would be very difficult, and is not very important. But one thing, I think, is discernible, and that is, that his manners were very gracious and graceful.

I dwell upon this, because I conceive it was a characteristic of the race; and no one will estimate this characteristic lightly, who has observed how very rare, even in the centres of civilized life, it is to find people of fine manners, so that in great capitals but very few persons can be pointed out who are at all transcendent in this respect. The gracious delight which Montezuma had in giving was particularly noticeable; and the impression which he made upon Bernal Diaz may be seen in the narrative of this simple soldier, who never speaks of him otherwise as 'the great Montezuma'; and, upon the occasion of his death, remarks that some of the Spanish soldiers who had known him mourned for him as if he had been a father, 'and no wonder,' he adds, 'seeing that he was so good.'

---

6. I am not ignorant that it has been asserted that Montezuma received the rite of baptism at the hands of his Christian captors. See Bustamante's notes on Chimalpain's Translation of Gomara (*Historia de las Conquistas de Hernando Cortes*. Carlos Maria de Bustamante. Mexico, 1826, p. 287). But the objection raised by Torquemada—the silence of some of the best authorities, such as Oviedo, Ixlilxochitl, *Histoire des Chichimeques*, and of Cortes himself; and, on the other hand, the distinctly opposing testimony of Bernal Diaz (see cap. 127), and the statement of Herrera, who asserts that Montezuma, at the hour of his death, refused to quit the religion of his fathers. ("*No se queria apartar de la Religion de sus Padres.*" *Hist. de las Indias*, dec. II. lib. x, cap. 10), convinces me that no such baptism took place.

Cortes sent out the body to the new king, and Montezuma was mourned over by the Spaniards, to whom he had always been gracious, and probably, by his own people; but little could be learned of what the Mexicans thought, or did, upon the occasion, by the Spaniards, who only saw that Montezuma's death made no difference in the fierceness of the enemy's attack.

Meanwhile the situation of the Spaniards was indescribable. There was mutiny and rebellion among them. The soldiers of Narvaez, who looked for a pleasant promenade through a land of peace and plenty, were appalled. There was daily, desperate fighting. The Mexicans had manned the temple of the war-god which overlooked the Spanish *pueblo*, and Cortes determined to capture it. With a large body of chosen men he attempted its escalade. It was crowded to the very top with the most resolute Aztecs, and they fought for it with the courage of fanaticism and despair itself. The feather shields were no match for the steel *cuirasses*. The wooden clubs, stuck full of sharp pieces of obsidian, could not compete on equal terms with the Toledo blades. Step by step, terrace by terrace, the Spaniards fought their way to the very top. As if by mutual consent, the contests in the streets stopped and all eyes were turned upon this battle in the air.

Arriving at the great *plateau* upon the crest, the Spaniards were met by five hundred of the noblest Aztecs, who, animated by their priests, made the last desperate stand for the altars of their gods.

And how can men die better,
Than in facing fearful odds,
For the ashes of their Fathers,
And the temples of their Gods?

In the course of the terrific conflict which ensued, two of the bravest leaped upon Cortes, wrapped their arms around him, and attempted to throw themselves off the top of the temple, devoting themselves to death, if so be, they might compass their bold design. It was on the very verge of eternity that Cortes tore himself free from them. Singled out for attack because of his position and because of his fearlessness in battle, his life was saved again and again by his followers, until it seemed to be miraculously preserved.

After a stupendous struggle the summit of the temple was carried. Amid the groans of the populace, the Spaniards tumbled down from its resting-place the hideous image of the war-god, and completed in Aztec eyes the desecration of the temple. They were victorious, but they had paid a price. Dead Spaniards dotted the terraces, the sunlight, gleaming on their armour, picking them out amid the dark, naked bodies of the Mexicans. Of those who had survived the encounter, there was scarcely one but had sustained one or more wounds, some of them fearful in character. The Mexicans had not died in vain.

Leaving a guard at the temple, Cortes came back to the garrison. The attack was resumed at once by the natives. Attempts were made to burn the thatched roofs of the *pueblo*. A rain of missiles was poured upon it. The Spaniards made sally after sally, inflicting great slaughter, but losing always a little themselves. The Aztecs would sometimes seize a Spaniard and bear him off alive to sacrifice him on some high pyramid temple in full view of his wretched comrades below. The Spaniards fired cannon after cannon, but to no avail. They were starving, they were becoming sick, and they were covered with wounds; their allies, who took part gallantly in all the hard fighting, suffered frightful losses. It was at last reluctantly agreed among the leaders that their only salvation was the evacuation of the city.

11. The Melancholy Night

Although the course thus thrust upon them was indeed a hard one, there was nothing else to be done. Sick, wounded, starving, dying, they could by no means maintain themselves longer in the city. Fight as they might and would, the end would come speedily, and would mean annihilation. Happy in that event would be those who died upon the field, for every living captive, whatever his condition, would be reserved for that frightful sacrifice to the war-god, in which his body would be opened, and his reeking heart torn, almost while still beating, from his breast. To retreat was almost as dangerous as it was to remain. It was certain, however, that some would get through in that attempt, although it was equally certain that many would not.

Cortes, mustering his soldiers and allies, after a day of heart-breaking fighting, disclosed the situation to them in blunt soldier-like words, although they all knew it as well as he, and then the hasty preparations began. A vast treasure had been amassed by the Spaniards. Making an effort to preserve the fifth portion of it, which by law belonged to the King, Cortes threw open the treasure chamber and bade the rest help themselves. He cautioned them, however, that those who went the lightest, would have the greatest prospects for escape, a warning which many, especially among those who had come to the country with Narvaez, chose to disregard.

The causeway along which they determined to fly and which connected Mexico with the mainland was pierced at intervals to admit passage from one portion of the lake to the other. The bridges which usually covered these openings had been taken away by the Aztecs. Cortes caused a temporary bridge or pontoon to be built which was to be carried with the fugitives to enable them to pass the openings.

The night was the first of July, 1520. It was pitch dark and a heavy rain was falling. The forces consisted of twelve hundred and fifty Spaniards, of whom eighty were mounted, and six thousand Tlascalans. They were divided into three divisions. The advance was under the command of Juan Valesquez, Cortes led the main body, and the rear was put in the charge of the rash, cruel, but heroic Alvarado. The less severely wounded were supported by their comrades, and those unable to walk were carried on litters or mounted on horses. Montezuma had died the night before. Any lingering hopes of being able to effect peace through his influence had departed. Leaving everything they could not carry, the Spaniards, after prayer, confession and absolution, threw open the gates,[7] and entered the city.

Midnight was approaching. The streets and avenues were silent and deserted. The retreat proceeded cautiously for a little way, unmolested, when suddenly a deep, booming sound roared like thunder over the heads of the Spaniards, through the black night, filling their hearts with alarm. Cortes recognized it at once. The Aztecs were awake and ready. The priests in the great *teocallis*, or temple pyramids, were beating the great drum of the war-god, Huitzilopocahtli. Lights appeared here and there in the town, the clashing of arms was heard here and there on the broad avenues. Under the lights farther up the streets could be seen files of troops moving. The hour was full of portent.

Dragging their artillery, carrying their wounded, bearing their treasure, the Spaniards and their allies passed rapidly through the streets. Before the advance reached the first opening in the causeway it was already hotly engaged. The water on either side of the cause-way suddenly swarmed with canoes. Spears, javelins, arrows, heavy war-clubs with jagged pieces of obsidian were hurled upon the Spaniards on the causeway. In front of them, almost, it seemed, for the whole length, the Indians were massed. Step by step, by the hardest kind of hand-to-hand fighting, the Spaniards and their allies arrived at the first

---

7. These gates they had made themselves. The Aztecs had not learned the art of making gates or doors. The exits and entrances of their houses were closed, if at all with *portières*.

opening. Their loss had been frightful already. They were surrounded and attacked from all sides. Indians scrambled up the low banks in the darkness, seized the feet of the flying Spaniards and strove to draw them into the water.

Many a white man, many a Tlascalan locked in the savage embrace of some heroic Aztec, stumbled or was dragged into the lake and was drowned in the struggle. The frightened horses reared and plunged and created great confusion. The golden treasure with which many had loaded themselves proved a frightful incumbrance. Those who could do so, flung it away; those too bitterly occupied in fighting for their lives could do little but drive, thrust, hew, hack and struggle in the dark and slippery way.

But the army did advance. Arriving at the brink of the first opening, the bridge was brought up and the division began its passage. It had scarcely crossed the gap when under the pressure of tremendous fear, the second division, in spite of all that could be done to refrain and control them by Cortes and his officers—and there were no braver men on earth—crowded on the frail bridge. The structure which was sufficiently strong for ordinary and orderly passage, gave way, precipitating a great mass of Spaniards and Indians into the causeway. Cortes with his own hands, assisted by a few of the cooler veterans, tried to lift up the shattered remains of the bridge but was unable to do anything with it. It was ruined beyond repair, and sank into a splintered mass of timber under the terrific pressure to which it had been subjected. A passage at that gap was afforded to those who came after because it was filled level with dead bodies of Spaniards, Indians and horses, to say nothing of guns, baggage and equipment.

By this time the advance guard was again heavily engaged. The Spaniards and their allies staggered along the dyke, fighting desperately all the time. Velasquez, leading the advance division was killed at the brink of the second opening. The wretched fugitives were driven headlong into the second opening which was soon choked with horses and men as the first had been. Over this living, dying bridge the survivors madly ploughed. Some of them led by Cortes himself found a ford on the side. Although they were cut down by the hundreds, there seemed to be no end to the Aztecs. The rain still fell. The drum of the war-god mingled with frightful peals of thunder, and the shrill cries of the Mexicans rose higher and higher. The Spaniards were sick, wounded, beaten and terrified. Only Cortes and his captains and a few of his veterans preserved the slightest semblance of organization.

The third gap was passed by the same awful expedient as the other two had been. There was not a great distance from the third opening to the mainland. The few who had passed over rushed desperately for the shore. Way back in the rear, last of all, came Alvarado. There was a strange current in the lake, and as he stood all alone at the last opening, confronting the pursuers, his horse having been killed under him, a swift movement of the water swept away the gorged mass of bodies. Torches in the canoes enabled the Aztecs to recognize Alvarado, Tonatiuh, the child of the sun. His helmet had been knocked off and his fair hair streamed over his shoulders. He indeed would be a prize for their sacrifice, second only to Cortes himself. With furious cries, the most reckless and intrepid leaped upon the dyke and rushed at him. At his feet lay his neglected lance. Dropping his sword, he seized his spear, swiftly plunged the point of it into the sand at the bottom of the pass, and, weighted though he was with his armour, and weak from his wounds and from the loss of blood, leaped to safety on the other side. To this day, this place of Alvarado's marvellous leap is pointed out. Like Ney, Alvarado was the last of that grand army, and like the French commander, also, he might properly be called the bravest of the brave.

Darkness was not the usual period for Aztec fighting. It was this alone that saved the lives of the remaining few for, having seen Alvarado stagger to freedom along the causeway, the Aztecs concluded that they had done enough and returned to the city rejoicing. They took back with them many Spaniards and Tlascalans as captives for sacrifice and the cannibalistic feast which followed.

When day broke, Cortes sitting under a tree, which is still to be seen in Mexico,[8] ordered the survivors to pass in review before him. They numbered five hundred Spaniards and two thousand Tlascalans and a score of horses. Seven hundred and fifty Spaniards had been killed or taken captive and four thousand Tlascalans. All the artillery had been lost, seven *arquebuses* had been saved, but there was no powder. Half the Spaniards were destitute of any weapons and the battle-axes and spears which had been saved were jagged and broken. Their armour was battered and the most important parts, as helmets, shields, breastplates, had been lost. Some of the Tlascalans still preserved their

---

8. It is growing very old and is badly decayed. The newspapers report that efforts are being made by experts to try a course of treatment which will preserve this venerable and interesting forest relic, already nearly four hundred years old, but it is not believed that success will attend their endeavours.

savage weapons. There was scarcely a man, Spanish or Tlascalan who was not suffering from some wound.

It is no wonder that when Cortes saw the melancholy and dejected array, even his heart of steel gave way and he buried his face in his hands and burst into tears. This terrible night has always been known in history as *la noche triste*—the melancholy night. Melancholy indeed it was. Surely the situation of a man was never more desperate. If the Mexicans had rejoiced in the leadership of a Cortes, they would have mustered their forces and fallen upon the Spaniards without the delay of a moment, and the result could only have been annihilation. But the Mexicans themselves had suffered terrifically. They had won a great victory, but they had paid a fearful price for it. Now they wanted to enjoy it. They wished to sacrifice their captives to their gods, and they thought that there was no hope for the Spaniards, and that they might overwhelm them at their leisure.

This is Sir Arthur Helps' vivid description of the awful retreat:

A little before midnight the stealthy march began. The Spaniards succeeded in laying down the pontoon over the first bridge-way, and the vanguard with Sandoval passed over; Cortes and his men also passed over; but while the rest were passing, the Mexicans gave the alarm with loud shouts and blowing of horns. 'Tlaltelulco![9] Tlaltelulco!' they exclaimed, 'come out quickly with your canoes; the *teules* are going; cut them off at the bridges.' Almost immediately after this alarm, the lake was covered with canoes. It rained, and the misfortunes of the night commenced by two horses slipping from the pontoon into the water.

Then, the Mexicans attacked the pontoon-bearers so furiously that it was impossible for them to raise it up again. In a very short time the water at that part was full of dead horses, Tlascalan men, Indian women, baggage, artillery, prisoners, and boxes (*petacas*) which, I suppose, supported the pontoon. On every side the most piteous cries were heard: 'Help me! I drown!' 'Rescue me! They are killing me!' Such vain demands were mingled with prayers to the Virgin Mary and to Saint James. Those that did get upon the bridge and on the causeway found hands of Mexicans ready to push them down again into the water.

9. "Tlaltelulco" was the quarter of the town where the market was situated.

143

At the second bridge-way a single beam was found, which doubtless had been left for the convenience of the Mexicans themselves. This was useless for the horses, but Cortes diverging, found a shallow place where the water did not reach further than up to the saddle, and by that he and his horsemen passed (as Sandoval must have done before). He contrived, also to get his foot-soldiers safely to the mainland, though whether they swam or waded, whether they kept the line of the causeway, or diverged into the shallows, it is difficult to determine. Leaving the vanguard and his own division safe on shore, Cortes with a small body of horse and foot, returned to give what assistance he could to those who were left behind.

All order was now lost, and the retreat was little else than a confused slaughter, although small bodies of the Spaniards still retained sufficient presence of mind to act together, rushing forward, clearing the space about them, making their way at each moment with loss of life, but still some few survivors getting onward. Few, indeed, of the rear-guard could have escaped. It is told as a wonder of Alvarado, that, coming to the last bridge, he made a leap, which has by many been deemed impossible, and cleared the vast aperture. When Cortes came up to him, he was found accompanied by only seven soldiers and eight Tlascalans, all covered with blood from their many wounds.

They told Cortes that there was no use in going further back, that all who remained alive were there with him. Upon this the General turned; and the small and melancholy band of Spaniards pushed on to Tlacuba, Cortes protecting the rear. It is said that he sat down on a stone in the village called Popotla near Tlacuba, and wept; a rare occurrence, for he was not a man to waste any energy in weeping while aught remained to be done. The country was aroused against them, and they did not rest for the night till they had fortified themselves in a temple on a hill near Tlacuba, where afterward was built a church dedicated, very appropriately, to Our Lady of Refuge (à *Nuestra Señora de los Remedios*).

There is an old story of a Roman general, who after a most terrific defeat, a defeat due largely to his own incompetency, not only escaped censure but was officially thanked by the senate, because he declared publicly that he did not despair of the republic. Of that same temper was Cortes.

Exhorting his men in the face of this awful peril which menaced them to conduct themselves as white men, as Spaniards, and as soldiers of the Cross, Cortes led his army toward Tlascala. Upon the position of that republic absolutely depended the future. It depends upon the way you look at the situation as to how you estimate the conduct of these dusky allies of the unfortunate conqueror. Had there been any national feeling among them, had their hatred of the Aztecs been less, they might have broken their agreements with the Spaniards and overwhelmed them, but the hatred of the Tlascalans did not permit them to look beyond the present day. They decided to maintain the alliance they had entered into with Cortes and welcomed him with open arms. They gave him a chance to recuperate, to get something to eat, and to dress the wounds of his men. All the Spaniards wanted was time to bring about the inevitable downfall of Mexico and the Mexicans.

Among the men who had followed Narvaez was a Negro who had brought with him the germs of smallpox, which were communicated to the Aztecs in the city. It spared neither rich nor poor, as one of the first victims was their leader, Cuitlahua. The electors chose his nephew to succeed him, the youthful Guatemoc, or, as he was commonly called, Guatemotzin. In some respects in spite of the lack of the sagacity and farsightedness of Cuitlahua, he was a better man for the problem, for he at once mustered his forces and launched them upon Cortes and the Tlascalans in the valley of Otumba. The Tlascalans had furnished shelter and provisions to Cortes, and had resolved to stand by their treaty with him, but they had not yet furnished him with any great assistance. A strong party in the council had been entirely opposed to doing anything whatever for him. Cortes practically had to fight the battle alone and the battle had to be won. He and his fought, as the saying is, with halters around their necks.

All day long the Spaniards and their few allies fought up and down the narrow valley. Defeat meant certain death. They must conquer or be tortured, sacrificed and eaten. It was Cortes himself who decided the issue. With Alvarado and a few of the other captains, he finally broke through the Aztec centre, with his own hand killed the Aztec general, to whom Guatemoc had committed the battle, and seized the Aztec standard. At the close of the long hours of fighting the natives broke and fled, and the supremacy of Cortes and the Spaniards was once more established.

Wavering Tlascala decided for Cortes and he was received with generous, royal and munificent hospitality, which accorded him everything he asked. Messengers were despatched to Hispaniola for reinforcements and every preparation made for the renewal of the campaign. During the fall, troops, horses, men, guns and thousands of the flower of the Tlascalan army were placed at Cortes's disposal. He occupied them by sending expeditions in every direction, thus restoring their morale and punishing the savage tribes who had revolted against the Spanish rule and had returned to their old allegiance to the Aztec emperor. The punishments were fearful. The resources of the Mexicans were gradually cut off and by the end of the year the Aztecs realized that they would have to fight their last battle alone. These successful campaigns re-established the prestige which the Spaniards had lost. The people everywhere knew that they were no longer gods, but they now enjoyed a higher reputation, that of being invincible.

Cortes was resolved to attack Mexico. With a prudence as great as his determination he decided to neglect no precaution which would insure his success. He caused to be built a number of *brigantines* by which he could secure the command of the lake, and thereby give access to the city for his troops and allies. These *brigantines* were built at Tlascala under the supervision of the sailors of the expedition. The rigging of the ships, which had been destroyed, was useful in fitting them out. They were built in pieces and arrangements were made to carry them over the mountains and put them together at the lake when the campaign began. Guns and provisions were also amassed. Powder was brought from Cuba and it was also made by means of the sulphur deposits of the volcanoes round about. The troops were daily drilled and trained. Daily prayers were held, and every effort was made to give the forthcoming campaign the spirit of a crusade. The strictest moral regulations were promulgated. In short, nothing was left undone to bring about the downfall of Mexico.

On his part, Guatemoc was not idle. He summoned to his assistance all the tribes that remained loyal to him, especially those to the west, not subjected to the Spanish attack. He strove by bribery to detach those who had given their adherence to Cortes. Vast numbers of allies assembled in Mexico, which was provisioned for a siege. Everything that occurred to the minds of these splendid barbarians was done. After having done all that was possible, with resolution which cannot be commended too highly, they calmly awaited the onset of the Spaniards.

On Christmas day, 1520, Cortes took up the march over the mountains again for the great city of the cactus rock.

12. The Siege and Destruction of Mexico

It was April of the next year when Cortes at last arrived before the city and began the siege. The force which he had mustered for this tremendous undertaking consisted of seven hundred Spanish infantry, one hundred and twenty *arquebuses*, eighty-six horsemen, twelve cannon, and a countless multitude of Tlascalan fighters together with numbers of slaves and servants.

As the city was connected with the mainland by three causeways, it was necessary to invest it on three sides. The army was divided into three equal divisions. He himself commanded the force that was to attack along the south causeway; with him was Sandoval, his most trusted and efficient lieutenant; Alvarado led that which was to advance over the west causeway and Olid was to close the north causeway. The *brigantines* were brought over the mountains by hand by thousands of Tlascalans. There were no vehicles or highways of any sort in Mexico; the Mexicans not having domesticated any animals there was no use for anything broader than a footpath, a fact which throws an interesting side-light on their civilization, by the way. These Spanish boats were put together on the shores of the lake and when they were launched they served to close the ring of steel which surrounded the doomed city.

The three great tribal divisions of the Aztec empire were the Aztecs themselves, the Cholulans and the Tezcocans. Cholula had been conquered and with Tezcoco at this critical juncture went over to the Spaniards, leaving Guatemoc and his Aztecs to fight the last fight alone. Besides the forces enumerated, each Spanish division was accompanied by formidable bodies of Tlascalans. The Tlascalans were nearly, if not quite, as good fighters as the Aztecs; perhaps they were better fighters, so far as their numbers went, when led and supported by the white people.

The first thing that Cortes did was to cut the aqueduct which carried fresh water into the city. The lake of Tezcoco in which Mexico stood was salt. By this one stroke, Cortes forced the inhabitants to depend upon a very meagre, scanty supply of water from wells in the city, many of which were brackish and unpalatable. The shores of the lake were swept bare by the beleaguerers. Iztatapalan, a rocky fortress was taken by storm and on April 21, 1521, the first attack was

147

delivered along the causeways. The Mexicans met the advance with their customary intrepidity. The water on either side of the causeway swarmed with canoes. Thousands of warriors poured out of the city. The canoes swept down the lake intending to take the Spaniards in reverse and then pour in a terrible flank fire of missiles as they had done on the Melancholy Night. Cortes sustained this fire for a short time in order to draw the canoes as far toward him as possible, then he let loose the brigantines.

These *brigantines* were boats propelled by oars and sails on a single mast. They carried about a score of armed men and were very well and stoutly built. I suppose them to have been something like a modern man-o'-war cutter. They played havoc with the frail canoes. Their solid construction, their higher free-board, that is, the height they were above the water-line, the armour of their crews and the fact that the wind happened to be favourable and they could sail instead of row that morning, all contributed to the utter and complete destruction of the Indian flotilla. Canoes were splintered and sunk. Men were killed by the hundreds. They strove to climb up the slippery sides of the causeways and dykes. The Spaniards thrust them off into the deep water with their spears or cut them to pieces with their swords. The battle along the causeways, which were narrow, although quite wide enough for a dozen horsemen abreast, was terrible. The Aztecs literally died in their tracks, disdaining to fly. The Spaniards made their way over a floor of dead and writhing bodies.

Bare breasts, however resolute the hearts that beat beneath them, were no match for the steel *cuirasses*. The wooden shields did not even blunt the edge of the Toledo blade; the obsidian battle-axes could not contest with the iron maces. The jewelled feather work of the proudest noble was not equal even to the steel-trimmed leather jerkin of the poorest white soldier. The Spaniards literally cut their way, hewed, hacked, thrust their way into the city.

Here the fighting was slightly more equalized. The low roofs of the houses and *pueblos* swarmed with warriors. They rained missiles down upon the Spaniards' heads, while a never diminishing mob hurled itself into the faces of the white men. The Aztecs could have done more damage if they had not sacrificed everything in order to capture the Spaniards alive. In some instances they succeeded in their purpose. The fighting which was the same in all three of the causeways lasted all day and then the Spaniards retired to their several camps.

Save for the fact that they afterward cleared the lake of the canoes by the aid of the *brigantines*, one day's fighting was like another. The Spaniards would march into the city, slaughter until their arms were weary. They would lose a few here and there every day. The Tlascalans who took their part in all the fighting lost many. The end of the day would see things *in statu quo*. There were enough of the Indians even to sacrifice one hundred of them to one Spaniard and still maintain the balance of power. Cortes observed that he might fight this way until all of his army had melted away by piecemeal and have taken nothing.

He determined upon the dreadful expedient of destroying the city as he captured it. After coming to this decision, he summoned to his aid large bodies of the subject tribes. Thereafter, while the Spaniards and the Tlascalans fought, the others tore down that portion of the city which had been taken. The buildings were absolutely razed to the ground and nothing whatever was left of them. Canals were filled, gardens were ruined, trees cut down and even the walls of the city torn apart. In short, what once had been a teeming populous quarter of the city, abounding in parks, gardens and palaces, was left a desert. There was not enough power left in the Aztec Confederacy to rebuild the devastated portions over night and the Spaniards daily pressed their attack on every side with relentless rigor.

The Mexicans were slowly constricted to an ever narrowing circle. The Spaniards seized and choked up the wells. The Mexicans were dying of thirst. The *brigantines* swept the lake and prevented any re-enforcements reaching them, which cut off their supply of provisions. They were dying of hunger. After every day's fighting Cortes offered amnesty. To do him justice, he begged that peace might be made and the fighting stopped before the city was ruined and all its inhabitants were killed. He was no mere murderer, and such scenes of slaughter horrified him. He had a genuine admiration for the enemy too. He tried his best to secure peace. His offers were repudiated with contempt. In spite of the fact that they were starving, the Aztecs in bravado actually threw provisions in the faces of the advancing Spaniards. They declared to the Tlascalans that when there was nothing left to eat they would eat them, and if there was nothing else, they would live on one another until they were all dead. They mocked and jeered at the tribes tearing down the houses, and with grim humour pointed out to them that they would have to rebuild the city whoever was successful in the strife, for either the Aztecs or the Spaniards would compel them to do so. So the fighting went on through the long days.

13. A DAY OF DESPERATE FIGHTING

On one occasion the soldiers, tiring of this, demanded, and Cortes in compliance with their wishes projected, an attack which was hoped would capture the narrow circle of defence by storm. In his own words the story of this day's fighting is now related. It will be seen how he narrowly escaped with his life:

The day after mass,[10] in pursuance of the arrangements already mentioned, the seven *brigantines* with more than three thousand canoes of our allies left the encampment; and I, with twenty-five horses and all the other force I had, including the seventy-five men from the division at Tacuba, took up the line of march and entered the city, where I distributed the troops in the following manner: There were three streets leading from where we entered to the market-place, called by the Indians Tianguizco, and the whole square in which it is situated is called Tlaltelulco; one of these streets was the principal avenue to the marketplace, which I ordered Your Majesty's treasurer and auditor to take, with seventy men and more than fifteen or twenty thousand of our allies, and rear-guard consisting of seven or eight horses.

I also directed that, whenever a bridge or entrenchment was taken, it should be immediately filled up; and for this purpose they had twelve men with pick-axes, together with many more of our allies who were very useful in this kind of work. The two other streets also lead from that of Tacuba to the market-place, and are narrower and full of causeways, bridges, and water-streets (or canals). I ordered two captains,[11] to take the wildest of these with eighty men and more than ten thousand of our Indian allies; and at the head of the street of Tacuba I placed two heavy cannon with eight horse to guard them. With eight other horse and about one hundred foot, including twenty-five or more bowmen and musketeers, and an innumerable host of our allies, I took up the line of march along the other narrow street, intending to penetrate as far as possible.

At its entrance I caused the cavalry to halt, and ordered them by no means to pass from there, nor to come in my rear, un-

10. Archbishop Lorenzana, in his note on this passage, greatly extols the pious fervour of Cortes, who, he says, "whether in the field or on the causeway, in the midst of the enemy or toiling by night or day," never omitted the celebration of the mass.
11. They were Andres de Tapia and George de Alvarado, a brother of the more famous Pedro, Tonatiuh.

less I first sent them orders to that effect; and then I alighted from my horse, and we came to an entrenchment that had been raised in front of a bridge, which we carried by means of a small field-piece, and the archers and musketeers, and then proceeded along the causeway, which was broken in two or three places, where we encountered the enemy. So great was the number of our allies, who ascended the terraces and other places, that it did not appear possible anything could stop us. When we had gained the two bridges, the entrenchments and the causeways, our allies followed along the street without taking any spoils; and I remained behind with about twenty Spanish soldiers on a little island, for I saw that some of our Indians were getting into trouble with the enemy; and in some instances they retreated until they cast themselves into the water, and with our aid were enabled to return to the attack.

Besides this, we were on the watch to prevent the enemy from sallying forth out of the cross-streets in the rear of the Spaniards, who had advanced on the main street and at this time sent us word that they had made much progress, and were not far from the great square of the market-place; adding, that they wished to push forward, for they already heard the noise of the combat in which the Alguazil mayor and Pedro de Alvarado were engaged on their side of the city. I answered them that they must by no means go forward without leaving the bridges well filled up, so that, if it became necessary to beat a retreat, the water might present no obstacle or impediment, for in this consisted all the danger. They sent to me a message in reply, the amount of which was that the whole they had gained was in good condition, and that I might go and see if it was not so. But suspecting that they had disregarded the orders and left the bridges imperfectly filled up, I went to the place and found they had passed a breach in the road ten or twelve paces wide, and the water that flowed through it was ten or twelve feet deep.

At the time the troops had passed this ditch, thus formed, they had thrown in it wood and reed-canes, and as they had crossed a few at a time and with great circumspection, the wood and canes had not sunk beneath their weight; and they were so intoxicated with the pleasure of victory that they imagined it to be sufficiently firm. At the moment I reached this bridge of troubles, I discovered some Spaniards and many of our allies

151

flying back in great haste, and the enemy like dogs in pursuit of them; and when I saw such a rout, I began to cry out, 'Hold, hold!' and on approaching the water, I beheld it full of Spaniards and Indians in so dense a mass that it seemed as if there was not room for a straw to float. The enemy charged on the fugitives so hotly, that in the *mêlée* they threw themselves into the water after them; and soon the enemy's canoes came up by means of the canal and took the Spaniards alive.

As this affair was so sudden, and I saw them killing our men, I resolved to remain there and perish in the fight. The way in which I and those that were with me could do the most good was to give our hands to some unfortunate Spaniards who were drowning, and draw them out of the water; some came out wounded, others half-drowned, and others without arms, whom I sent forward. Already such multitudes of the enemy pressed upon us, that they had completely surrounded me and the twelve or fifteen men who were with me; and being deeply interested in endeavouring to save those that were sinking, I did not observe nor regard the danger to which I was exposed.

Several Indians of the enemy had already advanced to seize me and would have borne me off, had it not been for a captain of fifty men whom I always had with me, and also a youth of his company, to whom next to God, I owed my life; and in saving mine, like a valiant man, he lost his own.[12] In the meantime the Spaniards who had fled before the enemy, pursued their course along the causeway, and as it was small and narrow, and on the same level as the water, which had been effected by those dogs on purpose to annoy us; and as the road was crowded also with our allies who had been routed, much delay was thereby occasioned, enabling the enemy to come up on both sides of the water, and to take and destroy as many as they pleased.

The captain who was with me, Antonio de Quinones, said to me: 'Let us leave this place and save your life, since you know that without you none of us can escape'; but he could not induce me to go. When he saw this, he seized me in his arms, that he might force me away; and although I would have been

---

12. Antonio de Quinones was the captain and Francisco de Olea, the youth, according to Gomara; who says that the latter cut off at one blow the arms of the men that had seized Cortes, and was himself immediately slain by the enemy. Cortes was then rescued by Quinones.—*Cron. Nuev. Esp.* cap., 138.

better satisfied to die than to live, yet by the importunity of this captain and of my other companions, we began to retreat, making our way with our swords and bucklers against the enemy, who pressed hard upon us.

At this moment there came up a servant of mine and made a little room; but presently he received a blow in his throat from a lance thrown from a low terrace, that brought him to the ground. While I was in the midst of this conflict, sustaining the attacks of the enemy, and waiting for the crowd on the narrow causeway, to reach a place of safety, one of my servants brought me a horse to ride on. But the mud on the causeway, occasioned by the coming and going of persons by water, was so deep that no one could stand, especially with the jostling of the people against one another in their effort to escape.

I mounted the horse, but not to fight, as this was impossible on horseback; but if it had been practicable I should have found on the little island opposite the narrow causeway, the eight horsemen I had left there, who were unable to do more than effect their return; which indeed, was so dangerous that two mares, on which two of my servants rode fell from the causeway into the water; one of them was killed by the Indians, but the other was saved by some of the infantry.

Another servant of mine Cristobal de Guzman, rode a horse that they gave him at the little island to bring to me, on which I might make my escape; but the enemy killed both him and the horse before they reached me; his death spread sorrow through the whole camp, and even to this day his loss is still mourned by those who knew him. But after all our troubles, by the blessing of God, those of us who survived, reached the street of Tlacuba, which was very wide; and collecting the people, I took my post with nine horsemen in the rear-guard. The enemy pressed forward with all the pride of victory, as if resolved that none should escape with life; but falling back in the best manner I could, I sent word to the treasurer and auditor to retreat to the public square in good order.

I also sent similar orders to the two captains who had entered the city by the street that led to the market-place, both of whom had fought gallantly, and carried many entrenchments and bridges, which they had caused to be well filled up, on account of which they were able to retire without loss. Before the retreat of the treasurer and auditor some of the enemy threw in their way two or three heads of Christian men from the upper part of the entrenchment where they were fighting, but it was not known whether they were persons belonging to the camp of Pedro de Alvarado, or our own. All being assembled in the square, so large a multitude of the enemy charged upon us from all directions that we had as much as we could do to keep them back; and that, too, in places where, before this defeat, the enemy would have fled before three horse and ten foot. Immediately after, in a lofty tower filled with their idols that stood near the square, they burned perfumes and fumigated the air with certain gums peculiar to this country, that greatly resembled *anime*, which they offer to their idols in token of victory. Although we endeavoured to throw obstacles in the way of the enemy, it was out of our power, as our people were hurrying back to the camp.

In this defeat thirty-five or forty Spaniards, and more than a thousand of our allies, were slain by the enemy, besides more than twenty Christians wounded, among whom was myself in the leg. We lost the small field-piece that we had taken with us, and many crossbows, muskets and other arms. Immediately after their victory in order to strike terror into the Alguazil mayor and Pedro de Alvarado, the enemy carried all the Spaniards, both living and dead, whom they had taken, to the Tlaltelulco which is the market-place, and in some of the lofty towers that are situated there they sacrificed them naked, opening their breasts and taking out their hearts to offer them to the idols. This was seen by the Spaniards of Alvarado's division from where they were fighting, and from the whiteness of the naked bodies which they saw sacrificed they knew them to be Christians; but although they suffered great sorrow and dismay at the sight, they effected a retreat to their camp after having fought gallantly that day, and carried their conquests almost to the market-place, which would have been taken if God, on account of our sins, had not permitted so great a disaster.

We returned to our camp, such was the grief we felt, somewhat earlier than had been usual on other days; and in addition to our other losses, we had been told that the brigantines had fallen into the hands of the enemies, who attacked them in their canoes from the rear; but it pleased God this was not true, although the *brigantines* and the canoes of our allies had been seen in danger enough, and even a brigantine came near being lost, the captain and the master of it being wounded, the former of whom died eight days afterward."

This modest account of the brave soldier scarcely does justice to the situation, his peril and his courage. Therefore, I supplement it by Helps' description of the same day of desperate fighting:

The impatience of the soldiers grew to a great height, and was supported in an official quarter—by no less a person than Alderete, the King's Treasurer. Cortes gave way against his own judgment to their importunities. There had all along been a reason for his reluctance, which, probably, he did not communicate to his men; namely, that he had not abandoned the hope that the enemy would still come to terms. 'Finally,' he says, 'they pressed me so much that I gave way.'

The attack was to be a general one, in which the divisions of Sandoval and Alvarado were to cooperate; but Cortes, with that knowledge of character which belonged to him, particularly explained that, though his general orders were for them to press into the market-place, they were not obliged to gain a single difficult pass which laid them open to defeat; 'for,' he says, 'I knew, from the men they were, that they would advance to whatever spot I told them to gain, even if they knew that it would cost them their lives.'

On the appointed day, Cortes moved from his camp, supported by seven *brigantines*, and by more than three thousand canoes filled with his Indian allies. When his soldiers reached the entrance of the city, he divided them in the following manner. There were three streets which led to the market-place from the position which the Spaniards had already gained. Along the principal street, the King's Treasurer, with seventy Spaniards, and fifteen or twenty thousand allies was to make his way. His rear was to be protected by a small guard of horsemen.

The other streets were smaller, and led from the street of Tlacuba to the market-place. Along the broader of these two streets, Cortes sent two of his principal captains, with eighty Spaniards and the thousand Indians; he himself with eight horsemen, seventy-five foot-soldiers, twenty-five musketeers, and an 'infinite number' of allies, was to enter the narrower street. At the entrance to the street of Tlacuba, he left two large cannon with eight horsemen to guard them, and at the entrance of his own street, he also left eight horsemen to protect the rear.

The Spaniards and their allies made their entrance into the city with even more success and less embarrassment than on previous occasions. Bridges and barricades were gained, and the three main bodies of the army moved forward into the heart of the city. The ever-prudent Cortes did not follow his division, but remained with a small body-guard of twenty Spaniards in a little island formed by the intersection of certain water streets, whence he encouraged the allies, who were occasionally beaten back by the Mexicans, and where he could protect his own troops against any sudden descent of the enemy from certain side streets.

He now received a message from these Spanish troops who had made a rapid and successful advance into the heart of the town, informing him that they were not far from the market-place, and that they wished to have his permission to push forward, as they already heard the noise of the combats which the Alguazil mayor and Pedro de Alvarado were waging from their respective stations. To this message Cortes returned for answer that on no account should they move forward without first filling up the apertures thoroughly. They sent an answer back, stating that they had made completely passable all the ground they had gained; and that he might come and see whether it were not so.

Cortes, like a wise commander, not inclined to admit anything as a fact upon the statement of others which could be verified by personal inspection, took them at their word, and did move on to see what sort of a pathway they had made; when, to his dismay, he came in sight of a breach in the causeway, of considerable magnitude, being ten or twelve paces in width, and which, far from being filled up with solid material, had been passed upon wood and reeds, which was entirely insecure in case of retreat. The Spaniards, 'intoxicated with victory,' as their Commander describes them, had rushed on, imagining that they left behind them a sufficient pathway.

There was now no time to remedy this lamentable error, for when Cortes arrived near this 'bridge of affliction,' as he calls it, he saw many of the Spaniards and the allies retreating toward it, and when he came up close to it, he found the bridge-way broken down, and the whole aperture so full of Spaniards and Indians, that there was not room for a straw to float upon the surface of the water. The peril was so imminent that Cortes not only thought that the conquest of Mexico was gone, but that the term of his life as well as that of his victories had come; and he resolved to die there fighting. All that he could do at first was to help his men out of the water; and meanwhile, the Mexicans charged upon them in such numbers, that he and his little party were entirely surrounded.

The enemy seized upon his person, and would have carried him off, but for the resolute bravery of some of his guard, one of whom lost his life there in succouring his master. The greatest aid, however, that Cortes had at this moment of urgent peril, was the cruel superstition of the Mexicans, which made them wish to take the Malinche alive, and grudged the death of an enemy in any other way than that of sacrifice to their detestable gods. The captain of the body-guard seized hold of Cortes, and insisted upon his retreating, declaring that upon his life depended the lives of all of them. Cortes, though at that moment he felt that he should have delighted more in death than life, gave way to the importunity of his captain, and of other Spaniards who were near, and commenced a retreat for his life. His flight was along a narrow causeway at the same level as the water, an additional circumstance of danger, which to use his expression about them, those 'dogs' had contrived against the Spaniards.

The Mexicans in their canoes approached the causeway on both sides, and the slaughter they were thus enabled to commit, both among the allies and the Spaniards, was very great. Meanwhile, two or three horses were sent to aid Cortes in his retreat, and a youth upon one of them contrived to reach him, although the others were lost. At last he and a few of his men succeeded in fighting their way to the broad street of Tlacuba, where, like a brave captain, instead of continuing his flight, he and the few horsemen that were with him turned around and formed a rear-guard to protect his retreating troops. He also sent immediate orders to the King's Treasurer and the other commanders to make good their escape; orders the force of which was much heightened by the sight of two or three Spanish heads which the Mexicans, who were fighting behind a barricade, threw amongst the besiegers.

We must now see how it fared with the other divisions. Alvarado's men had prospered in their attack, and were steadily advancing toward the marketplace, when, all of a sudden, they found themselves encountered by an immense body of Mexican troops, splendidly accoutred, who threw before them five heads of Spaniards and kept shouting out, 'Thus we will slay you, as we have slain Malinche and Sandoval, whose heads these are.' With these words they commenced an attack of such fury, and came so close to hand with the Spaniards, that they could not use their cross-bows, their muskets, or even their swords. One thing, however, was in their favour. The difficulty of their retreat was always greatly enhanced by the number of their allies; but on this occasion, the Tlascalans no sooner saw the bleeding heads and heard the menacing words of the Mexicans, than they cleared themselves off the causeway with all possible speed.

The Spaniards, therefore, were able to retreat in good order; and their dismay did not take the form of panic, even when they heard, from the summit of the Temple, the tones of that awful drum, made from the skin of serpents, which gave forth the most melancholy sound imaginable, and which was audible at two or three leagues' distance. This was the signal of sacrifice, and at that moment ten human hearts, the hearts of their companions, were being offered up to the Mexican deities.

A more dangerous, though not more dreadful sound was now to be heard. This was the blast of a horn sounded by no less a personage than the Mexican King—which signified that his captains were to succeed or die. The mad fury with which the Mexicans now rushed upon the Spaniards was an 'awful thing' to see; and the historian, who was present at the scene, writing in his old age, exclaims that, though he cannot describe it, yet, when he comes to think of it, it is as if it were 'visibly' before him, so deep was the impression it had made upon his mind.

But the Spaniards were not raw troops; and terror however great, was not able to overcome their sense of discipline and their duty to each other as comrades. It was in vain that the Mexicans rushed upon them 'as a conquered thing'; they reached their station, served their cannon steadily—although they had to renew their artillery-men—and maintained their ground.

The appalling stratagem adopted by the Mexicans—of throwing down before one division of the Spanish army some of the heads of the prisoners they had taken from another division, and shouting that these were the heads of the principal commanders—was pursued with great success. They were thus enabled to discourage Sandoval, and to cause him to retreat with loss toward his quarters. They even tried with success the same stratagem upon Cortes, throwing before his camp, to which he had at last retreated, certain bleeding heads, which they said, were those of 'Tonatiuh' (Alvarado), Sandoval, and the other *teules*. Then it was that Cortes felt more dismay than ever, 'though,' says the honest chronicler, who did not like the man, no matter how much he admired the soldier, 'not in such a manner that those who were with him should perceive in it much weakness.'

After Sandoval had made good his retreat, he set off, accompanied by a few horsemen, for the camp of Cortes, and had an interview with him, of which the following account is given: 'O *Señor Captain!* what is this?' exclaimed Sandoval; 'are these the great counsels, and artifices of war which you have always been wont to show us? How has this disaster happened?' Cortes replied, 'O Don Sandoval! my sins have permitted this; but I am not so culpable in the business as they may make out, for it is the fault of the Treasurer, Juan de Alderete, whom I charged to fill up that difficult pass where they routed us; but he did not do so, for he is not accustomed to wars, nor to be commanded by superior officers.'

At this point of the conference, the Treasurer himself, who had approached the captains in order to learn Sandoval's news, exclaimed that it was Cortes himself who was to blame; that he had encouraged his men to go forward; that he had not charged them to fill up the bridges and bad passes—if he had done so, he (the Treasurer) and his company would have done it; and, moreover, that Cortes had not cleared the causeway in time of his Indian allies. Thus they argued and disputed with one another; for hardly any one is generous, in defeat, to those with whom he has acted. Indeed, a generosity of this kind, which will not allow a man to comment severely upon the errors of his comrades in misfortune, is so rare a virtue, that it scarcely seems to belong to this planet.

There was little time, however, for altercation, and Cortes was not the man to indulge in more of that luxury for the unfortunate than human nature demanded. He had received no tidings of what had befallen the Camp of Tlacuba, and thither he despatched Sandoval, embracing him and saying, 'Look you, since you see that I cannot go to all parts, I commend these labours to you, for, as you perceive, I am wounded and lame. I implore you, take charge of these three camps. I well know that Pedro de Alvarado and his soldiers will have behaved themselves as cavaliers, but I fear lest the great force of those dogs should have routed them.'

The scene now changes to the ground near Alvarado's camp. Sandoval succeeded in making his way there, and arrived about the hour of Vespers. He found the men of that division in the act of repelling a most vigorous attack on the part of the Mexicans, who had hoped that night to penetrate into the camp and carry off all the Spaniards for sacrifice. The enemy were better armed than usual, some of them using the weapons which they had taken from the soldiers of Cortez. At last, after a severe conflict, in which Sandoval himself was wounded, and in which the cannon shots did not suffice to break the serried ranks of the Mexicans, the Spaniards gained their quarters, and, being under shelter, had some respite from the fury of the Mexican attack.

There, Sandoval, Pedro de Alvarado, and the other principal captains, were standing together and relating what had occurred to each of them, when, suddenly, the sound of the sacrificial drum was heard again, accompanied by other musical instruments of a similar dolorous character. From the Camp of Tlacuba the great Temple was perfectly visible, and the Spaniards looked up at it for the interpretation of these melancholy tones; they saw their companions driven by blows and buffetings up to the place of sacrifice. The white-skinned Christians were easily to be distinguished amidst the dusky groups that surrounded them.

When the unhappy men about to be sacrificed had reached the lofty level space on which these abominations were wont to be committed, it was discerned by their friends and late companions that plumes of feathers were put upon the heads of many of them, and that men, whose movements in the distance appeared like those of winnowers, made the captive dance before the image of Huitzilopochtli. When the dance was concluded, the victims were placed upon the sacrificial stones; their hearts were taken out and offered to the idols; and their bodies hurled down the steps of the temple.

At the bottom of the steps stood 'other butchers' who cut off the arms and legs of the victims, intending to eat these portions of their enemy. The skin of the face with the beard was preserved. The rest of the body was thrown to the lions, tigers, and serpents. 'Let the curious reader consider,' says the chronicler, 'what pity we must have had for these, our companions, and how we said to one another, 'Oh, thanks be to God, that they did not carry me off today to sacrifice me.' And certainly no army ever looked on a more deplorable sight.

There was no time, however, for such contemplation: for, at that instant, numerous bands of warriors attacked the Spaniards on all sides, and fully occupied their attention in the preservation of their own lives.

Modern warfare has lost one great element of the picturesque in narrative, namely, in there being no interchange, now, of verbal threats and menaces between the contending parties; but in those days it was otherwise, and the Mexicans were able to indulge in the most fierce and malignant language. 'Look,' they said, 'that is the way in which all of you have to die, for our Gods have promised this to us many times.' To the Tlascalans their language was more insulting and much more minutely descriptive. Throwing to them the roasted flesh of their companions and of the Spanish soldiers, they shouted, 'Eat of the flesh of these *teules*, and of your brethren, for we are quite satiated with it; and, look you, for the houses you have pulled down, we shall have to make you build in their place much better ones with stone and plates of metal, likewise with hewn stone and lime; and the houses will be painted. Wherefore continue to assist these *teules* all of whom you will see sacrificed.'

The Mexicans, however, did not succeed in carrying off any more Spaniards for sacrifice that night. The Spanish camp had some few hours of repose, and some time to reckon up their losses, which were very considerable. They lost upward of sixty of their own men, six horses, two cannon, and a great number of their Indian allies. Moreover the *brigantines* had not fared much better on this disastrous day than the land forces. But the indirect consequences of this defeat were still more injurious than the actual losses. The allies from the neighbouring cities on the lake deserted the Spaniards, nearly to a man. The Mexicans regained and strengthened most of their positions; and the greatest part of the work of the besiegers seemed as if it would have to be done over again. Even the Tlascalans, hitherto so faithful, despaired of the fortunes of their allies, and could not but believe, with renewed terror, in the potency of the Mexican deities, kindred to, if not identical with, their own.

14. The Last Mexican

The courage of the Aztecs was beyond all question. Their heroism awakens a thrill of admiration, although we are fully aware of their fearful and ferocious and degrading religious rites. Again and again the heart-sick Spaniards saw lifted up before the hideous gods on the temple pyramids, the white, naked bodies of their unfortunate comrades who had been captured for that awful sacrifice. Both parties were wrought up to a pitch of furious rage.

No valour, no heroism, no courage, no devotion could prevail against thirst, hunger, smallpox, pestilence, the fever of besieged towns, with the streets filled with unburied dead. On August 13, 1521, the city fell. There was no formal surrender, the last defender had been killed. The old, weak and feeble were left. Only a small portion of the city, the cheapest and poorest part, was left standing. Into this ghastly street rode the Spaniards.

Where was Guatemoc? A wretched, haggard, worn, starved figure, having done all that humanity could do, and apparently more, in the defence of his land, he had striven to escape in a canoe on the lake. One of the *brigantines* overhauled him. The commander was about to make way with the little party when someone informed him that the principal captive was no less than Guatemotzin. The unfortunate young emperor, after vainly trying to persuade Garcia Holguin to kill him then and there, demanded to be led to Cortes. He found that great captain on one of the house-tops, watching the slaughter of the men and women and children by the furious Tlascalans who were at last feeding fat their revenge by indiscriminate massacre.

"Deal with me as you please," said the broken-hearted Mexican, as he touched the dagger which hung by Cortes's side. "Kill me at once," he implored.

He had no wish to survive the downfall of his empire, the devastation of his city, and the annihilation of his people. Cortes spared his life and at first treated him generously. He afterward marred his reputation by yielding him and the *Cacique* of Tlacuba to torture at the urgent and insistent demand of the soldiery. There was no treasure found in the city. It had been spirited away or else buried forever beneath the ruins of the town.[13] The soldiers, their greed for treasure excited, insisted upon the torture of the noble Guatemoc and his comrade. The *Cacique* of Tlacuba, unable through weakness to sustain the torture, which consisted of burning the soles of their feet with boiling oil, broke into lamenting reproaches, some of them addressed to the emperor.

"And am I taking pleasure in my bath, do you think?" proudly replied the young chief, while the soles of his feet were being immersed in the same dreadful cauldron.

He was lame and more or less helpless for the rest of his life. I have no doubt that he often wished that he had been cut down in the final moment of his defeat. He dragged on a miserable existence until Cortes put him to death by hanging several years after the conquest while in Honduras on an expedition. The charge against him, so Cortes writes to Charles V., was conspiracy. The evidence was flimsy enough, yet it is probable that Cortes believed it. The expedition was far from Mexico, surrounded by hostile nations, and Cortes, as usual, was in great danger. Helps thus describes the bitter end of the noble young emperor:

When led to execution, the King of Mexico exclaimed, 'O Malinche, I have long known the falseness of your words, and have foreseen that you would give me that death which, alas! I did not give myself, when I surrendered to you in my city of Mexico. Wherefore do you slay me without justice? May God demand it of you!'

The King of the Tlacuba said that he looked upon his death as welcome, since he was able to die with his Lord, the King of Mexico. After confession and absolution, the two kings were hanged upon a *ceyba* tree in Izzancanac, in the province of Acalan, on one of the carnival days before Shrovetide, in the year 1525. Thus ended the great Mexican dynasty—itself a thing compacted by so much blood and toil and suffering of countless

---

13. I wonder where it is! There may be a great amount of it somewhere.

human beings. The days of deposed monarchs—victims alike to the zeal of their friends and the suspicions of their captors—are mostly very brief; and perhaps it is surprising that the King of Mexico should have survived as long as four years the conquest of his capital, and have been treated during the greater part of that time with favour and honour.

Some writers have supposed that Cortes was weary of his captives, and wished to destroy them, and that the charge of conspiracy was fictitious. Such assertions betray a total ignorance of the character of this great Spaniard. Astute men seldom condescend to lying. Now, Cortes was not only very astute, but, according to his notions, highly honourable. A genuine hidalgo, and a thoroughly loyal man, he would as soon have thought of committing a small theft as of uttering a falsehood in a despatch addressed to his sovereign.

15. THE END OF CORTES

Cortes received a full reward for his conquest, at least for a time. He was received in high favour by Charles V., whom he visited in Spain, and who made him Marques of the Valley of Mexico.

There is on record a single sentence of the Emperor's that must have been addressed to Cortes in some private interview, which shows the gracious esteem in which he was held by his sovereign. Borrowing a metaphor from the archery-ground, and gracefully, as it seems, alluding to a former misappreciation of the services of Cortes, the Emperor said that he wished to deal with him as those who contend with the crossbow, whose first shots go wide of the mark, and then they improve and improve, until they hit the centre of the white. So, continued His Majesty, he wished to go on until he had shot into the white of what should be done to reward the Marquis' deserts; and meanwhile nothing was to be taken from him which he then held.

It was very pleasing to find that Cortes did not forget his old friends the Tlascalans, but dwelt on their services, and procured from the Emperor an order that they should not be given *encomienda* to His Majesty, or to any other person.

The only reward the Tlascalans got from the Emperor was that, when the other Mexicans were made slaves, they were left at least nominally free, but their republic soon fell into decay and the city in which they had so proudly maintained themselves in their independence, became a desolate ruin. A dirty and squalid village today marks the place.

Marina, who had served the Spaniards for the love of the great captain with such fidelity and such success, was cast off by Cortes and compelled to marry one of his officers, whom she scarcely knew. This crushed her spirit. She abandoned her husband and sank into wretched and miserable obscurity, and died at an early age of a broken heart.

Cortes conducted other expeditions, most of them without any great success, as that to Honduras, where he hanged the last of the Aztec Kings. Jealousy arose in the great state which he had founded, and he fell out of favour with the Emperor, who refused to see him, and he was received with cold and bitter reproaches by his wife, whom he married after the death of his former wife, and who had never proved a comfort to him. An admirable marriage which he had arranged for his daughter with one of the highest nobility of Spain failed, his last days were sad and miserable, and he died old, lonely and broken-hearted. I again quote Helps concerning these closing scenes:

> The poets say, '*Care sits behind a man and follows him wherever he goes.*' So does ill-success; and henceforward the life of Cortes was almost invariably unsuccessful. There is an anecdote told of him (resting upon no higher authority than that of Voltaire) which, although evidently untrue, tells in a mythical way the reception which Cortes met at the Spanish Court; and his feelings as regards that reception.
> One day he broke through the crowd which surrounded the carriage of the Emperor and jumped on the step.
> 'Who are you?' asked the Emperor in astonishment.
> 'I am the man,' replied Cortes fiercely, 'who has given you more provinces than your ancestors have left you cities.'
> Quitting fiction, however, and returning to fact, there is a letter extant addressed by Cortes to the Emperor, Charles V., which conveys more forcibly than even a large extent of narrative could do, the troubles, vexations, and disappointments which Cortes had to endure at this latter period of his life, and his feelings with regard to them. It is one of the most touching letters ever written by a subject to a sovereign. I will here translate some of it, greatly condensing those parts of the letter which relate to the business in hand, and which would be as wearisome to the

reader to read, as they were to the writer to write; for doubtless, it was not the first time, by many times, that Cortes had
set down the same grievance in writing. The letter bears date,
Valladolid, the 3rd. of February, 1544. It begins thus:—

'Sacred Cesarian Catholic Majesty:—I thought that having labored in my youth, it would so profit me that in
my old age I might have ease and rest; and now it is forty
years that I have been occupied in not sleeping, in eating
ill, and sometimes eating neither well nor ill, in bearing armour, in placing my person in danger, in spending
my estates and my life, all in the service of God, bringing sheep into his sheep-fold—which were very remote
from our hemisphere, unknown, and whose names are
not written in our writings—also increasing and making
broad the name and patrimony of my King—gaining
for him, and bringing under his yoke and Royal sceptre, many and very great kingdoms and many barbarous
nations, all won by my own person, and at my own ex-
pense; without being assisted in anything, on the contrary, being much hindered by many jealous and evil and
envious persons who, like leeches, have been filled to
bursting with my blood.'

He then proceeds to say that for the part which God has had in
his labours and watchings he is sufficiently paid, because it was
His work; and it was not without a reason that Providence was
pleased that so great a work should be accomplished by so weak
a medium, in order that it might be seen that to God alone the
good work must be attributed.

Cortes then says that for what he has done for the King, he has
always been satisfied with the remuneration he has received.
The King has been grateful to him, has honoured him, and has
rewarded him, and he adds that His Majesty knows that the
rewards and honours which the Emperor offered were, in the
opinion of Cortes, so far greater than his merits, that he refused
to receive them.

What, however, His Majesty did mean him to receive, he has
not received. That which His Majesty has given has been so
completely without fruit, that it would have been better for
Cortes not to have had it, but that he should have taken care
of his own estate, and not spent the fruit of that in defending

himself against 'the Fiscal of Your Majesty, which defence has been, and is, a more difficult undertaking than to win the land of the enemy.'

He then implores His Majesty that he will be pleased to render clear the good will which he had shown to reward him. 'I see myself,' he exclaims, 'old, poor and indebted. Not only have I no repose in my old age, but I can foresee labour and trouble until my death.' And he adds, 'Please God that the mischief may not go beyond death; but may finish with the body, and not exist forever, since whosoever has such toil in defending his bodily estate, cannot avoid injuring his soul.'

All that he asks is that his appeal may be heard; that members of the King's Council be added to the Council of the Indies; and that the cause may be determined, and judgment given, without further delay. 'For, otherwise, I must leave it and loose it, and must return to my home, as I am no longer of the age to go about to hostelries; and should withdraw myself to make my account clear with God, since it is a large one that I have, and little life is left to me to discharge my conscience; and it will be better for me to lose my estate than my soul.' He concludes by saying that 'he is of Your Catholic Majesty the very humble servant and *vassal*, who kisses your very royal feet and hands—the Marquis del Valle.'

In addition to these vexations he had a domestic trouble which doubtless caused him much mortification. His daughter, Donna Maria, was engaged to one of the greatest nobles in Spain; but ultimately the young man refused to fulfil the engagement. Some say that this caused the death of Cortes. But this is not so. He was broken, alike in health and in spirits, by reason of the many reverses he had met with in these his latter days.

We live, to a great measure, upon success; and there is no knowing the agony that an unvarying course of ill-success causes to a sanguine and powerful mind which feels that, if only such and such small obstacles were removed out of its way, it could again shine forth with all its pristine force and brightness.

To meet this rejected daughter, who was coming from New Spain, Cortes went to Seville. There he was taken ill, and, being molested by the importunity of many persons who came to see him on business, he retired to a small village, about half a league from Seville, called Castillaje de la Cuesta. He also sought retirement for the purpose, as Bernal Diaz says, of making his will and preparing his soul for death. 'And when he had settled his worldly affairs, our Lord Jesus Christ was pleased to take him from his troublesome world.' He died on the 2nd of December, 1547, being then sixty-two years of age.

His bones were interred in Mexico. During the civil wars of the last century, his bones were taken away and hidden. It is reported that only the other day, (as at time of first publication), the place of his sepulchre had been discovered. Some monument to his memory should be erected to match the statue of Guatemoc, which is one of the principal adornments of Mexico.

As is well said by William H. Johnson:

To the honour of Spain be it said, her rule in Mexico was firm and kind. The Indians became thoroughly incorporated into the national life, enjoying the opportunities of advancement as Spaniards. In the present Republic of Mexico the greatest name has been that of Benito Juarez, the president who upheld the national cause during the French-Austrian usurpation. He was of pure Aztec blood. Porfirio Diaz, the gallant soldier who led the army of the Republic during the same trying period, and who, as its president, is a model of a strong and wise ruler, is also, in part, a descendant of the ancient race.

With the following tributes to the great captain the story of his amazing adventures is ended. Says Helps:

He was the mighty conqueror of one of the most compact and well-ordered barbaric nations of the world—a conqueror who, with a few hundreds of his fellow-countrymen, not all of them his partisans, overcame hundreds of thousands of fanatic and resolute men fighting against him with immense resources, and with a resolution nearly equal to his own. Let us give him the benefit of his sincere belief in Christianity, and his determination to substitute that beneficent religion for the hideous and cruel superstition of the people he was resolved to conquer. And let us echo the wish of that good common soldier, Bernal Diaz, who, though having his grievances against Cortes, as all of the other *Conquistadores* thought they had, could yet, after watching every turn in the fortunes of the great Marquis, and knowing almost every sin that he had committed, write most tenderly of the great captain whose plume he had so often followed to victory.

After saying that, subsequently to the conquest of Mexico, Cortes had not had good fortune either in his Californian or his Honduras expedition, or indeed in anything else he had undertaken, Bernal Diaz adds, 'Perhaps it was that he might have felicity in heaven. And I believe it was so, for he was an honourable cavalier, and a devoted worshipper of the Virgin, the Apostle St. Peter and other Saints. May God pardon his sins, and mine too, and give me a righteous ending, which things are of more concern than the conquests and victories that we had over the Indians.'

Writes MacNutt:

His sagacity, his foresight, and his moderation have caused critical historians to rank him higher as a statesman than as a soldier. In virtue of his pre-eminent qualities both as a statesman and as a general, as well as because of the enduring importance of his conquest, Fernando Cortes occupies an uncontested place amongst the heroes of the nations.

However we may sympathize with the Aztecs, we cannot escape from the fact that it was much better that there should be a Spanish rule instead of an Aztec rule in Mexico, and that the civilization of the former should supplant the so-called civilization of the latter. That does not prevent us from wishing that the supersession might not have been so harsh and ruthless, but in view of the times, and the men, both Aztecs and Christians, it was not to be expected.

Personally, I love the memory of Guatemoc for his heroism and his devotion. I also have a warm feeling for Cortes. It is true, as has been stated, that he was a child of his age, but he was the best child of his age, and it was not his fault altogether that in some respects it was the worst age. The Spanish rule in Mexico was better than the Spanish rule in Peru, and Cortes and his successors, by the side of Pizarro and his successors, were almost angels of light.

I close with these noble words of John Fiske in his great and highly valued *Discovery of North America*:

A great deal of sentimental ink has been shed over the wickedness of the Spaniards in crossing the ocean and attacking people who had never done them any harm, overturning and obliterating a 'splendid civilization,' and more to the same effect. It is undeniable that unprovoked aggression is an extremely hateful thing, and many of the circumstances attendant upon the Spanish conquest in America were not only heinous in their atrocity, but were emphatically condemned, as we shall presently see, by the best moral standards of the sixteenth century. Yet if we are to be guided by strict logic, it would be difficult to condemn the Spaniards for the mere act of conquering Mexico without involving in the same condemnation our own forefathers who crossed the ocean and overran the territory of the United States with small regard for the proprietary rights of Algonquins, or Iroquois, or red men of any sort.

Our forefathers, if called upon to justify themselves, would have replied that they were founding Christian states and diffusing the blessings of a higher civilization; and such, in spite of much alloy in the motives and imperfection in the performance, was certainly the case. Now if we would not lose or distort the historical perspective, we must bear in mind that the Spanish conquerors would have returned exactly the same answer. If Cortes were to return to the world and pick up some history book in which he is described as a mere picturesque adventurer, he would feel himself very unjustly treated. He would say that he had higher aims than those of a mere fighter and gold-hunter; and so doubtless he had.

In the complex tangle of motives that actuated the mediaeval Spaniard—and in his peninsula we may apply the term mediaeval to later dates than would be proper in France or Italy—the desire of extending the dominion of the Church was a very real and powerful incentive to action. The strength of the missionary and crusading spirit in Cortes is seen in the fact that where it was concerned, and there only, was he liable to let zeal overcome prudence.

There can be no doubt that, after making all allowances, the Spaniards did introduce a better state of society into Mexico than they found there. It was high time that an end should be put to those hecatombs of human victims, slashed, torn open and devoured on all the little occasions of life. It sounds quite pithy to say that the Inquisition, as conducted in Mexico, was as great an evil as the human sacrifices and the cannibalism; but it is not true. Compared with the ferocious barbarism of ancient

Mexico, the contemporary Spanish modes of life were mild, and this, I think, helps further to explain the ease with which the country was conquered.

In a certain sense the prophecy of Quetzalcoatl was fulfilled and the coming of the Spaniards did mean the final dethronement of the ravening Tezcatlipoca. The work of the noble Franciscan and Dominican monks who followed closely upon Cortes, and devoted their lives to the spiritual welfare of the Mexicans, is a more attractive subject than any picture of military conquest. To this point I shall return hereafter, when we come to consider the sublime character of Las Casas. For the present we may conclude in the spirit of one of the noble Spanish historians, Pedro de Cieza de Leon, and praise God, that the idols are cast down.

1

The Yarn of the "Essex", Whaler

Among marine disasters there is none more extraordinary in character or more appalling in consequence, than the loss of the whaleship *Essex*.

The *Essex* was a well-found whaler of two hundred and thirty-eight tons. James Pollard was her captain, with Owen Chase and Matthew Joy as mates. Six of her complement of twenty were Negroes. Thoroughly overhauled and provisioned for two and one-half years, on the 17th of August, 1819, she took her departure from Nantucket. On the 17th of January, 1820, she reached St. Mary's Island, off the coast of Chili, near Conception, a noted whaling ground.

They cruised off these coasts for some time, being lucky enough to take several large whales, and finally, the season being over, having about one thousand barrels of oil in the hold, they struck boldly westward. On the 16th of November, being a few minutes south of the line in Long. 118 degrees W., a school of sperm whales was sighted, and three boats were lowered in chase.

Chase, the mate—the first mate is always the mate *par excellence*—soon got fast to a huge bull-whale who, when he felt the deadly harpoon in his vitals, swiftly turned and struck the whale-boat a terrific blow with his tail, smashing it into kindling wood and hurling the men in every direction. After that splendid exhibition of power, he got away scot-free save for the rankling iron and the dangling line which he took with him. The boat's crew were picked up, no one being much the worse for the encounter, strange to say, and were brought back to the ship by the other boats.

On the 20th of November, being then just about 40 minutes south of the equator, and in Long. 119 degrees W., at eight o'clock in the morning the lookout at the masthead shouted the welcome signal:

"There she blows!"

It was evident that they were in the presence of a large school. The ship was headed toward them, and when within half a mile the mainyard was backed, and three boats, under the charge of the captain and the first and second mates, respectively, were lowered. Their only other boat was a spare one, lashed amidships on chocks.

Arriving at the spot where they had been sighted at the ship, the men discovered that the whales had sounded and vanished. The boats, thereupon, separated widely, and the men lay on their oars and waited. Presently a great bull rose lazily, spouting in front of the mate's boat, and lay idly wallowing in the tumbling sea. Approaching cautiously, the harpooneer drove in the terrible weapon.

In his agony, the great *cetacean*, instead of sounding, threw himself blindly toward the boat. So close were they, and so unexpected was the whale's movement in spite of his vast bulk, that, although the order, "Stern all!" had been promptly given, they were unable to win clear of him. The tip of his massive tail, as he thrashed about in his rage, struck the side of the light, clinker-built boat and smashed a hole in it. Then the whale started to run, towing the boat, which immediately began to fill with water under the terrible drag to which it was subjected. There was nothing to do but cut the line. Two or three jackets were stuffed into the aperture, and while some bailed, the others rowed back to the ship. The captain's and second mate's boats, meanwhile, were seeking the school, which had risen and was swimming away from the ship.

As soon as the wrecked boat was run up to the davits, the mate swung the mainyard and got under way, following the other boats. He first determined to break out the spare boat, but after investigating the damaged boat, he concluded that he could save time by nailing a patch of canvas over the broken place, which would serve temporarily to keep out the water, in case they went in search of another whale in her. While he was about this, an immense sperm-whale, about eighty-five feet long, "breached"—that is, coming from a great depth, he shot out of the water his whole length and then fell back with a tremendous splash—about fifty fathoms from the ship. After he fell back, he spouted three or four times, sounded, and once more appeared, this time about a ship's length off the weather bow of the *Essex*. Evidently, it was the whale they had just struck. He was angry, and he meant business, for as soon as he came to the surface he started for the ship.

Under the light air the vessel was making about three knots. The

173

whale was going at the same speed. The mate saw at once that if he did not change his course, the whale would strike his ship. Dropping the hammer, he shouted to the boy at the helm to put it hard up, and himself sprang across the deck to re-enforce his order. The unwieldy ship paid off slowly, and before her head had been fairly turned to leeward the whale deliberately rammed her right under the forechains.

The concussion was terrible. The ship came to a dead stop, as if she had run upon a rock, while the whale bumped along under the keel. Some of those aboard were thrown to the deck. The masts quivered and buckled under the shock, but fortunately nothing was carried away. The onset was so unexpected that the men were dazed for a moment. When the mate recovered his wits, he immediately sounded the well, and found that the ship was leaking badly. He then ordered the men to the pumps, and set signals for the recall of the boats, each of which had got fast to a whale.

In spite of all they could do, the ship began settling rapidly by the head. She was badly stove in, and making water fast. While some of the men toiled at the pumps, others cleared away the extra boat. There was no longer time to repair the other. At this juncture one of the men discovered the same whale about two hundred and fifty fathoms to leeward. He was in a fit of convulsive rage terrible to look upon; leaping, turning, writhing, threshing about in the water, beating it with his mighty tail and great flukes, thundering upon it with all his force, and all the while opening and shutting his enormous jaws, "smiting them together," in the words of the mate, as if distracted with wrath and fury.

There was no time to watch the whale in the exigency of their peril, and observing him start out with great velocity to cross the bows of the ship to leeward, the men turned their attention to the more serious duty at the pumps and the boat. But a few moments had elapsed, when another man forward observed the whale again.

"Here he is!" he shouted. "He's making for us again."

The great *cachalot* was now directly ahead, about two hundred fathoms away, and coming down upon them with twice his ordinary speed. The surf flew in all directions about him. "His course was marked by a white foam a rod in width which he made with the continual thrashing of this tail." His huge head, boneless but almost as solid and as hard as the inside of a horse's hoof, most admirably designed for a battering-ram, was almost half out of the water. The mate made one desperate attempt to get out of his way. Again the helm was put up and

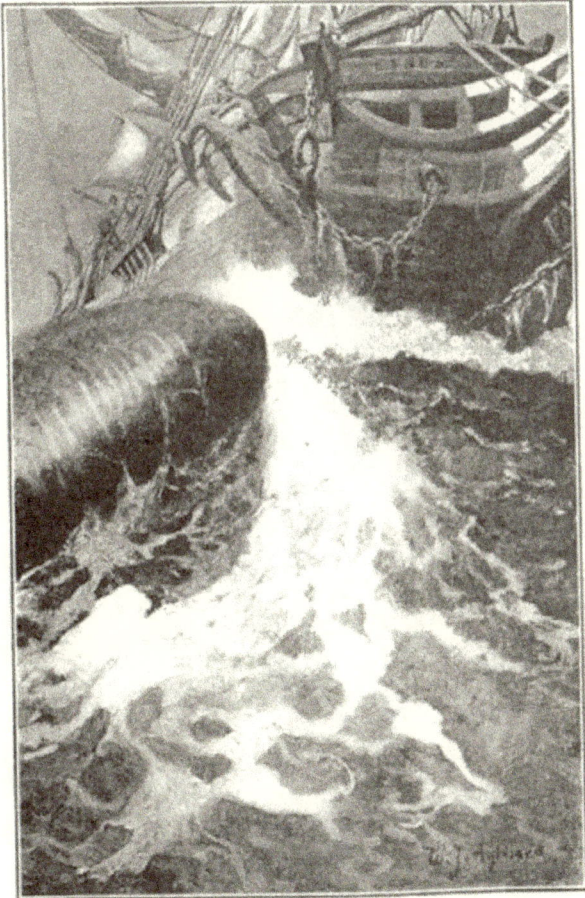

"THE SHIP CAME TO A DEAD STOP"

"THE KILLING OF ALEXANDER HAMILTON BY AARON
BURR, AT WEEHAWKEN, NEW JERSEY, JULY 11, 1804"

the men ran to the braces, but the water-laden ship, already well down by the head, and more sluggish than ever, had fallen off only one point when the whale leaped upon her with demoniac energy, and—so it appeared to the seamen—rammed her with maleficent passion.

This time he struck the ship just under the weather cathead. He was going not less than six knots an hour to the ship's three, and the force of the blow completely stove in the bows of the *Essex*. Those on board could feel the huge bulk scraping along beneath the keel a second time, and then, having done all the damage he could, he went hurtling off to windward. He had exacted a complete revenge for their attack upon him.

Working with the energy of despair, for the ship seemed literally sinking under their feet, the men succeeded in clearing away the spare boat and launching it. The steward saved two quadrants, two Bow-ditch's *Practical Navigators,* the captain's chest and that of the first mate, with two compasses which the mate had snatched from the binnacle. They shoved off, but had scarcely made two lengths from the ship when she fell over to windward and settled low in the water on her beam-ends, a total wreck.

The captain and second mate, seeing the signal for the recall of the boats flying, had cut loose from their whales and were rowing toward the ship. They knew something had happened, but what it was, they could not tell. The captain's boat was the first to reach the mate's. He stopped close by, so completely overpowered that for a space he could not utter a syllable.

"My God! Mr. Chase," he gasped out at last; "what is the matter?"

"We have been stove in by a whale, sir," said the mate, telling the whole appalling story.

By the captain's direction, the boats rowed to the sinking ship, and with their hatchets the men managed to cut away the masts, where-upon she rose two-thirds of the way to an even keel. They scuttled the deck—chopped holes through her, that is—and succeeded in com-ing at some six hundred pounds of unspoiled hard bread, which they divided among the three boats, and sufficient fresh water to give each boat sixty-five gallons in small breakers—being all they dared to take in each one. They also procured a musket, two pistols, some powder and bullets, some tools and six live turtles. From the light spars of the ship they rigged two masts for each boat and with the light canvas provided each one with two spritsails and a jib. They also got some light cedar planking used to repair the boats, and with it built the gunwales up six inches all around.

On the 22nd of November, being then in 120 W. Long., and just north of the equator, the officers took counsel together as to what to do. The nearest lands were the Marquesas Islands, fifteen hundred miles away; the Society Islands, twenty-four hundred miles away, and the Sandwich Islands, three thousand miles away. They knew little about the first two groups, save that they were inhabited by fierce and treacherous savages from whom they had as much to fear as from the perils of the sea. The Sandwich Islands were too far away, and they would be apt to meet hurricanes, prevalent at that season, should they attempt to reach them. After a long deliberation they decided to take advantage of the southeast trades by sailing by the wind until they reached the twenty-fifth parallel of south latitude. Then falling in with westerly and variable winds, they could turn east and run for the coast of Chili or Peru. This course involved the longest voyage, but it also promised the greatest chance for success.

Sometimes they made good progress with favourable winds. At other times they lay immobile in the blazing tropic sunlight which was almost unbearable. Often they were buffeted by fierce squalls or wild storms, especially as they left the equator. Only the important incidents of their unparalleled voyage can be dwelt upon. Most of the events mentioned happened in the mate's boat, but the experience of the boat epitomes that of the others.

The mate's boat was the smallest. He was allotted five men. The other two boats each contained one more man. The men were put on an allowance of one sea-biscuit, weighing about one pound and a quarter, and a pint of water a day. In the mate's boat the provisions were kept in his chest, which he locked. The men behaved in the most exemplary manner. In only one instance did anyone ever attempt to steal provisions. They ran into a storm on the 24th, which wet some of their biscuit, and as it was necessary to get rid of the damaged bread as soon as possible, the daily allowance was taken from the spoiled portion exclusively. The soaked biscuit were very salt and greatly increased their thirst.

During the long and exhausting voyage, a plank started in the mate's boat, and it was with difficulty that they heeled it over in the water, at the risk of their lives, to get to the place and nail it up. One night the captain's boat was attacked by a species of fish known as a "killer" (*Orca*), and its bows were stove in. This also they managed to patch up. On December 3rd, they ate the last of the spoiled salt bread, and their relief when they began on the other was amazing. Their thirst was terrible, especially as it became necessary to cut the allowance of food and water in half. They tried from time to time to catch rain water by means of the sails, but the canvas had been so often drenched by the spray that the water they caught was as salt as the sea.

One day they caught half a dozen flying fish, which they ate raw. Mr. Chase remarks on the delicacy and daintiness of the mouthfuls which these little fish afforded the starving mariners. They fished for dolphins and porpoises, but they never caught any, perhaps because they had nothing with which to bait the hooks. One day, seeking to alleviate the pangs of thirst by wetting their bodies, three of the men dropped into the water alongside and clung to the gunwale. One of them discovered that the boat's bottom was covered with barnacles. They were ravenously devoured, but proved of little value as food. The men in the water were so weak that had it not been for the efforts of three who had remained in the boat, sceptical as to the utility of the bath, they would never have been able to regain their positions. During all these experiences, discipline was maintained—indeed, it was maintained to the very last.

On the 15th of December, they reached Ducie Island, in Long. 124 degrees 40 minutes W., Lat. 24 degrees 40 minutes S., having come some seventeen hundred miles in twenty-three days in these open boats. They landed on the island and found a few shell-fish, birds, and a species of pepper-grass, but no water. The famished men soon consumed everything eatable they could come at on the island. They hunted high and low, but it was not until the 22nd that they found a spring of water. The island was almost desolate. Nothing was to be gained by remaining there, so the majority concluded to sail for Easter Island, some nine hundred miles southward. Three men decided to stay on the island. They all spent a melancholy Christmas there, repairing their boats and filling their water-breakers, and on the 27th the others took their departure.

On the 14th of January, 1821, they found that they had been driven to the south of Easter Island, and that it was not practicable to beat up to it. They therefore determined to head for Juan Fernandez— Robinson Crusoe's Island—some two thousand miles south-eastward. On the 10th, the second mate, Matthew Joy, died from exposure, and was buried the next morning. On the 12th in the midst of a terrible storm, the boats separated.

First we will follow the course of the mate's boat. On the 20th, Peterson, a black man, died and was buried. On the 8th of February, Isaac Cole, a white seaman, died. The men on the boat were by this time in a frightful condition, weak and emaciated to the last degree. Their provisions were almost gone. But two biscuit to a man remained. They were still over a thousand miles from land. They came to a fearful determination. The body of Cole was not buried. They lived on him from the 9th to the 14th. On the 15th and 16th, they consumed the last vestige of their biscuit.

On the 17th, driving along at the mercy of wind and wave, for there was not a man strong enough to do anything, they caught sight of the Island of Massafuera. They were helpless to bring the boat near to the Island. Whale-boats were steered by an oar. There was not a single man able to lift an oar. In addition to starvation, thirst, weakness, mental anguish, their legs began to swell with a sort of scurvy, giving them excessive pain. Their condition can scarcely be imagined. The breath of life was there, nothing more.

However, they had at last reached the end of their sufferings, for on the morning of the 19th of February, 1821, in Lat. 35 degrees 45 minutes S., Long. 81 degrees 03 minutes W., the three surviving men were picked up by the brig *Indian*, of London, Captain William Crozier. On the 25th of February, they arrived at Valparaiso, ninety-six days and nearly four thousand miles from the sinking of the ship!

The other two boats managed to keep together for a little while after they lost sight of the mate's boat. On the 14th of February, provisions in the second mate's boat gave out entirely. On the 15th, Lawson Thomas, a black man, died in that boat and was eaten. The captain's boat ran out of provisions on the 21st. On the 23rd Charles Shorter, another Negro, died in the second mate's boat and was shared between the two boats. On the 27th another black man died from the same boat, furnishing a further meal for the survivors. On the 28th, Samuel Reed, the last black man, died in the captain's boat and was eaten like the rest. Singular that all the Negroes died first!

On the 29th, in a storm, these two boats separated. When they parted the second mate's boat had three living white men in her. Nothing was ever heard of her.

It might be inferred from the fact that the surviving men had had something to eat, that they were in fair physical condition. That is far from the truth. The men who had died were nothing but skin and bone, and all that the survivors got from their ghastly meals was the bare prolongation of a life which sank steadily to a lower and lower ebb. We may not judge these people too harshly. Hunger and thirst make men mad. They scarcely realized what they did.

There was worse to come. On the 1st of February, 1821, being without food or drink of any sort, the four men in the captain's boat cast lots as to which should die for the others. There is something significant of a spirit of fair play and discipline, not without its admirable quality, that under such circumstances, the weaker were not overpowered by the stronger, but that each man had an equal chance for life. The lot fell upon Owen Coffin,[1] the captain's nephew. He did not repine. He expressed his willingness to abide by the decision. No man desired to be his executioner. They cast lots, as before, to determine who should kill him, and the lot fell upon Charles Ramsdale. By him Coffin was shot.

Thus they eked out a miserable existence until the 11th of February, when Barzilla Ray died. On the 23rd of February, the two remaining men, the captain and Ramsdale, just on the point of casting lots as to which should have the last poor chance for life, were picked up by the Nantucket whaler, *Dauphin*, Captain Zimri Coffin. They had almost reached St. Mary's Island, ten miles from the coast of Chili. On the 17th of March, these two survivors joined the three from the mate's boat in Valparaiso.

In the harbour was the United States frigate, *Constellation*, Captain Charles G. Ridgeley, U. S. N. As soon as her commander heard of the three left on Ducie Island, he arranged with Captain Thomas Raines, of the British merchant ship, *Surrey*, to touch at the island on his voyage to Australia and take off the men. Captain Raines found them still alive, but reduced to the last gasp.

Thus of the twenty men, five reached Valparaiso; three were saved on the island, three were lost in the second mate's boat, two died and were buried; six died and were eaten, and one was shot and eaten.

So ends this strange tragedy of the sea.

---

1. A tradition still current in Nantucket has it that the lot fell to the captain, whereupon his nephew, already near death, feeling that he could not survive the afternoon, offered and insisted upon taking his uncle's place. I doubt this.

2

Some Famous American Duels

We are accustomed to regard our country as peculiarly law-abiding and peaceful. This, in spite of the fact that three presidents have been murdered within the last forty-five years, a record of assassination of chief magistrates surpassed in no other land, not even in Russia. We need not be surprised to learn that in no country was the serious duel, the *combat à l'outrance*, so prevalent as in the United States at one period of our national development. The code of honour, so-called, was most profoundly respected by our ancestors; and the number of eminent men who engaged in duelling—and of whom many lost their lives on the field—is astonishing. Scarce any meeting was without its fatal termination, perhaps owing to the fact that pistols and rifles were generally used, and Americans are noted for their marksmanship.

There has been a revulsion of public sentiment which has brought about the practical abolition of duelling in America. Although the practice still obtains in continental European countries, it is here regarded as immoral, and it is illegal as well. For one reason, in spite of the apparent contradiction above, we are a law-abiding people. The genius of the Anglo-Saxon—I, who am a Celt, admit it—is for the orderly administration of the law, and much of the evil noted comes from the introduction within our borders of an imperfectly assimilated foreign element which cherishes different views on the subject. Another deterrent cause is a cool common sense which has recognized the futility of trying to settle with blade or bullet differences which belong to the courts; to this may be added a keen sense of humour which has seen the absurdity and laughed the practice out of existence. The freedom of the press has also been a contributing factor. Perhaps the greatest deterrent, however, has been the development of a sense of responsibility for life and its uses to a Higher Power.

As General Grant has put it, with the matchless simplicity of greatness: "I do not believe I ever would have the courage to fight a duel. If any man should wrong me to the extent of my being willing to kill him, I should not be willing to give him the choice of weapons with which it should be done, and of the time, place, and distance separating us when I executed him. If I should do any other such a wrong as to justify him in killing me, I would make any reasonable atonement within my power, if convinced of the wrong done."

With this little preliminary, I shall briefly review a few of the most noted duels in our history.

1. A TRAGEDY OF OLD NEW YORK

On Wednesday, the 11th of July, 1804, at seven o'clock on a bright, sunny, summer morning, two men, pistol in hand, confronted each other on a narrow shelf of rocky ground jutting out from the cliffs that overlook the Hudson at Weehawken, on the Jersey shore. One was a small, slender man, the other taller and more imposing in appearance. Both had been soldiers; each faced the other in grave quietude, without giving outward evidence of any special emotion.

One was at that time the Vice-president of the United States; the other had been Secretary of the Treasury, a general in command of the army, and was the leading lawyer of his time. The Vice-president was brilliantly clever; the ex-Secretary was a genius of the first order.

A political quarrel had brought them to this sorry position. Words uttered in the heat of campaign, conveying not so much a personal attack as a well-merited public censure, had been dwelt upon until the Vice-president had challenged his political antagonist. The great attorney did not believe in duels. He was a Christian, a man of family; he had everything to lose and little to gain from this meeting. Upon his great past he might hope to build an even greater future. He was possessed of sufficient moral courage to refuse the meeting, but had, nevertheless, deliberately accepted the other's challenge. It is believed that he did so from a high and lofty motive; that he felt persuaded of the instability of the Government which he had helped to found, and that he realized that he possessed qualities which in such a crisis would be of rare service to his adopted country. His future usefulness, he thought—erroneously, doubtless, but he believed it—would be impaired if anyone could cast a doubt upon his courage by pointing to the fact that he had refused a challenge.

Thirty months before, his son, a bright lad of eighteen, fresh from Columbia College, had been shot dead in a duel which he had brought upon himself by resenting a public criticism of his father. He had fallen on that very spot where his father stood. I think that the tragedy must have been in the great statesman's mind that summer morning.

The word was given. The two pistols were discharged. The Vice-president, taking deliberate aim, fired first. The ex-Secretary of the Treasury, who had previously stated to his second that he did not intend to fire at his adversary, discharged his pistol in the air. He had been hit by the bullet of his enemy, and did not know that as he fell, by a convulsive movement, he had pulled the trigger of the weapon in his hand.

That was the end—for he died the next day after lingering agonies—of Alexander Hamilton, the greatest intellect and one of the greatest personalities associated with the beginning of this Government. It was also the end of his successful antagonist, Aaron Burr, for thereafter he was a marked man, an avoided, a hated man. When abroad in 1808, he gave Jeremy Bentham an account of the duel, and said that he "was sure of being able to kill him."

"And so," replied Bentham, "I thought it little better than a murder."

"Posterity," the historian adds, "will not be likely to disturb the judgment of the British philosopher."

2. Andrew Jackson as a Duellist

Comparatively speaking, the next great duel on my list attracted little more than local attention at the time. Years after, when one of them who took part in it had risen to national fame, and was a candidate for the Presidency, it was revived and made much of. On Friday, the 30th of May, 1806, Charles Dickinson, a young man of brilliant abilities, born in Maryland and residing in Tennessee, met Andrew Jackson, of the latter state, near the banks of a small stream called the Red River, in a sequestered woodland glade in Logan County, Ky., a day's ride from Nashville.

Unwittingly, and with entire innocence on the part of both parties, Andrew Jackson had placed his wife in an equivocal position by marrying her before a divorce had separated her from her husband[1]. Absolutely no blame, except, perhaps, a censure for carelessness, attaches to Jackson or his wife, and their whole life together was an example of conjugal affection. However, his enemies—and he had many—found it easy to strike at him through this unfortunate episode. There did not live a more implacable and unforgiving man, when his wife was slandered, than Andrew Jackson.

---

1. The reader may consult my book *The True Andrew Jackson* for a detailed account of this interesting transaction.

Dickinson, who was a political rival, spoke slurringly of Mrs. Jackson. He apologized for it on the plea that he had been in his cups at the time, but Jackson never forgave him. A political difference as an ostensible cause of quarrel soon developed. Dickinson sent a challenge which was gladly accepted. The resulting duel was probably the most dramatic that ever occurred in the United States. Dickinson was a dead shot. So, for that matter, was Jackson, but Dickinson was remarkable for the quickness of his fire, while Jackson was slower. The arrangements stipulated that the combatants should be placed at the close distance of eight paces; that the word "fire!" should be given, after which each was to fire one shot at will. Rather than be hurried and have his aim disturbed, Jackson determined to sustain Dickinson's fire and then return it at his leisure.

"What if he kills you or disables you?" asked his second.

"Sir," replied Jackson deliberately, "I shall kill him though he should hit me in the brain!"

This is no *gasconade* or bravado, but simply an evidence of an intensity of purpose, of which no man ever had a greater supply than Andrew Jackson.

Dickinson fired instantly the word was given. A fleck of dust arose from the loose coat which covered the spare form of the General, but he stood apparently untouched. Dickinson, amazed, shrank back from the peg indicating his position. Old General Overton, Jackson's second, raised his pistol.

"Back to the mark, sir!" he thundered, as the unhappy young man exclaimed in dismay.

"Great God! Have I missed him?"

Dickinson recovered himself immediately, stepped back to the mark, and folded his arms to receive Jackson's fire. The hammer of the Tennessean's pistol stopped at half-cock. He deliberately re-cocked his weapon, took careful aim again, and shot Dickinson through the body. Seeing his enemy fall, Jackson turned and walked away. It was not until he had gone one hundred yards from the duelling ground and was hidden by the thick poplar trees, that his second noticed that one of his shoes was filled with blood. Dickinson had hit the General in the breast, inflicting a severe wound, and might have killed him had not the bullet glanced on a rib. The iron-nerved Jackson declared that his reason for concealing his wound was that he did not intend to give Dickinson the satisfaction of knowing that he had hit his enemy before he died.

Twenty-two years after, as Jackson stood by his dead wife's body, he "lifted his cane as if appealing to heaven, and by a look commanding silence, said, slowly and painfully, and with a voice full of bitter tears:

"'In the presence of this dear saint I can and do forgive all my enemies. But those vile wretches who have slandered her must look to God for mercy!'"

3. THE KILLING OF STEPHEN DECATUR

The idol of the American Navy was Stephen Decatur. James Barron, a disgraced officer under suspension for his lack of conduct during the famous affair between the British ship *Leopard* and the American ship *Chesapeake*, had taken no part in the war of 1812, for causes which afforded him sufficient excuse; but subsequently he sought re-employment in the navy. Decatur, who had been one of the court which tried and sentenced him before the war, and who was now a naval commissioner, opposed his plea. The situation brought forth a challenge from Barron. Decatur was under no necessity of meeting it. As commissioner, he was in effect, Barron's superior, and Washington had laid down a rule for General Greene's guidance in a similar case that a superior officer is not amenable to challenge from a junior officer whom he has offended in course of duty. The principle is sound common sense, as everybody, even duellists, will admit. Nevertheless, such was the state of public opinion about questions of "honour" that Decatur felt constrained to accept the challenge.

The two naval officers met on the duelling ground at Bladensburg, "the cockpit of Washington duellists," on the 22nd of March, 1820. Barron was near-sighted, and insisted upon a closer distance than the usual ten paces. They were placed a scant eight paces apart. Decatur, who was a dead shot, did not wish to kill Barron; at the same time he did not deem it safe to stand his adversary's fire without return. Therefore he stated to his second that he would shoot Barron in the hip. Before the duel, Barron expressed the hope that if they met in another world they might be better friends. Decatur replied gravely that he had never been Barron's enemy. Under such circumstances it would appear that the quarrel might have been composed without the shedding of blood.

At the word "two" the men fired together, Decatur's bullet struck Barron in the hip, inflicting a severe but not mortal wound. At the same instant Barron's bullet passed through Decatur's abdomen, inflicting a wound necessarily fatal then, probably so, even now. As he lay on the ground the great commodore said faintly:

"I am mortally wounded—at least, I believe so—and I wish I had fallen in defence of my country."

He died at ten o'clock that night, regretted by all who love brave men the world over.

4. An Episode in the Life of James Bowie

Of a different character, but equally interesting, was an encounter in August, 1829, which has become famous because of one of the weapons used with deadly effect. On an island in the Mississippi River, opposite Natchez, which was nothing but a sand bar with some undergrowth upon it, a party of men met to witness and second a duel between a Dr. Maddox and one Samuel Wells. The spectators were all interested in one or the other combatant, and had taken part in a neighbourhood feud which arose out of a speculation in land.

The two principals exchanged two shots without injury, whereupon the seconds and spectators, unable to restrain their animosity, started a free fight. Judge Crane, of Mississippi, was the leader on one side; James Bowie, of Georgia, the principal man on the other. Crane was armed with a brace of duelling pistols; Bowie had nothing but a knife. Bowie and a friend of his, named Currey, attacked Crane after the Maddox-Wells duel had been abandoned. Crane was wounded in the left arm by a shot from Currey; he thereupon shot Currey dead and with his remaining pistol he wounded Bowie in the groin. Nevertheless, Bowie resolutely came on. Crane struck him over the head with his pistol, felling him to the ground. Undaunted, Bowie scrambled to his feet and made again for Crane.

Major Wright, a friend of Crane's, now interposed, and thrust at Bowie with a sword cane. The blade tore open Bowie's breast. The terrible Georgian, twice wounded though he was, caught Wright by the neck-cloth, grappled with him, and threw him to the ground, falling upon him.

"Now, Major, you die," said Bowie coolly, wrenching his arm free and plunging his knife into Wright's heart.

The knife had been made by Bowie's brother Rezin out of a blacksmith's rasp. It was shaped in accordance with his own ideas, and James Bowie used it with terrible effect. It was the first of the celebrated "Bowie knives" which played so great a part in frontier quarrels.

In the general *mêlée* which followed the death of Wright and Currey, six other men were killed and fifteen severely wounded. Bowie was a noted duellist in his day, and died heroically in the famous siege of the Alamo[2].

On one occasion he was a passenger on a Mississippi steamboat with a young man and his bride. The young man had collected a large sum of money for friends and employers, which he gambled away on the boat. Bowie kept him from suicide, took his place at the gaming-table, exposed the cheating of the gamblers, was challenged by one of them, fought him on the hurricane deck of the steamer, shot him into the river, and restored the money to the distracted husband.

Brief reference may be made to an affair between Major Thomas Biddle, of the United States Army, and Congressman Spencer Pettis, of Missouri, on August 27, 1831. The cause of the duel was a political difficulty. The two men stood five feet apart, their pistols overlapping. Both were mortally wounded. This was nothing less than a double murder, and shows to what length men will go under the heat of passion or the stimulus of a false code of honour.

5. A Famous Congressional Duel

On February the 24, 1838, at a quarter after three o'clock on the Marlborough Road in Maryland, just outside the District of Columbia, two members of Congress, Jonathan Cilley of Maine, and William J. Graves of Kentucky, exchanged shots with rifles at a distance of ninety yards three times in succession. At the third exchange, Cilley was shot and died in three minutes. Of all the causes for deadly encounters, that which brought these two men opposite each other was the most foolish. Cilley, on the floor of the House, had reflected upon the character of a newspaper editor in the discussion of charges which had been made against certain Congressmen with whom he had no personal connection. The newspaper editor, whose subsequent conduct showed that he fully merited even more severe strictures than Cilley had passed upon him, sent a challenge to the gentleman from Maine by the hand of Congressman Graves.

Cilley took the justifiable position that his language had been proper and privileged, and that he did not propose to accept a challenge or discuss the matter with anyone. He assured Graves that this declination to pursue the matter further was not to be construed as a reflection upon the bearer of the challenge. There was no quarrel whatever between Cilley and Graves. Nevertheless, Graves took the

---

2. See my *Border Fights and Fighters* in this series for an account of this dramatic and heroic adventure.

ground that the refusal to accept the challenge which he had brought was a reflection upon him. He thereupon challenged Cilley on his own behalf. Efforts were made to compose the quarrel but Cilley was not willing to go further than he had already done. He positively refused to discuss the editor in question. He would only repeat that he intended no reflection upon Mr. Graves, whom he respected and esteemed, by refusing the editor's challenge. This was not satisfactory to Graves, and the duel was, accordingly, arranged.

During its course, after each fruitless exchange of shots, efforts were made to end the affair, but Graves refused to accept Cilley's statement, again repeated, that he had no reflection to cast upon Mr. Graves, and Cilley refused to abandon the position he had taken with regard to the editor. Never did a more foolish *punctilio* bring about so terrible a result. Aside from accepting the challenge, Cilley had pursued a dignified and proper course. Graves, to put it mildly, had played the fool. He was practically a disgraced man thereafter. The Congressional committee which investigated the matter censured him in the severest terms, and recommended his expulsion from Congress. Perhaps the public indignation excited by this wretched affair did more to discredit duelling than any previous event.

6. The Last Notable Duel in America

The last notable American duel was that between United States Senator Broderick, of California, and ex-Chief Justice Terry, of the Supreme Court of the same state, on September 13, 1859. This, too, arose from political differences. Broderick and Terry belonged to different factions of the growing Republican party, each struggling for control in California. Broderick was strongly anti-slavery, and his opponents wanted him removed. Terry was defeated in his campaign for reflection largely, as he supposed, through Broderick's efforts. The two men had been good friends previously. Broderick had stood by Terry on one occasion when everybody else had been against him and his situation had been critical. In his anger over his defeat, Terry accused Broderick of disgraceful and underhand practices. Broderick was provoked into the following rejoinder:

I see that Terry has been abusing me. I now take back the remark I once made that he is the only honest judge in the Supreme Court. I was his friend when he was in need of friends, for which I am sorry. Had the vigilance committee disposed of him as they did of others, they would have done a righteous act.

He alluded to Terry's arrest by the Vigilantes in August, 1856, charged with cutting a man named Sterling A. Hopkins, in the attempt to free from arrest one Reuben Maloney. Had Hopkins died, Terry would probably have been hung. As it was, it took the strongest influence—Masonic, press and other—to save him from banishment.

Terry, after some acrimonious correspondence, challenged Broderick. A meeting on the 12th of September was stopped by the Chief of Police of San Francisco. The police magistrate before whom the duellists were arraigned, discharged them on the ground that there had been no actual misdemeanour.

Next day the principals and the seconds met again at the foot of Lake Merced, about twelve miles from San Francisco. About eighty spectators, friends of the participants, were present. The distance was the usual ten paces. Both pistols had hair triggers, but Broderick's was more delicately set than Terry's, so much so that a jar might discharge it. Broderick's seconds were inexperienced men, and no one realized the importance of this difference.

At the word both raised their weapons. Broderick's was discharged before he had elevated it sufficiently, and his bullet struck the ground about six feet in front of Terry. Terry was surer and shot his antagonist through the lung. Terry, who acted throughout with cold-blooded indifference, watched his antagonist fall and remarked that the wound was not mortal, as he had struck two inches to the right. He then left the field.

When Broderick fell, one of the bystanders, named Davis, shouted out:

"That is murder, by God!"

Drawing his own weapon, he started for Terry, exclaiming: "I am Broderick's friend. I'm not going to see him killed in that way. If you are men you will join me in avenging his death!"

Some cool heads in the multitude restrained him, pointing out that if he attacked Terry there would be a general *mêlée*, from which few on the ground would escape, and they finally succeeded in getting him away.

Broderick lingered for three days.

"They have killed me," he said, "because I was opposed to slavery and a corrupt administration."

Colonel Edward D. Baker, who was killed at Ball's Bluff in the Civil War, received his friend's last words.

"I tried to stand firm when I was wounded, but I could not. The blow blinded me."

Terry was tried for murder, but by influence and other means he was never convicted, and escaped all punishment save that inflicted by his conscience.

In judging these affairs, it must be remembered that many of the most prominent Americans of the past—Benton, Clay, Calhoun and Houston among them—fought duels. And it is well known that only Abraham Lincoln's wit and humour saved him from a deadly encounter with General James Shields, whose challenge he accepted.

3

The Cruise of the Tonquin

A FORGOTTEN TRAGEDY IN EARLY AMERICAN HISTORY

On the morning of the 8th of September, 1810, two ships were running side by side before a fresh south-westerly breeze off Sandy Hook, New York. One was the great United States ship *Constitution*, Captain Isaac Hull; the other was the little full-rigged ship *Tonquin*, of two hundred and ninety tons burden.

This little vessel was captained by one Jonathan Thorn, who was at the time a lieutenant in the United States Navy. He had obtained leave of absence for the purpose of making a cruise in the *Tonquin*. Thorn was a thoroughly experienced seaman and a skilled and practised navigator. He was a man of magnificent physique, with a fine war record.

He was with Decatur in the *Intrepid* when he put the captured *Philadelphia* to flames six years before. In the subsequent desperate gunboat fighting at Tripoli, Midshipman Thorn had borne so distinguished a part that he received special commendation by Commodore Preble. As to his other qualities, Washington Irving, who knew him from infancy, wrote of him to the last with a warm affection which nothing could diminish.

Mr. John Jacob Astor, merchant, fur-trader, financier, had pitched upon Thorn as the best man to take the ship bearing the first representatives of the Pacific Fur Company around the Horn and up to the far north-western American coast to make the first settlement at Astoria, whose history is so interwoven with that of our country.

Mr. Astor already monopolized the fur trade of the Far West south of the Great Lakes. His present plan was to form a fur company and establish a series of trading posts along the Missouri River, reaching overland across the Rocky Mountains until they joined the posts on the Pacific. The place he selected for his Pacific depot was the mouth of the Columbia River.

The principal rival of the Astor Fur Trading Company was the Northwest Company. Astor tried to persuade the company to join him in his new venture. When it refused to do so as an organization, he approached individual employees of the Company, and in 1810 formed the Pacific Fur Company. Among the incorporators were four Scottish Canadians, Messrs. McKay, McDougall, David Stuart, and Robert, his nephew. There were several other partners, including Wilson Price Hunt, of New Jersey.

It was planned that Hunt should lead an overland expedition from St. Louis, while the four Scotsmen mentioned went around the Horn, and that they should meet at the mouth of the Columbia River, where the trading post was to be situated. Most of the employees of the company were Canadians who had enjoyed large experience in the fur business. Among these were included a large number of French *voyageurs*.

Thus the *Tonquin*, owned by a German, captained by an American, with a crew including Swedes, French, English, Negroes, and Americans, carrying out a party of Scottish and French Canadians and one Russian, started on her memorable voyage to establish a trading post under the American flag! The crew of the *Tonquin* numbered twenty-three men. The number of passengers was thirty-three.

The story of her voyage is related in the letters of the captain to Mr. Astor, and more fully in a quaint and curious French journal published at Montreal in 1819, by M. Gabriel Franchere, one of the Canadian clerks who made the voyage.

The *Tonquin* was pierced for twenty guns, only ten small ones being mounted. The other ports were provided with imposing wooden dummies. She had a high poop and a topgallant forecastle. The four partners, with James Lewis, acting captain's clerk, and one other, with the two mates, slept in the cabin or wardroom below the poop. Forward of this main cabin was a large room extending across the ship, called the steerage, in which the rest of the clerks, the mechanics, and the Canadian boatmen were quartered.

Thorn seems to have felt to the full all the early naval officer's utterly unmerited contempt for the merchant service. It is also the habit of the Anglo-Saxon to hold the French in slight esteem on the sea. The Canadians were wretched sailors, and Thorn despised them.

Thorn also cherished a natural hatred against the English, who were carrying things with a high hand on our coast. He began the voyage with a violent prejudice against the four partners on his ship. Indeed, the *Constitution* had convoyed the *Tonquin* to sea because it was rumoured that a British brig-o'-war intended to swoop down upon her and take off the English subjects on board. It was quite evident that war would shortly break out between England and the United States, and the Scottish partners had surreptitiously consulted the English consul as to what they should do if hostilities began. They were informed that in that case they would be treated as British subjects—a fine situation for an American expedition!

With such a spirit in the captain, and such a feeling on the part of the passengers, the relations between them were bound to become strained. Hostilities began at once. The first night out Thorn ordered all lights out at eight bells. This in spite of all the remonstrances of the four partners, who, as representing Mr. Astor, considered themselves, properly enough, as owners of the ship. These gentlemen did not wish to retire at so early an hour, nor did they desire to spend the intervening time in darkness. They remonstrated with Thorn, and he told them, in the terse, blunt language of a seaman, to keep quiet or he would put them in irons. In case he attempted that, they threatened to resort to firearms for protection. Finally, however, the captain allowed them a little longer use of their lights. Thus was inaugurated a long, disgraceful wrangle that did not cease while life lasted.

There was doubtless much fault on both sides, but, in spite of the brilliant advocate who has pleaded Thorn's cause, I cannot but admit that he was decidedly the more to blame. He carried things with a high hand, indeed, treating the partners as he might a graceless lot of undisciplined midshipmen.

A voyage around the Horn in those days was no slight matter. The *Tonquin* was a remarkably good sailer, but it was not until the 5th of October that they sighted the Cape Verde Islands. There they struck the Trades, and went booming down the African coast at a great rate. There, also, they were pursued by a large man-o'-war brig. On the third day she drew so near that Thorn prepared for action, whereupon the brig sheered off, and left them.

On the 11th of October they ran into a terrific storm, which prevailed until the 21st, when they found themselves off the River Plate. While the storm was at its height the man at the wheel was thrown across the deck by a sudden jump of the wheel and severely injured, breaking three of his ribs and fracturing his collar-bone[1]. Thorn's seamanship during the trying period was first class. After the gale blew itself out, a fresh breeze succeeded, which enabled them rapidly to run down their southing. The water supply had grown very low, and it was determined to run in to the Falkland Islands to fill the casks.

They made a landfall on the 3rd of December, got on shore on one of the smaller islets on the 4th, found no water, and were driven to sea to seek an offing on the 5th by a gale. On the 6th they landed at Point Egmont on the West Falkland, and found a fine spring of fresh water. As it would take several days to fill the casks, all the passengers went ashore and camped on the deserted island. They amused themselves by fishing, shooting and rambling about. On the 11th of the month the captain, having filled his water-casks, signalled for every man to come aboard, by firing a gun. Eight passengers, including McDougall and Stuart, happened to be on shore at the time. They had wandered around to the other side of the island, and did not hear the report of the gun. Thorn, after waiting a short time, weighed anchor and filled away from the island, firmly resolved to leave the men ashore, marooned and destitute of supplies on that desolate and uninhabited spot, where they must inevitably perish of starvation and exposure.

Some of the abandoned passengers happened to see the *Tonquin* fast leaving the island. In great alarm they hastily summoned all the other wanderers, and the eight got into a small boat twenty feet long, which had been left with them, and rowed after the rapidly receding ship. They had not the slightest hope of catching her unless she waited for them, but they pulled for her with furious energy, nevertheless. As the *Tonquin* got from under the lee of the land the breeze freshened and she drew away from them with every passing moment in spite of their manful work at the oars. When they had about given up in exhaustion and despair, the ship suddenly changed her course and stood toward them.

Franchere says that it was because young Stuart put a pistol to the captain's head and swore that he would blow out his brains unless he went back for the boat. The captain's account to Mr. Astor is that a sudden shift of wind compelled him to come about and this gave the boat an opportunity to overhaul him. There was a scene of wild recrimination when the boat reached the ship, shortly after six bells (3 p. m.), but it did not seem to bother Thorn in the least.

---

1. I have seen a man at the wheel of the old *Constellation* on one of my own cruises similarly injured.

On the 18th of December, they were south and east of Cape Horn. The weather was mild and pleasant, but before they could make headway enough against the swift easterly current to round that most dangerous point it came on to blow a regular Cape Horn gale. After seven days of hard beating they celebrated Christmas under pleasanter auspices in the southern Pacific.

Their run northward was uneventful, and on the 11th of February, 1811, they sighted the volcano of Mauna Loa in the Sandwich Islands. They landed on the 12th and spent sixteen days among the different islands, visiting, filling the water-casks, and buying fresh meat, vegetables, and live-stock from Kamehameha I.

While Captain Thorn was hated by the passengers, he was not loved by his officers. Singularly enough, he seems to have been well liked by the crew, although there were some exceptions even there. Anderson, the boatswain, left the ship at Hawaii. There had been difficulties between them, and the captain was glad to see him go. A sample of Thorn's method of administering discipline is interesting.

The day they sailed a seaman named Aymes strayed from the boat party, and was left behind when the boat returned to the ship. In great terror Aymes had some natives bring him aboard in a canoe. A longboat loaded with fodder for the live-stock lay alongside. As Aymes clambered into the long-boat, the captain, who was furiously angry, sprang down into the boat, seized Aymes with one hand and a stout piece of sugar-cane with the other. With this formidable weapon the unfortunate sailor was beaten until he screamed for mercy. After wearing out the sugarcane upon him, with the remark that if he ever saw him on the sloop again, he would kill him, the captain pitched him into the water. Aymes, who was a good swimmer, made the best of his way to the shore, and stayed there with Anderson. Twenty-four natives were shipped at Hawaii, twelve for the crew and twelve for the new settlement.

On the 16th of March they ran into another storm, of such violence that they were forced to strike their topgallant masts and scud under double-reefed foresail. As they were nearing the coast, the ship was hove to at night. Early on the morning of the 22nd of March, they sighted land, one hundred and ninety-five days and twenty thousand miles from Sandy Hook. The weather was still very severe, the wind blowing in heavy squalls and the sea running high, and the captain did not think it prudent to approach the shore nearer than three miles. His navigation had been excellent, however, for before them lay the mouth of the Columbia River, the object of their long voyage. They could see the waves breaking over the bar with tremendous force as they beat to and fro along the coast.

Thorn, ignorant of the channel, did not dare take the ship in under such conditions. He therefore ordered First-Mate Ebenezer Fox to take Sailmaker Martin and three Canadians into a boat and find the channel. It was a hazardous undertaking, and the despatch of the small boat under such circumstances was a serious error in judgment.

There had been bad blood between the captain and the mate, and Fox did not wish to go. If he had to go, he begged that his boat might be manned with seamen instead of Canadians. The captain refused to change his orders. Fox appealed to the partners. They remonstrated with the captain, but they could not alter his determination. The boat was pulled away and was lost to sight in the breakers. Neither the boat nor any member of the crew was ever seen or heard of again. The boat was ill-found and ill-manned. She was undoubtedly caught in the breakers and foundered.

The next day the wind increased in violence, and they cruised off the shore looking for the boat. Everyone on board, including the captain, stern and ruthless though he was, was very much disturbed at her loss.

On the 24th the weather moderated somewhat, and running nearer to the shore, they anchored just outside Cape Disappointment, near the north shore of the river mouth. The wind subsiding, Mumford, the second mate, with another boat, was sent to search for the passage, but finding the surf still too heavy, he returned about noon, after a terrible struggle with the breakers.

In the afternoon McKay and Stuart offered to take a boat and try to get ashore to seek for Fox and the missing men. They made the endeavour, but did not succeed in passing the breakers, and returned to the ship. Later in the afternoon a gentle breeze sprang up from the west, blowing into the mouth of the river, and Thorn determined to try and cross the bar. He weighed anchor, therefore, and bore down under easy sail for the entrance of the river. As he came close to the breakers he hove to and sent out another boat, in charge of Aitkin, a Scottish seaman, accompanied by Sailmaker Coles, Armourer Weeks and two Sandwich Islanders.

The breakers were not quite so rough as they had been, and Aitkin proceeded cautiously some distance in front of the ship, making soundings and finding no depth less than four fathoms. In obedience to his signals, the ship came bowling on, and the fitful breeze suddenly freshening, she ran through the breakers, passing Aitkin's boat to starboard in pistol-shot distance. Signals were made for the boat to return, but the tide had turned, and the strong ebb, with the current of the river, bore the boat into the breakers in spite of all her crew could do. While they were watching the boat, over which the waves were seen breaking furiously, the ship, the wind failing, was driven seaward by the tide, and struck six or seven times on the bar. The breakers, running frightfully high, swept over her decks again and again. Nothing could be done for the boat by the ship, their own condition being so serious as to demand all their efforts.

Thorn at last extricated the *Tonquin* from her predicament. The wind favoured her again, and she got over the bar and through the breakers, anchoring at nightfall in seven fathoms of water. The night was very dark. The ebb and current threatened to sweep the ship on the shore. Both anchors were carried out. Still the holding was inadequate and the ship's position grew more dangerous. They passed some anxious hours until the turn of the tide, when in spite of the fact that it was pitch dark, they weighed anchor, made sail, and succeeded in finding a safe haven under the lee of Cape Disappointment, in a place called Baker's Bay. The next day the captain and some of the partners landed in the morning to see if they could find the missing party. As they were wandering aimlessly upon the shore, they came across Weeks, exhausted and almost naked.

He had a sad story to tell. The boat had capsized in the breakers and his two white companions had been drowned. He and the Kanakas had succeeded in righting the boat and clambering into her. By some fortunate chance they were tossed outside the breakers and into calmer waters. The boat was bailed out, and the next morning Weeks sculled her ashore with the one remaining oar. One of the Sandwich Islanders was so severely injured that he died in the boat, and the other was probably dying from exposure. The relief party prosecuted their search for the Kanaka and found him the next day almost dead.

The loss of these eight men and these two boats was a serious blow to so small an expedition, but there was nothing to be done about it, and the work of selecting a permanent location for the trading-post on the south shore, unloading the cargo, and building the fort was rapidly carried on, although not without the usual quarrels between captain and men. After landing the company, Thorn had been directed by Mr. Astor to take the *Tonquin* up the coast to gather a load of furs.

He was to touch at the settlement which they had named Astoria, on his way back, and take on board what furs the partners had been able to procure and bring them back to New York. Thorn was anxious to get away, and on the 1st of June, having finished the unloading of the ship, and having seen the buildings approaching completion, accompanied by McKay as supercargo, and James Lewis of New York, as clerk, he started on his trading voyage.

That was the last that anybody ever saw of Thorn or the *Tonquin* and her men. Several months after her departure a Chehalis Indian, named Lamanse, wandered into Astoria with a terrible story of an appalling disaster. The *Tonquin* made her way up the coast, Thorn buying furs as he could. At one of her stops at Gray's Harbour, this Indian was engaged as interpreter. About the middle of June, the *Tonquin* entered Nootka Sound, an ocean estuary between Nootka and Vancouver Islands, about midway of the western shore of the latter. There she anchored before a large Nootka Indian village, called Newity.

The place was even then not unknown to history. The Nootkas were a fierce and savage race. A few years before the advent of the *Tonquin*, the American ship *Boston*, Captain Slater, was trading in Nootka Sound. The captain had grievously insulted a native chieftain. The ship had been surprised, every member of her crew except two murdered, and the ship burned. These two had been wounded and captured, but when it was learned that one was a gunsmith and armorer, their lives were preserved and they had been made slaves, escaping long after.

Every ship which entered the Sound thereafter did so with the full knowledge of the savage and treacherous nature of the Indians, and the trading was carried on with the utmost circumspection. There had been no violent catastrophes for several years, until another ship *Boston* made further trouble. Her captain had shipped twelve Indian hunters, promising to return them to their people on Nootka Sound when he was finished with them. Instead of bringing them back, he marooned them on a barren coast hundreds of miles away from their destination. When they heard of his cruel action, the Nootkas swore to be revenged on the next ship that entered the Sound. The next ship happened to be the ill-fated *Tonquin*.

Now, no Indians that ever lived could seize a ship like the *Tonquin* if proper precautions were taken by her crew. Mr. Astor, knowing the record of the bleak north-western shores, had especially cautioned Thorn that constant watchfulness should be exercised in trading. Thorn felt the serenest contempt for the Indians, and took no precautions of any sort. Indeed, the demeanor of the savages lulled even the suspicions of McKay, who had had a wide experience with the aborigines. McKay even went ashore at the invitation of one of the chiefs and spent the first night of his arrival in his lodge.

The next day the Indians came aboard to trade. They asked exorbitant prices for their skins, and conducted themselves in a very obnoxious way. Thorn was not a trader; he was a sailor. He offered them what he considered a fair price, and if that was not satisfactory, why, the vendor could go hang, for all he cared. One old chief was especially persistent and offensive in his bargaining for a high price. He followed Thorn back and forth on the deck, thrusting a roll of skins in front of him, until the irascible captain at last lost the little control of his temper he ordinarily retained. He suddenly grabbed the skins and shoved them—not to say rubbed them—in the face of the indignant and astonished Indian. Then he took the Indian by the back of the neck and summarily rushed him along the deck to the gangway. It is more than likely that he assisted him in his progress by kicking him overboard.

The other Indians left the ship immediately. The interpreter warned McKay that they would never forgive such an insult, and McKay remonstrated with the captain. His remonstrances were laughed to scorn, as usual. Not a precaution was taken. Ships trading in these latitudes usually triced up boarding nettings fore and aft to prevent savages from swarming over the bulwarks without warning. Thorn refused to order these nettings put in position. McKay did not think it prudent to go on shore that night.

Early the next morning a large canoe containing some twenty Indians, all unarmed, came off to the ship. Each Indian held up a bundle of furs and signified his desire to trade. Thorn in great triumph admitted them to the ship, the furs were brought on deck, and bargaining began. There was no evidence of resentment about any of them. Their demeanour was entirely different from what it had been the night before. On this occasion the Indians were willing to let the white men put any value they pleased on the furs.

While they were busily buying and selling, another party of unarmed Indians made their appearance alongside. They were succeeded by a second, a third, a fourth, and others, all of whom were welcome to the ship. Soon the deck was crowded with Indians eager to barter. Most of them wanted hunting or butcher knives in return, and by this means, no one suspecting anything, nearly every one of the savages became possessed of a formidable weapon for close-quarter fighting. McKay and Thorn appeared to have gone below temporarily, perhaps to break out more goods to exchange for furs, when the Indian interpreter became convinced that treachery was intended. Whoever was in charge at the time—perhaps Lewis—at the interpreter's instance [insistence?], sent word to the captain, and he and McKay came on deck at once.

The ship was filled with a mob of Indians, whose gentle and pleasant aspect had given way to one of scowling displeasure and menace. The situation was serious. McKay suggested that the ship be got under way at once. The captain for the first time agreed with him. Orders were given to man the capstan, and five of the seamen were sent aloft to loose sail. The wind was strong, and happened to be blowing in the right direction. With singular fatuity none of the officers or seamen were armed, although the ship was well provided with weapons. As the cable slowly came in through the hawse-pipe, and the loosed sails fell from the yards, Thorn, through the interpreter, told the Indians that he was about to sail away, and peremptorily directed them to leave the ship. Indeed, the movements of the sailors made his intentions plain.

It was too late. There was a sharp cry—a signal—from the chief, and without a moment's hesitation the Indians fell upon the unprepared and astonished crew. Some of the savages hauled out war-clubs and tomahawks which had been concealed in bundles of fur; others made use of the knives just purchased. Lewis was the first man struck down. He was mortally wounded, but succeeded in the subsequent confusion, in gaining the steerage. McKay was seriously injured and thrown overboard. In the boats surrounding the ships were a number of women, and they despatched the unfortunate partner with their paddles. The captain whipped out a sailor's sheath knife which he wore, and made a desperate fight for his life. The sailors also drew their knives or caught up belaying-pins or handspikes, and laid about them with the energy of despair, but to no avail. They were cut down in spite of every endeavour. The captain killed several of the Indians with his knife, and was the last to fall, overborne in the end by numbers. He was hacked and stabbed to death on his own deck.

The five sailors aloft had been terrified and helpless witnesses to the massacre beneath them. That they must do something for their own lives they now realized. Making their way aft by means of the rigging, they swung themselves to the deck and dashed for the steerage hatch. The attention of the savages had been diverted from them by the *mêlée* on deck. The five men gained the hatch, the last man down, Weeks the armourer being stabbed and mortally wounded, although he, too, gained the hatch.

At this juncture the Indian interpreter, who had not been molested, sprang overboard, and was taken into one of the canoes and concealed by the women. His life was spared, and he was afterward made a slave, and eventually escaped. The four unhurt men who had gained the steerage, broke through into the cabin, armed themselves, and made their way to the captain's cabin, whence they opened fire upon the savages on deck. The Indians fled instantly, leaving many of their dead aboard the ship. The decks of the *Tonquin* had been turned into shambles.

The next morning the natives saw a boat with four sailors in it pulling away from the ship. They cautiously approached the *Tonquin* thereupon, and discovered one man, evidently badly wounded, leaning over the rail. When they gained the deck, he was no longer visible. No immediate search appears to have been made for him, but finding the ship practically deserted, a great number of Indians came off in their canoes and got aboard. They were making preparations to search and pillage the ship, when there was a terrific explosion, and the ill-fated *Tonquin* blew up with all on board. In her ending she carried sudden destruction to over two hundred of the Indians.

It is surmised that the four unwounded men left on the ship realized their inability to carry the *Tonquin* to sea, and determined to take to the boat in the hope of reaching Astoria by coasting down the shore. It is possible that they may have laid a train to the magazine—the *Tonquin* carried four and a half tons of powder—but it is generally believed, as a more probable story, on account of the time that elapsed between their departure and the blowing up of the ship, that Lewis, who was yet alive in spite of his mortal wounds, and who was a man of splendid resolution and courage as well, realizing that he could not escape death, remained on board; and when the vessel was crowded with Indians had revenged himself for the loss of his comrades by firing the magazine and blowing up the ship.

Again, it is possible that Lewis may have died, and that Weeks, the armourer, the other wounded man, made himself the instrument of his own and the Indians' destruction. To complete the story, the four men who had escaped in the boats were pursued, driven ashore, and fell into the hands of the implacable Indians. They were tortured to death.

Such was the melancholy fate which attended some of the participants in the first settlement of what is now one of the greatest and most populous sections of the Union.

4

John Paul Jones

Being Further Light on His Strange Career[1]

One hundred and eighteen years ago, (as at time of first publish, a little man who had attracted the attention of two continents, and who, in his comparatively brief career of forty-five years, had won eternal fame for himself among the heroes of the world, died in Paris, alone in his room. He had been ill for some time, and his physician, calling late in the evening, found him prone upon his bed, sleeping a sleep from which no call to battle would ever arouse him. Like Warren Hastings, John Paul Jones was at rest at last; "in peace after so many storms, in honour after so much obloquy."

He was buried in a Protestant cemetery in Paris, which was officially closed in January, 1793. The exact location of his grave there was forgotten. For many years even the fact that he was buried there was forgotten. The other day the cable flashed a message which gladdened every American heart. Under the inspiration, and at the personal charges, of General Horace Porter, United States Ambassador to France, a search had been instigated and the body was found and completely identified. It is a service of sentiment that General Porter has rendered us, but not the less valuable on that account. To love the hero, to recall the heroic past, is good for the future.

The remains of the great captain came back to the United States. On the decks of such a battleship as even his genius never dreamed

---

1. My reason for including in this volume a paper on this great sailor whose career has already been discussed in *Revolutionary Fights and Fighters* (q. v.), (also published by Leonaur), is because this present article contains a new and original contribution to history, never before published in book form, which absolutely and finally settles one phase of the much mooted question as to why John Paul assumed the surname Jones, as will be seen hereafter.

of, surrounded by a squadron that could have put to flight all the sea-fighters of the world before the age of steam and steel, the body of the little commodore was brought back to his adopted country to repose on the soil of the land he loved, for whose liberty he fought, whose honour he maintained in battle; and a suitable monument is to be raised by our people to commemorate his services, to inspire like conduct in years to come.

Commodore John Paul Jones, the first of the great American fighters, and not the least splendid in the long line, was born of humble origin in a southern county of Scotland. His family was obscure, his circumstances narrow, his advantages meagre, his opportunities limited. At the age of twelve he became a sailor. Genius rose, superior to adverse circumstances, however, and before he died he was one of the most accomplished officers who ever served the United States. The greatest men of America and France took pleasure in his society and were proud of his friendship.

He progressed rapidly in his chosen career. At nineteen he was chief mate of a slaver, a legitimate occupation in his day but one that filled him with disgust. At twenty-one he was captain of a trader. In 1773 he came to America, forsook the sea and settled in Virginia.

1. THE BIRTH OF THE AMERICAN NAVY

He was still poor and still obscure when on December 7, 1775, he was appointed a lieutenant in the new Continental Navy, In that capacity he was ordered to the *Alfred*, a small converted merchantman, the flagship of Commodore Hopkins. He joined the ship immediately, and in the latter part of December he had the honour of hoisting with his own hands the first naval flag of an American squadron. This was the famous yellow silk banner with a rattlesnake and perhaps a pine tree emblazoned upon it, and with the significant legend, "Don't tread on me!"

Hopkins made an abortive expedition to New Providence, in which Jones had but one opportunity to distinguish himself. At the peril of his commission, when the regular pilots refused to do so, he volunteered to take the *Alfred* through a difficult and dangerous channel. Needless to say, he succeeded—he always succeeded!

His first independent command was the little schooner *Providence*, of seventy men and twelve four-pound guns. In the Fall of 1775 he made a notable cruise in this schooner; he skirmished with, and escaped from, by seamanship and daring, two heavy frigates, the *Solebay* and the *Milford*; in four months he captured sixteen vessels, eight of which were sent in as prizes, five burned, three returned to certain poor fishermen; and he destroyed property aggregating a million dollars.

Later, in command of the *Alfred*, with a short crew of one hundred and fifty, when he should have had three hundred, he made another brilliant cruise in which he burned several British transports, captured one store-ship, laden to the gunwales with priceless munitions of war and supplies, cut out three of the supply fleet from under the guns of the *Flora* frigate, and had another smart brush with the *Milford*.

2. JONES FIRST HOISTS THE STARS AND STRIPES

Commissioned captain on the 14th of June, 1777, in the same resolution which established an American flag, he was ordered to the *Ranger*, a little ship-rigged corvette of three hundred tons. In her, on the 4th of July of the same year, he hoisted the first stars and stripes that had ever waved over a ship-of-war. In Quiberon Bay—famous as one of the battle-grounds of the world—on the evening of the 14th of February, 1778, in the *Ranger*, he received the first formal recognition ever given by a foreign fleet to the United States in a salute to the American flag. As it was after sunset when the salutes were exchanged, and in order that there should be no mistake about it, the next morning, the 15th of February, Jones transferred his flag to the *Independence*, a small privateer, and deliberately sailed through La Motte Picquet's great fleet of towering line-of-battle-ships, saluting and receiving salutes again.

Still on the *Ranger*, on the 24th of April, he fought the British sloop-of-war *Drake*, of equal force and larger crew, to a standstill in an hour and five minutes. When the *Drake* struck her flag, her rigging, sails and spars were cut to pieces. She had forty-two killed and wounded— more than one-fifth of her crew—and was completely helpless. The *Ranger* lost two killed and six wounded.

In 1779 Jones hoisted his flag on the *Duc de Duras*, a condemned East Indiaman, which would have been broken up had he not turned her into a makeshift frigate by mounting forty guns in her batteries— fourteen twelve-pounders, twenty nines and six eighteens. This, in honour of Franklin, he named the *Bonhomme Richard*. Accompanied by the fine little American-built frigate *Alliance* and the French ship *Pallas*, with the brig *Vengeance*, and the cutter *Cerf*, he cruised around England, taking several prizes, and striking terror all along the shore.

3. The Battle With the *Serapis*

On the evening of the 23rd of September he fell in with the Baltic convoy. He was accompanied at the time by the *Alliance* and the *Pallas*. The Baltic convoy was protected by the *Serapis* and the *Scarborough*. The *Serapis* was a brand-new, double-banked frigate of eight hundred tons, carrying twenty eighteen-pounders, twenty nines and ten sixes. Inasmuch as the eighteen-pounders on the *Richard* burst and were abandoned after the first fire, the *Serapis* could and did discharge near-ly twice as many pounds' weight of broadside as the *Richard*, say three hundred pounds to one hundred and seventy-five. The *Pallas* grappled with the *Scarborough*—a more equal match—and Jones attacked the *Serapis*, which was not unwilling—quite the contrary—for the fight.

The battle was one of the most memorable and desperate ever fought upon the ocean. The *Richard* was riddled like a sieve. Her rot-ten sides were literally blown out to starboard and port by the heavy batteries of the *Serapis*. Jones had several hundred English prisoners on board. The master-at-arms released them, but, with great readiness and presence of mind, Jones sent them to the pumps, while he continued to fight the English frigate, his own ship kept afloat by their efforts.

Captain Pearson, of the *Serapis*, was as brave a man as ever drew a sword, but he was no match for the indomitable personality of the American commander. After several hours of such fighting as had scarcely been seen before on the narrow seas, he struck his flag. The *Alliance*, accompanied by a jealous and incapable Frenchman, had con-tributed nothing to Jones's success. Indeed, she had twice poured her broadsides into the *Richard*. The American vessel was so wrecked be-low and aloft that she sank alongside, and Jones had to transfer the survivors of his crew to the English frigate. The aggregate of the two crews was nearly seven hundred, of which about three hundred and fifty were killed or wounded.

It is the greatest pity that the poverty of America did not permit Jones to get to sea in a proper frigate, or in a ship of the line, before the close of the war. After the Revolution, in which he had borne so conspicuous a part, so much so that his exploits had electrified both continents, he took service under Catherine of Russia, carefully reserving his American citizenship. In her service he fought four bril-liant actions in the Black Sea, in which he had to contend with the usual discouragement of indifferent personnel and wretched material, and in which he displayed all his old-time qualities, winning his usual successes, too.

Worn out in unrequited service, disgusted with Russian court intrigues of which he was the victim, resentful of the infamous Potemkin's brutal attempts at coercion, he asked leave of absence from Catherine's service and went to Paris, where, in the companionship of his friends, and in the society of the beautiful Aimèe de Telison, the one woman he loved, he lived two years and died at the age of forty-five.

4. A Hero's Famous Sayings

Besides the memory of his battles, Paul Jones left a collection of immortal sayings, which are the heritage of the American Navy and the admiration of brave men the world over. When the monument which is to be erected shall be ready for inscriptions, these may with propriety be carved upon it:

"I do not wish to have command of any ship that does not sail fast, for I intend to go in harm's way!" Brave little captain.

"I have ever looked out for the honour of the American flag!" It is the truth itself.

"I can never renounce the glorious title of a citizen of the United States!" The title was one which Paul Jones signally honoured.

Last, but not least, that curt phrase which comes ringing through the centuries like a trumpet call to battle; the words with which he replied to the demand of the astonished Pearson, who saw his enemy's ship beaten to a pulp, and wondered why he did not yield:

"I have not yet begun to fight!"

That was the finest phrase, under the circumstances, that ever came from the lips of an American sailor. "It was no new message. The British had heard it as they tramped again and again up the bullet-swept slopes of Bunker Hill; Washington rang it in the ears of the Hessians on the snowy Christmas morning at Trenton; the hoof-beats of Arnold's horse kept time to it in the wild charge at Saratoga; it cracked with the whip of the old wagoner Morgan at the Cowpens; the Maryland troops drove it home in the hearts of their enemies with Greene at Guilford Court House; and the drums of France and America beat it into Cornwallis's ears when the end came at Yorktown. There, that night, in that darkness, in that still moment of battle, Paul Jones declared the determination of a great people. His was the expression of an inspiration on the part of a new nation. From this man came a statement of our unshakeable determination, at whatever cost, to be free! A new Declaration of Independence, this famous word of warning to the brave sailor of the British king."

5. What Jones Did for His Country

Never in his long career did Jones have a decent ship or a respectable crew. His materials were always of the very poorest. His officers, with the exception of Richard Dale, were but little to boast of. What he accomplished, he accomplished by the exercise of his own indomitable will, his serene courage, his matchless skill as a sailor, and his devotion to the cause he had espoused. After his death, among his papers, the following little memorandum, written in his own hand, was found:

> In 1775, J. Paul Jones armed and embarked in the first American ship of war. In the Revolution he had twenty-three battles and solemn *rencontres* by sea; made seven descents in Britain, and her colonies; took of her navy two ships of equal, and two of superior force, many store-ships, and others; constrained her to fortify her ports; suffer the Irish Volunteers; desist from her cruel burnings in America and exchange, as prisoners of war, the American citizens taken on the ocean, and cast into prisons of England, as 'traitors, pirates, and felons!'

Indeed a truthful and a brilliant record. Paul Jones was accused of being a pirate. The charge was a long time dying, but it is today generally disavowed. When recently his bones were returned to American shores, may we not believe that from some Valhalla of the heroes, where the mighty men of the past mingle in peace and amity, he saw and took pride in the great if tardy outpouring of our fellow citizens to greet this first sea-king of our flag?

Now, this story of the magnificent career of John Paul Jones, so briefly summarized, has been often told, and its details are familiar to every schoolboy. There is one mystery connected with his life, however, which has not yet been solved. I purpose to make here an original contribution toward its solution. No one knows positively—it is probable that no one ever will know, why John Paul assumed the name of Jones. Of course the question is not vital to Jones's fame, for from whatever reason he assumed the name by which he is remembered, he certainly honoured it most signally; but the reason for the assumption is nevertheless of deep interest to all lovers of history. There have been two explanations of this action.

6. Why Did He Take the Name of Jones?

Five years ago two biographies of Jones appeared simultaneously.

One I had the honour of writing myself. The other was from the pen of that gifted and able author, the late Colonel Augustus C. Buell. Our accounts were in singular agreement, save in one or two points, and our conclusions as to the character of Jones in absolute harmony. In Colonel Buell's book he put forth the theory—which, so far as I know, had not before been formulated—that John Paul assumed the name of Jones in testamentary succession to his brother William Paul, who had preceded him to America; and that William Paul had himself taken the name in testamentary succession to one William Jones, a childless old planter of Middlesex County, Virginia, who bequeathed to the said William Paul an extensive plantation on the Rappahannock, some nine miles below Urbana, at a place called Jones's Wharf, on condition that he call himself Jones. In 1805 this Jones property was owned by members of the Taliaferro family, who had received it from Archibald Frazier, who claimed to have received it from John Paul Jones, although there are no records of transfer extant.

My theory, which Colonel Buell facetiously characterized— doubtless in all good humour—as "Tar-heel mythology," stated that John Paul assumed the name of Jones out of friendship and regard for the justly celebrated Jones family of North Carolina, and especially for Mrs. Willie Jones, who is not unknown in history, and who was one of the most brilliant and charming women of the colonies. Members of this family had befriended him and assisted him pecuniarily, and had extended to him the bounteous hospitality of the famous plantations, Mount Gallant and The Groves, near Halifax. It was through their influence with Congressman Hewes that Jones received his commission as a lieutenant in the Continental Navy. In further explanation it was suggested that on casting his lot with the rebellious colonies John Paul, who was somewhat erratic as well as romantic and impulsive, determined to take a new name and begin life over again.

Here are two utterly irreconcilable theories. I at once wrote to Colonel Buell asking him to inform me what was his authority for his statement. I quote, with his permission given me before his lamented death, from several letters that he wrote me:

My first authentic information on the subject was from a gentleman named William Louden, whom I met in St. Louis in 1873, when I was attached to the *Missouri Republican*. Mr. Louden was a great-grandson of Mary Paul Louden, sister of John Paul Jones. He was the only surviving blood-relative of

Paul Jones in this country, being his great-grandnephew. He told me substantially the history of the change of names as related in my first volume.

Two years later I met the late General Taliaferro of Virginia in Washington, and he corroborated the version, together with the history of the Jones plantation.[2]

One would naturally judge that the great-grandnephew of the man himself, and the gentleman who had subsequently owned the property, ought to know something about the antecedents of both the man and the land.... I doubt whether documentary evidence—such as would be admitted in court—can ever be found.

Colonel Buell also called my attention to the fact that in none of Paul Jones's letters to Joseph Hewes is there any reference to the North Carolina Jones family; and further, that Jones and Hewes became acquainted in commercial transactions before Jones settled in America.

7. Search for Historical Evidence

In an attempt to settle the matter I wrote to all the Virginia county clerks on both sides of the Rappahannock River, asking them if any copy of the will of William Paul, or that of William Paul Jones, could be found in their records. Most of these Virginia county records were destroyed during the Civil War. By great good fortune, however, those of Spottsylvania County, in which the city of Fredericksburg is situated, were preserved, and I herewith append a copy of the will of William Paul, in which he bequeaths his property, making no mention of any plantation and no mention of the name of William Jones, to his sister, Mary Young, who afterward married Louden.

In the name of God, Amen; I, William Paul, of the town of Fredericksburg and County of Spottsylvania in Virginia—being in perfect sound memory, thanks be to Almighty God, and knowing it is appointed unto all men to die, do make and ordain this my last Will and Testament in manner and form revoking all former will or wills by me herebefore made.

Principally and first of all, I recommend my soul to Almighty God who gave it, hoping through the merits of my blessed Saviour and Redeemer Jesus Christ to find Redemption, and as

---

2. Of which he (General Taliaferro) had become the owner.

to touching and concerning what worldly estate it has pleased God to bless me with, I dispose of it in the following manner:

Item—It is my will and desire that all my just debts and funeral expenses be first paid by my Executors hereafter named, who are desired to bury my body in a decent, Christian-like manner.

Item—It is my will and desire that my Lots and Houses in this Town be sold and converted into money for as much as they will bring, that with all my other estate being sold and what of my out-standing debts that can be collected, I give and bequeath unto my beloved sister Mary Young, and her two eldest children and their heirs in Arbiglon in Parish of Kirkbeen in Stewartry of Galloway, North Brittain, forever. I do hereby empower my Executors to sell and convey the said land, lots and houses and make a fee simple therein, as I could or might do in my proper person, and I do appoint my friends Mr. William Templeman and Isaac Heislop my Executors to see this my will executed, confirming this to be my last will and testament. In Witness whereof, I have hereunto set my hand and fixed my seal as my last act and deed this 22nd day of March, 1772.

William Paul (Seal).

William Paul having heard the above will distinctly read, declared the same to be his last will and testament in the presence of us:

John Atkinson,
Thomas Holmes,
B. Johnston.

William Paul evidently died in 1774, instead of 1773, as all the biographers of his famous brother have it, and the will was accordingly probated, as will be seen from the following transcript of the court records:

At a Court continued and held for Spottsylvania County, December the 16th, 1774.

The Last Will and Testament of William Paul, deceased, was proved by the oaths of John Atkinson, a witness thereto, and ordered to be certified, and the Executors therein named refusing to take upon themselves the burden of the execution thereof, on the motion of John Atkinson who made oath and together with John Walker, Jr., his security, entered into and acknowledged their bond in the Penalty of Five hundred Pounds as the law directs. Certificate is granted him for obtaining letter of administration on the said decedent's estate with his will aforesaid annexed in due form.

In further support of these facts, the grave of William Paul was recently discovered in St. George's churchyard, Fredericksburg, and his tombstone bears the date of 1774. This effectually disposes of Colonel Buell's contention. For whatever reason John Paul assumed the name of Jones it was not in testamentary succession to William Paul; for William Paul kept his inherited surname to the last.

It occurred to me that John Paul might have been empowered to represent his sister in the settlement of his brother's estate. A power-of-attorney which would have enabled him to attend to her affairs would not necessarily have been registered in the Scottish or American courts; yet, knowing the methodical habit of the Scottish bar, I caused search to be made in the private papers and records of those local advocates who might possibly have handled the business in Scotland; but with no results so far.

I also had search made for any conveyance of the property mentioned in the will by William Paul's administrators. I append a copy of a letter from Mr. J. P. H. Crismund, a county clerk of Spottsylvania County.

Spottsylvania, VA., June 7, 1901.
I have made the matter of John Paul Jones and William Paul and William Jones a matter of most careful study and search, but have not been able to find anything beyond the last will and testament of William Paul, a copy of which I send you. My first search was made to find the conveyance from William Paul's administration, with will annexed, conveying the houses and lots in Fredericksburg which are directed in William Paul's will to be sold, but the records nowhere show this. This seems and is strange, because some disposition must have been made of this property in some way, but I cannot find this here. I then followed the fiduciary indexes to see if I could find anything about the enlistment and service of John Paul to John Paul Jones—but this also was fruitless.

William Paul could not have assumed the name of Jones, as he leaves his last will and testament in the name of Paul, nor is there any will of record in the name of Paul, nor is there any will of record in the name of John Paul Jones. I have given this matter such thought and attention and work, but I cannot find a clue to anything named in your letter to me and concerning which you make inquiry.

As William Paul's property was in Fredericksburg, it may be that the settlement of his estate and the account of the sale of his effects is of record there. If you desire to write to the clerk of corporation court of that city as to that, he will courteously attend to your matter of inquiry.

Yours sincerely,

J. P. H. Crismund.

I wrote as Mr. Crismund suggested, but could get no further information.

8 THE JONESES OF NORTH CAROLINA

Now to revert to the North Carolina account. It comes down as straight as such a story could. Colonel Cadwallader Jones of North Carolina, in a privately printed genealogical history of his family, states that he was born in 1812. His grandmother, Mrs. Willie Jones, died in 1828. He lived with her for the first fifteen years of his life. He declares positively that she told him that John Paul had taken the name for the reasons mentioned. The matter was generally so stated and accepted in the family. Mrs. Willie Jones was a woman of unusual mental force and character, and preserved the full use of her faculties until her death.

The same statement is made independently by descendants of other branches of the Jones family. For instance, Mr. Armistead Churchill Gordon, of Staunton, Va., had it direct from his great-aunt, who was a kinswoman of Mrs. Jones, and who heard from her the circumstances referred to. And there are still other lines of tradition which create a strong probability in favour of the credibility of the theory.

For one thing, if Jones did represent his sister in the settlement of his brother's estate, it is probable that he would have to give bond for the proper performance of his trust, and it is sometimes stated that Willie and Allen Jones went on his bond for five hundred pounds—just the sum required of the Executors, by the way. It is also singular, in view of this will leaving property to his grandmother, that the Louden whom Mr. Buell knew—and who is said to have died in New Orleans 1887—should have been so mistaken in his statements; but on this point the evidence of the will is absolutely conclusive.

9. Paul Jones Never a Man of Wealth

Colonel Buell claims that John Paul Jones had riches and influence in Virginia after the death of his brother, but the claim is not tenable according to an exhaustive review of his book in the *Virginia Historical Magazine*. In the face of the present exhibit, and in the view of the fact that Jones himself spoke of living for two years in Virginia on fifty pounds, the story of his wealth cannot be credited. It is therefore entirely in harmony with the facts to accept the North Carolina tradition, in the absence of any evidence to the contrary. The direct statement coming to us in one instance through but one generation is entitled to respect. As a matter of fact both Colonel Buell's version of the matter and my own story rest upon tradition alone, with this difference—the evidence submitted absolutely excluded one of the accounts; the other, therefore, logically comes to the fore.

And thus, I think, I have contributed to clear up one mooted point in American history.

5

In the Caverns of the Pitt

One of the most distinguished of the minor soldiers of the Civil War, minor in the sense of being surpassed only by men of the stature of Grant, Sherman, Sheridan and Thomas, was George Crook. His exploits in the valley of the Shenandoah were brilliant, and his whole career was replete with instances of ability and courage which stamped him as a soldier of the first grade. A major-general of volunteers and a brevet major-general in the regular army, the year 1868 found him a colonel of infantry commanding the military district of Owyhee, a section of the country which included the south-eastern part of Oregon and the northeastern part of California.

In the adaptation of means to ends, so far as Indian affairs are concerned, the United States has usually been woefully lacking. With a few companies of cavalry and infantry not aggregating a full regiment, this eminent soldier was directed to hold the various scattered garrison points throughout a large extent of territory, and also to settle the Indians, who for some time had been indulging their propensities for savage slaughter almost unchecked, save for a few sporadic and ineffective efforts by volunteers and irregulars.

The far western representatives of the great Shoshone nation are among the meanest, most degraded, most despicable Indians on the continent. This did not hinder them from being among the most brutal and ferocious. They made the tenure of life and property more than precarious in that far-off section during and after the Civil War. They were not very numerous, nor were they a great race of fighters, except when cornered. The character of the country to the eastward of their ravaging ground, abounding in lava beds, desolate plains, inaccessible valleys and impassable mountain ranges, to which they could fly when they were hard pressed, rendered it difficult to bring any considerable number of them to action, and they enjoyed a certain immunity from punishment on that account.

The most important engagement between them and the troops, before the patience and perseverance of Crook and his handful, finally wore out the Indians, presents, perhaps, the one instance where they were brought fairly to bay and the soldiers had an opportunity to give them a thorough beating. This unique battle demonstrated also how desperately even a coward will fight when his back is against a wall. And it showed, as few other frontier fights have shown, the splendid courage of the regular American soldier in this arduous, unheeded service.

Early on the 26th of September, 1868, General Crook, with a small troop of cavalry, H of the First, numbering less than thirty men, together with about a score of mounted infantrymen from the Twenty-third Regiment, and perhaps as many Warm Spring Indian scouts under a leader named Donald Macintosh, with a small pack train, found himself on the south fork of Pitt River, in Modoc County, Cal., a few miles below its junction with the main stream. The country is wild, unsettled, largely unexplored to this day. There is no railroad even now nearer than one hundred and twenty-five miles. General Crook had been hunting and trailing Indians in the Warmer Mountains without success for several days. On this morning the Warm Spring Indian scouts reported that a large body of Indians was encamped in the valley upon which he was just entering.

The general direction of the river here was due north and south. Perhaps a mile from the bank of the river to the west, rose a high table-land which terminated in precipitous and generally insurmountable bluffs of black basalt, extending above the general level of the valley about twelve hundred feet. Projecting eastward from the side of these lofty cliffs was a singular rocky *plateau*, the outer lines of which roughly formed a half circle. This elevation was bordered on the south by a deep and broken *cañon*, on the north by a creek which ran through a forest of scattered juniper trees. The *plateau* rose in two gentle slopes to a height of about five or six hundred feet above the valley level, and was thus half as high as the bluff to the westward, which formed the base of the semi-circle. Near the northern part of the *plateau* the rocks were elevated in a series of irregular broken peaks, like the jagged ice hummocks of the higher latitudes. The whole *plateau* was covered

217

with enormous boulders, over which it was impossible even to lead a horse. On the lower reaches plots of grass, dotted with junipers, abounded. The valley of the river proper below the cliffs and the projecting plateau was a good place for a camp, although the ground near the banks was swampy and impassable.

The peaks mentioned, it was afterward learned, abounded with hidden caves and underground passages. By some curious freak of nature, the volcanic hummocks contained no less than four natural fortifications of varying sizes, which, supplemented by very slight efforts on the part of the Indians, had been turned into defensive works of the most formidable character.

They were connected by a perfect labyrinth of crevasses and underground passages and caves, so that the defenders could easily pass from one to the other. The northeast fort, which was the principal one of the chain, was surrounded by a natural gorge some fifty feet deep and twenty-five feet wide at the top. A sort of *banquette*, or balcony, making a practicable path several feet wide, extended around the fort between the wall and the edge of the ravine. The fort proper was enclosed by a wall of rock, partly natural, partly artificial, about eight feet high. An assailant crossing the ravine and gaining the crest of the peak would have ample standing ground between the edge and the wall. The broken ground around these forts on the *plateau* formed a series of natural rifle pits.

These works were held by no less than one hundred and twenty Shoshones belonging to the Piutes, Pitt Rivers, Modocs and Snakes. Their chief was Sa-hei-ta, one of the bravest and most brutal of the marauders. When they saw Crook's little force of fifty white soldiers and a score of Warm Spring Indians descending the bluff into the valley south of the rocky *cañon*, they laughed them to scorn. They were confident in the strength of their position and in their numbers, and they resolved to hold their ground. Indeed, after the first few moments there was nothing else for them to do, for Crook distributed his cavalry and infantry around the northern and southern sides, put his pack mules in camp in the valley on the east with a small guard, and threw the Warm Spring Indian scouts back of the forts between them and the cliffs. Thus he had the Indians surrounded, so far as seventy men could surround nearly twice their number in chosen fortifications. The whole place was popularly known as the Hell Caves of the Pitt River, although in the War Department and official records it is described more politely as the Infernal Caverns of the Pitt River.

Getting his men in position, Crook acted promptly. In long thin lines on the north and south, taking advantage of the abundant cover, the soldiers cautiously advanced, clearing out the rifle pits and driving the Indians back toward their stronghold. There was severe fighting all during the afternoon, in which First Sergeant Charles Brackett and Private James Lyons were killed and a number were wounded. The Warm Spring Indians, who were good scouts, did not fancy this sort of warfare, and they took practically no part in the battle. They were useful enough in one way, as they checked any retreat toward the bluffs, although as it turned out the Indians had no intention of leaving.

Finally, toward evening, the *plateau* was entirely cleared of Indians, who had all been forced back into the forts. Crook had sent a picket of soldiers to the edge of the basalt cliffs and these men, with long-range rifles, did some little execution on the defenders of the forts, although the distance was so great that their fire was largely ineffectual. Night found the soldiers ensconced behind boulders on the very rim of the ravine, the Indians in the forts. In little squads the soldiers were withdrawn from the battlefield and sent down to the camp in the valley to get something to eat. They had been without food or water since morning, and fighting is about the hottest, thirstiest work that a man can engage in. After they had refreshed themselves, they went back to the *plateau* to keep watch over the fort. Desultory firing took place all night long, the Indians blazing away indiscriminately—they had plenty of ammunition, it appeared—and the soldiers firing at the flashes of the guns. The voices of the medicine men and the chiefs could be heard exhorting them and promising victory.

Crook determined to storm the place at break of day. The darkness rendered it impossible to attempt the broken, precipitous descent and ascent of the ravine in the night. Light was needed for that. He had fought valiantly throughout the day, this major-general, as a common soldier in the ranks. He was a dead shot, and had used his Spencer carbine with effect whenever opportunity presented. He could assemble for the assault but forty men, twenty-two of the First Cavalry and eighteen of the Twenty-third Infantry. The Warm Spring auxiliaries refused to assault, such close work not being to their taste. There were several wounded men in the camp, and a small guard had to be kept there to protect them and the horses from the attacks of some of the Indians who had taken advantage of the night to escape from the stronghold to endeavour to stampede the herd, and who from various covers kept up a constant fire on the camp, so that Lieutenant Eskridge, quartermaster, had his hands full in holding his ground.

First Lieutenant W. R. Parnell, now of San Francisco, who commanded the cavalry, was directed to lead the assault. Second Lieutenant John Madigan, also of the cavalry, who had charge of the infantry, was ordered to support. The troops were directed to creep to the brink of the crevasses surrounding the fort and drop down it as quickly as possible. Arrived at the bottom, they were to scale the rocky counterscarp, and when they got to the platform they were to keep moving while they attempted to break the wall of the fort proper. Crook, who believed in intimidation, advised them to yell and cheer as much as possible. The general crawled around during the night from man to man, acquainting every soldier with his ideas and "talking to them as a father." He reminds me a little of Henry V. before the Battle of Agincourt.

The task he had set his soldiers was desperate in the extreme. It speaks well not only for the general's reliance upon them, but for the quality of the men also, that he conceived it possible and that they carried it out effectively. So soon as it was fairly dawn the soldiers at a given signal dashed at the crest. So suddenly did they appear that, although the Indians in the fort across the ravine opened a terrific rifle and arrow fire upon them, not one was injured. Without a moment's hesitation, the men plunged down the walls, and sliding, falling, any way, they reached the bottom. There they were safe from the fire of the Indians, for the platform around the wall of the fort prevented the Indians from shooting into the ravine.

Parnell's company immediately began the escalade of the cliffs. Madigan had not been so fortunate. Where he struck the ravine the wall happened to be absolutely sheer. Descent was not practicable. His men therefore stopped on the brink until he directed his infantrymen to circle the ravine until they found a practicable descent and there join Parnell's men. He had scarcely given the order when a bullet pierced his brain. Some of his men were also struck down, others retired behind the rocks, made a detour and followed Parnell.

The sides of the ravine were so precipitous that no man could scale them unaided. Two or three would lift up a fellow-soldier. After gaining a foothold he in turn would pull others up, and thus they slowly made their way to the edge of the cliffs, Crook climbing with the rest. They finally gained the *banquette*, or platform, after a difficult and exhausting climb. The Indians were behind the walls of the fort, the soldiers outside. Sergeant Michael Meara, leading the advance, peeped through a loop-hole, and was shot dead. Private Willoughby Sawyer, happening to pass by another orifice, was killed in the same way. In both cases the Indians were so close that the faces of both men were badly powder burned. A slug struck the wrist and an arrow pierced the body of Private Shea, hurling him to the bottom of the ravine.

But the soldiers were not idle. Guns from each side were thrust through every loophole or crevice and discharged blindly. In this desperate method of fighting, the Indians, being contracted within the circle, suffered the more. While some were fighting thus, others were tearing down the rocky wall with hands and bayonets. A breach was soon made, and through it the soldiers streamed. The Indians, after one hasty volley, fled precipitately. The last man to leave the fort was the chief, Sa-hei-ta. As he leaped over the wall Crook's unerring Spencer sent a bullet into his spine, and he fell dead at the bottom of the ravine. The fort had been defended by at least fifty Indians, and there were fifteen dead bodies in it. Among these was that of the chief medicine man.

The soldiers ran to the western wall, and through loopholes opened a fire upon the Indians, who had joined their fellows in the other forts. The fire was fiercely returned. About nine in the morning one of the infantrymen, peering through a small crevice in the rock, found his view obstructed by a small weed. In spite of Parnell's caution, he uprooted it, leaving quite an opening, in which he was completely exposed. He was shot through the head instantly and fell unconscious.[1]

The wounded, of which there were a number, were now taken to the camp about 11 a. m. The fire of the Indians having slackened, Crook, leaving a detachment in the fort, withdrew the rest of the men to the camp for breakfast. The Indians took advantage of this opportunity to charge the fort. The few defenders were driven out of the fortification and Sergeant Russler was killed, the third sergeant to lose his life that day! Rallying on the *banquette*, upon the return of the others, they in turn drove the Indians out of the fort. Neither party could occupy it all day long. The soldiers clung to the platform covering their dead in the fort on one side, while the Indians from the forts on the other side prevented the soldiers from re-entering.

It was not until nightfall that the dead could be withdrawn. The

---

1. He lived three weeks without regaining his senses, and eventually died at Camp Warner, Ore., over one hundred and fifty miles away, whither he was carried with the other wounded, after the battle.

soldiers reoccupied the fort at night, and although the Indians sent frequent volleys of arrows, which they shot into the air, hoping they would fall upon the soldiers, and kept up an irregular fire, culminating in a sustained discharge about midnight, they made no attempt seriously to take the fort, although the soldiers, confidently expecting an attack, lay on their arms all night. During the last half of it not a sound came from the Indians.

The next morning Crook prepared to resume the attack by assaulting the other forts, when his suspicions were awakened by a strange quiet, which continued in spite of several efforts to draw the Indian fire. Fearing some stratagem, he delayed until he could have speech with the interior forts by means of a wounded Indian squaw, whom they captured after cautious scouting. From this woman, whom they forced to speak by threatening to hang her, it was learned that the Indians had decamped during the night. The warriors had taken advantage of a long underground passage which led south and opened in a cave in the side of the *cañon*. This concealed way actually took them under the feet of Crook's soldiers, and sufficiently far from his camp and scouts to enable them, so quietly had they moved, to steal away undetected. They left their women and children in the caves. These caves were a perfect maze. To attempt to search them would have been impossible. Indeed, one soldier, Private James Carey, who saw the body of a dead Indian near the mouth of one of them, and who sought a scalp as a trophy, descended to the cave mouth and was shot dead by someone, probably a wounded brave, within the dark recesses.

The Indians' loss was about forty killed. Crook had lost nearly a moiety—50 *per cent.*—of his entire force, an appalling proportion! One officer, six soldiers, one civilian had been killed, twelve soldiers, including three corporals,[2] seriously wounded, two of them afterward died; and almost every survivor in the party had received some slight wound or had been badly bruised by falls in climbing over the broken rocks. Their clothing and shoes were cut to pieces, they were utterly worn out by two sleepless nights and two days' desperate fighting. They buried the brave soldiers in the valley, concealing their graves so that the Indians could not discover them and ravage them. Carrying their wounded in rude travels slung between horses and mules, and taking the body of brave young Madigan, who was buried in a lonely forgotten grave, one day's march from the battlefield, they returned to

2. The loss among non-commissioned officers was especially heavy, showing how well these brave men did their duty.

222

Camp Warner.

With a greatly inferior force Crook had assailed the Indians on ground of their own choosing, which they believed to be impregnable, and had administered a crushing defeat. The escalade of the wall of the ravine, the breaching of the rampart, the storming of the fort, its defence, its abandonment and recapture, was one of the most gallant and heroic exploits ever performed in American history. Although he had paid dearly for his victory, the lesson Crook had inflicted upon the savages was a salutary one, and the disastrous defeat of the Indians in the Infernal Caverns of the Pitt River was a great factor in bringing about the subsequent pacification of that section.

Today the exploit is forgotten. All the officers, save one, and I presume most of the men, who participated, are dead. It is from the papers of the surviving officer, Colonel Parnell, and from official reports and a few meagre published accounts in newspapers and books that this story of American heroism has been prepared.

6

Being a Boy Out West

I am in some doubt as to whether to call this particular reminiscence *"Pants That I Have Worn"* or *"Trousers Like Those Mother Used to Make."* For either name seems admirably suitable to the situation.

I was the oldest son in a numerous family, and therefore had the heritage of my father's clothes. He was an exceedingly neat and careful man, and never—to my sorrow be it said—did he ever wear out anything, unless it were an apple switch on me or my brothers. I had to wear out all his old clothes, it seemed to me. It was not a matter of choice but of necessity with me. My younger brother always escaped. By the time I had finished anything, there was no more of it. It went perforce to the ragman, if he would condescend to accept it.

There was a certain sad, plum-coloured, shad-bellied coat that flashes athwart my memory in hideous recollection, which wrapped itself portentously about my slim figure, to the great delectation of my young friends and companions, and to my corresponding misery. I can recall their satirical criticisms vividly even now. They enjoyed it hugely, especially the little girls. Think of a small—say "skinny"—little boy, about nine or ten years old, in a purple shad-bellied coat which had been made to fit (?) him by cutting off the sleeves, also the voluminous tails just below the back buttons!

I could never understand the peculiar taste my father manifested in his younger days, for when I recall the age which permitted me to wear cut-down clothing (and that age arrived at an extraordinary early period in my existence, it appeared to me), such a fearful and wonderful assortment of miscellaneous garments of all colours, shapes and sizes as were resurrected from the old chests in the garret, where they had reposed in peaceful neglect for half a generation, the uninitiated can scarcely believe.

The shad-bellied coat was bad enough—you could take that off, though—but there was something worse that stayed on. Fortunately there is one season in the year when coats in the small Western village, in which I lived, were at a discount, especially on small boys, and that was summer. But on the warmest of summer days the most recklessly audacious youngster has to wear trousers even in the most sequestered village.

One pair rises before me among the images of many and will not down. The fabric of which this particular garment was made was coloured a light cream, not to say yellow. There was a black stripe, a piece of round black braid down each leg, too, and the garment was as heavy as broadcloth and as stiff as a board. Nothing could have been more unsuitable for a boy to wear than that was. I rebelled and protested with all the strength of my infantile nature, but it was needs must—I had either to wear them or to remain in bed indefinitely. Swallowing my pride, in spite of my mortification, I put them on and sallied forth, but little consoled by the approving words and glances of my mother, who took what I childishly believed to be an utterly unwarranted pride in her—shall I say—adaptation or reduction? Those trousers had a sentimental value for her, too, as I was to learn later. As for me, I fairly loathed them.

Many times since then, I have been the possessor of a "best and only pair," but never a pair of such colour, quality and shape. They were originally of the wide-seated, peg-top variety, quite like the fashion of today, by the way—or is it yesterday, in these times of sudden changes?—and when they were cut off square at the knee and shirred or gathered or reefed in at the waist, they looked singularly like the typical "Dutchman's breeches." I might have worn them as one of Hendrik Hudson's crew in *Rip Van Winkle*—which was, even in those days, the most popular play in which Joseph Jefferson appeared. You can see how long ago it was from that.

Well, I put them on in bitterness of heart. How the other boys greeted me until they got used to them—which it seemed to me they never would! Unfortunately for them, anyway, they had only one day, one brief day, in which to make game of me; for the first time I wore them something happened.

There was a pond on a farm near our house called, from its owner, "Duffy's Pond." The water drained into a shallow low depression in a large meadow, and made a mudhole, a cattle wallow. Little boys have a fondness for water, when it is exposed to the air—that is, when it is muddy, when it is dirty—which is in adverse ratio to their zest for nice, clean water in a nice clean tub. To bathe and be clean does not seem instinctive with boys. And how careful we were not to wet the backs of our hands and our wrists except when in swimming! And how hard did our parents strive to teach us to distribute our ablutions more generally!

Well, Mr. Duffy did not allow boys to swim in his pond, which made it all the more inviting. It was a hot August day when I first put on those cream-colored pants. Naturally, we went in swimming. Having divested ourselves of our clothing—and with what joy I cast off the hideous garment!—we had to wade through twenty or thirty yards of mud growing deeper and more liquid with every step, until we reached the water. We were having a great time playing in the ooze when Mr. Duffy appeared in sight. He was an irascible old man, and did not love his neighbours' children! He had no sympathy at all with us in our sports; he actually begrudged us the few apples we stole when they were unripe and scarce, and as for watermelons—ah, but he was an unfeeling farmer!

Fortunately, he had no dog with him that morning, nothing but a gun—an old shotgun with the barrels sawed off at half their length, loaded with beans or bacon, or pepper or sand, I don't remember which—they were all bad enough if they hit you. The alarm was given instantly, and we made a wild rush for the tall grass through that mud. You can fancy how dirty we became, splashing, stumbling, wallowing in it. Mr. Duffy, firing beans at us from the rear, accelerated our pace to a frightful degree. Fortunately again, like Hamlet, he was "fat and scant o' breath," and we could run like deer, which we did. *En route* I grabbed my shirt with one hand and those cream-colored pants with the other.

The mud of that pond was the thick, black, sticky kind. It stained hideously anything light that it touched, as irrevocably as sin. Those trousers had been clasped against my boyish muddy breast or flapped against my muddy, skinny legs, and they were a sight to behold! There was no water available for miles where we stopped. We rubbed ourselves off with the burnt grass of August and dusty leaves as well as we could, dressed ourselves and repaired home.

I was a melancholy picture. The leopard could have changed his spots as easily as I. Yet I well remember the mixture of fierce joy and terrified apprehension that pervaded me. I arrived home about dinner-time. Father was there. "Wh—what!" he cried in astonishment.

226

"Where have you been, sir?"

"Those," sobbed my mother in anguished tones, "were your father's wedding trousers! I gave them to you with reluctance and as a great favour, you wretched boy, and—and—you have ruined them."

I was taken upstairs, thoroughly washed, scrubbed—in the tub, which was bad enough—and when sufficiently clean to be handed to my father, he and I had an important interview in the wood-shed—our penal institution—over which it were well to draw the curtain. There was a happy result to the adventure, however: I never wore the cream-colored pants again, and hence my joy. The relief was almost worth the licking.

Some of the material, however, was worked up into a patchwork quilt, and of the rest my mother made a jacket for my sister. My mother could not look upon those things without tears; neither could I! Why is it that grown people will be so inconsiderate about a little boy's clothes?

It was the fashion of many years before I was born for people—that is, men and boys—to wear shawls. There was a dearth in the family exchequer on one occasion—on many occasions, I may say, but this was a particular one. I had no overcoat, at least not one suitable for Sunday, and really it would have been preposterous to have attempted to cut down one of father's for me. That feat was beyond even my mother's facile scissors, and she could effect marvels with them, I knew to my cost. It was a bitter cold winter day, I remember, and my mother, in the kindness of her heart, brought to light one of those long, narrow, fringed, brilliantly coloured plaided shawls, so that I should not miss Sunday school. I was perfectly willing to miss it, then or any other time, for any excuse was a good one for that. But no, I was wrapped up in it in spite of my frantic protests and despatched with my little sister—she who wore the cream-colored trousers-jacket—to the church. Strange to say, she did not mind at all.

We separated outside the house door, and I ran on alone. I had evolved a deep, dark purpose. I went much more rapidly than she, and as soon as I turned the corner, and was safely out of sight, I tore off that hateful shawl and when I arrived at the meeting-house I ignominiously thrust it into the coal heap in the dilapidated shed in the corner of the lot. I was almost frozen by the time I arrived, but any condition was better than that shawl.

The Sunday school exercises proceeded as usual, but in the middle of them, the janitor who had gone into the coal house for the wherewithal to replenish the fires, came back with the shawl. I had rammed it rather viciously under the coal, and it was a filthy object. The superintendent held it up by finger and thumb and asked to whom it belonged.

"Why, that's our Johnny's" piped up my little sister amid a very disheartening roar of laughter from the school. There was no use in my denying the statement. Her reputation for veracity was much higher than mine, and I recognized the futility of trying to convince anyone that she was mistaken. At the close of the session I had to wrap myself in that coal-stained garment and go forth. I was attended by a large delegation of the scholars when the school was over. They did not at all object to going far out of their way to escort me home, and they left me at my own gate.

It was Sunday, and it was against my father's religious principles to lick us on Sunday—that was one of the compensations, youthful compensations of that holy day—but Monday wasn't far off, and father's memory was remarkably acute. Ah, those sad times, but there was fun in them, too, after all.

There was a little boy who lived near us named Henry Smith. He and I were inseparable. He had a brother three years older than himself whose name was Charles. Charles was of course much taller and stronger than Henry and myself, and he could attend to one of us easily. But both of us together made a pretty good match for him. Consequently we hunted in couples, as it were. Charles was unduly sensitive about his Christian name. I think he called it his unchristian name. Not the "Charles" part of it, that was all right, but his parents had inconsiderately saddled him with the hopeless additional name of Peter Van Buskirk Smith! All we had to do to bring about a fight was to approach him and address him as "Peter Van Buskirk." He bitterly resented it, which was most unreasonable of him. I recall times when the three of us struggled in the haymow for hours at a time, Peter Van Buskirk, furiously angry, striving to force an apology or retraction, and Henry and I having a glorious time refusing him.

We were safe enough while we were together, but when he caught us alone—O my! I can remember it yet. He was always Charles, at that time, but it was of no use. Yet notwithstanding the absolute certainty of a severe thrashing when he caught us singly, we never could refrain from calling him "Peter Van Buskirk" when we were together.

Why is it that parents are so thoughtless about the naming of their children? I knew a boy once named Elijah Draco and there was another lad of my acquaintance who struggled under the name of Lord Byron. That wasn't so bad, because we shortened it to "By," but "Elijah Draco" was hopeless, so we called him "Tommy," as a rebuke to his unfeeling parents.

Charles Peter Van Buskirk was a funny boy. He was as brave as a lion. You could pick him up by the ears, which were long—and shall I say handy?—and he never would howl. We knew that was the way to tell a good dog. "Pick him up by the ears; an' if he howls, he'll be no fighter!" And we thought what was a good test for a dog could not be amiss for a boy.

He had a dog once, sold to him for a quarter when it was a pup by a specious individual of the tramp variety, as one of the finest "King-Newf'un'lan'—Bull Breed." His appetite and his vices were in proportion to his descriptions, but he had no virtues that we could discover. With a boy's lack of inventiveness we called him "Tiger" although anything less ferocious than he would be hard to find. He was more like a sheep in spirit than anything else. But Charles thought he saw signs of promise in that pup, and in spite of our disparaging remarks he clung to him. Charles knew a lot about dogs, or thought he did, which was the same thing.

I remember we were trying to teach Tige to "lead" one day. He had no more natural aptitude for leading than an unbroken calf. The perverse dog at last flattened himself down on his stomach, spread-eagled himself on the ground, and stretched his four legs out as stiff as he could. We dragged him over the yard until he raised a pile of dirt and leaves in front of him like a plough in an untilled field. He would not "lead," although we nearly choked him to death trying to teach him. Then we tried picking him up by the ears, applying that test for courage and blood, you know! You might have heard that dog yelp for miles. He had no spirit at all. Charles Peter Van Buskirk was disgusted with him.

We got out a can of wagon-grease and spotted him artistically to make him look like a coach-dog, which was legitimate, as coach-dogs are notoriously remarkable for lack of courage. They are only for ornament. That was a pretty-looking animal when it rained. We changed his name, too, and called him "Kitty," regardless of his sex. It was the last insult to a dog, we thought, but he never seemed to mind it. I feel sorry for that dog as I look back at him now, and it rather provoked Charles when we subsequently asked his opinion of any other dog. This we did as often as there were enough of us together to make it safe.

When we felt very reckless, we used to go in swimming in the river, which was a very dangerous proceeding indeed, for the Missouri is a treacherous, wicked stream, full of "suck-holes" and whirlpools and with a tremendous current, especially during the June "rise." The practice was strictly forbidden by all right-minded parents, including our own. Frequently, however, in compliance with that mysterious sign, the first two fingers of the right hand uplifted and held wide apart, which all boys over a thousand miles of country knew meant "Will you go swimming?" we would make up a party after school and try the flood.

Father usually inspected us with a rather sharper eye, when we came sneaking in the back way after such exercises. For a busy man, father had a habit, that was positively maddening, of happening upon a boy at the wrong time. We used to think we had no privacy at all.

"Hum!" he was wont to say, looking suspiciously at our wet, sleek heads and general clean appearance—clean for us, that is, for the Missouri River, sandy though it was, was vastly cleaner than Duffy's Pond or puddles of that ilk—"been in swimming again, have you? In the river, I'll be bound."

Two little boys, my brother and I would choke out some sort of a mumbling evasion in lieu of a reply.

"How did you get your hair wet?" the old man would continue, rising and feeling two guilty little heads.

"Per-perspiration, sir," we would gasp out faintly.

"And that vile odour about you? Hey? Is that perspiration, too?" sniffing the air with a grim resolution that made our hearts sink.

We had been smoking drift-wood, the vilest stuff that anybody can put in his mouth. This was enough to betray us.

"It's no use, boys; you needn't say another word," father would add in the face of our desperate and awful attempts at an adequate explanation. "You know what I told you. Go to the wood-shed!"

Oh, that wood-shed! *"Abandon ye all hope who enter here"* should have been written over its door. Often mother would interfere—bless her tender heart!—but not always. Father was a small man of sedentary habits, not given to athletic exercises. A board across two barrels afforded a convenient resting-place for the arms and breast of the one appointed to receive the corporal punishment, and a barrel stave was an excellent instrument with which to administer it. I said father was a small, weak man. When he got through with us we used to think he would have made a splendid blacksmith. Our muscles were pretty strong, and our skin callous—"*the hand of little use hath the daintier touch!*"—but they were as nothing to his. We always tired of that game before he did, although we played it often.

Two of us, I recall, have carried large tubs up the steep bank from the river to the train at 4 a. m. on a summer morning, when the circus came to town. We were proud to be privileged to water the elephants, but it killed us to split wood for a day's burning in the kitchen stove. We never were good for anything except assisting the circus people, on circus day. School was torture, and it was generally dismissed.

Our father was mayor of the town, and the mayor's children usually got in free. On one occasion we yielded to the solicitations of our most intimate friends and assembled thirty of them in a body. This group of children of all ages and sizes—and there was even one lone "nigger" in it—we were to pass through the gate by declaring that we were the mayor's children.

"Great heavens!" cried the ticket man, appalled at the sight, "How many blame children has the mayor of the town got? Is he a Mormon, anyway, or what? An' how about that one?" pointing to the darky.

Father was standing near. We had not seen him. He turned and surveyed the multitude, including the black boy, that we had foisted upon him. It was a humorous situation, but father didn't see it that way. He sent all of us home with a few scathing words. My younger brother and I wanted to go to that circus more than we ever wanted to go to any circus before. We slept in a half-story room with windows opening on the porch roof. That night we climbed out on the roof and slid down the porch to the ground at the risk of breaking our necks.

Henry and Charles met us by appointment. We none of us had any money and we resolved to sneak in, our services at watering the elephants not being considered worthy of a ticket. My brother and I got in safely under the canvas in one place. Henry succeeded in effecting an entrance in another, but Charles Peter Van Buskirk got caught. A flat board in the hands of a watchman made a close connection with his anatomy. Charles was hauled back, well paddled and sent home. Circuses were a tabooed subject where he was concerned for some time thereafter.

William, my brother, and I clambered through the legs of the crowd on the seats after we got into the canvas tent. As luck would have it, we ran right into the arms of our father. I was paralyzed, but William burst out with a boldness that savoured of an inspiration, "Why father, you here? I thought you were going to prayer-meeting."

Everybody laughed, father said nothing; someone made room for us, and we watched the performance with mingled feelings of delight and apprehension. The wood-shed loomed up awfully black as we passed it that night. We held our breath. However, father never said anything to us but, "Goodnight, boys. I hope you had a good time."

We certainly had. And we escaped the usual licking, deserved though it was. And it wasn't Sunday, either.

But where was I? O, yes! Charles Peter Van Buskirk one Saturday morning announced his intention of going on an expedition across the river. Over the river from where we lived was "Slab Town," dilapidated little settlement of no social or moral consideration. The old captain, the pilot of the wheezy ferry-boat *Edgar*, was our sworn friend, and allowed us to ride free as often as we could get away. Charles intended crossing the river to get *pawpaws*. A *pawpaw* is an easily mashed fruit, three or four inches long, with a tough skin inclosing a very liquid pulp full of seeds, and about as solid as a cream puff, when it is dead ripe. It grows on a low, stunted bush-like tree.

We were mighty fond of *pawpaws*, but little fellows as we were didn't dare to cross the river and venture into "Slab Town" or its vicinity, for such an excursion within its territory usually provoked a fight with the young ruffians of that hamlet, who hated the village boys as aristocrats.

"You'd better not go over there, Charles," we advised him timorously. "Those Slab Town boys will take your *pawpaws* away from you."

I can see now the chesty movement with which Charles stuck out his breast, threw back his shoulders, curved inward and swung his arms, and went away basket in hand, remarking in a lordly manner; "Aw, who's goin' to take *my pawpaws?*"

It was evening when the rash youth returned. He came slinking up the back alley in a vain endeavour to elude observation, but we had a number of his and our friends on the watch for him—to see that he returned safely, of course—and we gave him a royal greeting. We had been true prophets, though without honour in Charles's sight. The Slab Town boys had taken his *pawpaws* in a spirit of aggressive appropriation, which was bad enough, but with rare and unusual generosity they had afterward returned them to Charles. They had not put them back in his basket, however, but had heaped them indiscriminately upon his person. It appears that he must have run for miles pursued by a howling mob of all the ruffians over there, engaged in the happy pastime of throwing soft, mushy *pawpaws* at him. Charles could hardly see; in fact he could hardly walk. He was plastered with *pawpaws* from his head to his feet.

Thereafter when we wanted to provoke a fight, all that was necessary when the unappreciated portion of his name was flung at him and was not sufficient to awaken his ire, was to throw out our chests, hold back our shoulders, curve our arms and say in a throaty voice, "Who's going to take *my pawpaws?*"

I feel tempted to use the old phrase in certain modern circumstances today when it seems to fit some bold and reckless endeavour. I have never forgotten Charles's "who's-goin'-to-take-*my*-pawp*a*ws" air!

We were sometimes able to get a little money together by doing odd jobs—not for our parents, however, but for the neighbours. We had plenty of odd jobs to do at home, but such work was a matter of obligation and not remunerative, nor was it interesting. With this money Henry and I each bought a game-chicken, which we kept cooped up separately in the back lot behind the stable. Neither father nor mother knew anything about it, of course.

We would let these two game-cocks out half a dozen times a day. They would rush at each other fiercely, but before the battle was fairly on, we would summarily part them, and put them back in their coops, which were placed opposite each other, when they would indulge in chicken-swearing and personalities as much as they desired. Their appetites for fighting were whetted indeed. In fact, there was so much animosity engendered between these two birds that they would rush together like two express trains trying to pass each other on the same track whenever they were turned loose. There was no time sparring for time or position. It was fight from the moment they saw each other, although we never let them strike more than one blow or two. A half-minute round was enough for us. I think it really scared us.

Charles, in spirit of revenge, let them out one day during our absence. When we got back from school we had only one chicken between us. It was a wonderful chicken, for it had beaten the other, although the conquered bird had fought until it had been killed. We burned him on a funeral pyre as a dead gladiator, with much ceremony and boyish speaking. We wanted to sacrifice to his *manes* a hen as his wife, but finally concluded to abandon that part of the ceremony; mother kept count of the hens, you see.

Of course, Julius Caesar (as we named him) had the run of the yard thereafter, there being no one to oppose him. He led a very peaceful life until our next door neighbour bought a large Shanghai rooster. I forgot now what particular breed our rooster was, but he was small, not much larger than a bantam. The Shanghai rooster, which was a huge monster, had the most provoking crow, large, loud and aggressive. An alley intervened between the yard where he held forth and our yard. One day we came home from school and looked for our chicken. He was gone!

We hunted everywhere for him, but could not find him. We missed the crowing of the Shanghai rooster, which had been frequent and exasperating, I have no doubt. The yard was very silent. We pursued our investigations with zeal and finally reached the alley. It had been raining heavily for almost a week, and the alley was a mass of black, sticky mud. Gazing anxiously over the fence, we heard a feeble chirp from a large gob of mud in the alley. It was our rooster!

The Shanghai had rashly ventured into supposed neutral ground in that alley and had crowed once too often. The little game cock had squeezed through the fence and come over to investigate the situation. They had fought there in the mud. The mud was too deep for the Shanghai to run and the bantam killed him. During the battle the victor had become so covered with mud that he could neither move nor crow nor see. He was in a worse state than Charles with the *pawpaws*, and indifferent to honours.

We took him and washed him. He seemed none the worse for his adventure, but that battle must have been a royal one. It was the second one we had not seen! We felt like the Roman public deprived of its "*Circenses.*" We really never did see that chicken fight, for he got the pip or something, a few days after, perhaps from the microbes in the alley, and in spite of our careful nursing, or possibly because of it, he died. He died just in time, too, for after we had put him away with more ceremony than we had used before, father who had got some inkling of the affair, suddenly broke out at supper: "Boys, are you keeping game-cocks in the back lot? Fighting-chickens, eh?"

"No, sir," we both answered meekly, with a clear conscience and a steady eye.

We had lots of pets in those days; some time they may serve for another story.

234

www.ingramcontent.com/pod-product-compliance
Lightning Source LLC
Chambersburg PA
CBHW032032090426
42733CB00029B/214